CELTIC
TREE MAGIC

About the Author

Danu Forest has been a practicing druid witch and Celtic shaman for more than twenty years, and has been teaching Celtic shamanism and witchcraft for more than a decade. Danu is an *Ard Bandrui* (Archdruidess) of the Irish Druid Clan of Dana and runs a druid group, the Grove of the Avalon Sidhe, in Glastonbury, UK. This is her third book.

To Write to the Author

If you wish to contact the author or would like more information about this book, please write to the author in care of Llewellyn Worldwide, and we will forward your request. Both author and publisher appreciate hearing from you and learning of your enjoyment of this book and how it has helped you. Llewellyn Worldwide cannot guarantee that every letter written to the author can be answered, but all will be forwarded. Please write to:

Danu Forest
⁒ Llewellyn Worldwide
2143 Wooddale Drive
Woodbury, MN 55125-2989

Please enclose a self-addressed stamped envelope for reply,
or $1.00 to cover costs. If outside the USA, enclose
an international postal reply coupon.

Many of Llewellyn's authors have websites with additional information and resources. For more information, please visit us at www.llewellyn.com.

CELTIC
TREE MAGIC

OGHAM LORE AND
DRUID MYSTERIES

DANU FOREST

Llewellyn Worldwide
Woodbury, Minnesota

FIRST EDITION
Eleventh Printing, 2023

Book design by Bob Gaul
Chapter art by Llewellyn Art Department
Cover design by Kevin R. Brown
Cover illustration by Chris Down
Edit by Laura Graves
Interior illustrations by Dan Goodfellow

Llewellyn Publications is a registered trademark of Llewellyn Worldwide Ltd.

Library of Congress Cataloging-in-Publication Data
Forest, Danu.
Celtic tree magic: Ogham lore and Druid mysteries/Danu Forest.—First Edition.
  pages cm
Includes bibliographical references and index.
  ISBN 978-0-7387-4101-7
1. Magic, Celtic. 2. Tree worship. 3. Ogham alphabet. 4. Mythology, Celtic.
5. Trees—Mythology—Ireland. 6. Druids and Druidism—Miscellanea. I. Title.
BF1622.C45F67 2014
299'.16—dc23

2014021888

Llewellyn Publications
A Division of Llewellyn Worldwide Ltd.
2143 Wooddale Drive
Woodbury, MN 55125-2989
www.llewellyn.com

Printed in the United States of America

For Dan Goodfellow—
ranger and a true man of the oak.

Contents

List of Figures

Acknowledgments

No book is ever the creation of only one person, and in writing this I am eternally grateful to so many people for their support and encouragement over many years; as I learnt my tree lore and spent hours in the woods, to those who walked with me under the trees in rain or shine, to those who spent long nights by the fire with me, and those who shared their knowledge and experience as I have grown along my own path, each of them allowing me to grow deep roots and tall branches in their esteemed company. Gratitude, honour and praise goes to Elysia Gallo for her amazing support, and to Penny Billington for opening the way. Thanks also go to Nicholas R. Mann for lending me treasure, Philip Shallcrass aka Greywolf of the BDO, Philip Carr-Gomm of OBOD, and Kristoffer Hughes of the Anglesey Druid Order. And finally I hold the greatest gratitude of all to my green kin, and to my husband and son, Dan and Gwyn, without whom I would not be.

Prayer to Ogma

Ogma sun face
shining one, illuminate my vision
that I may see the wisdom of trees.
Not hard shall be my ascent into the branches
and my understanding deep into the roots of being.
Champion my quest
bright one
light the way through the forest
that I may know the mysteries of the ogham
by hand and knife
by heart.
That I may be a wielder of knowledge
and a keeper of its secrets
upon the One Great Tree between the worlds.

—Danu Forest, 2013

Introduction

Trees are distinctly mysterious and magical beings. Few people are not moved by the deep presence felt in a forest grove or by the soothing hush of wind in branches. Regardless of religion or culture, humanity has long held trees to be beloved kin. Valuable for a host of practical reasons, they also are held sacred by many ancient peoples as wise elders and homes to spirits and otherworldly beings.

My first experiences of trees as spiritual, magical creatures were when I was a very small child. There was an old apple tree in my grandparents' garden, and for the first years of my life I remember it as a dear friend: long hours spent by its side, lost in conversations without words, joy bubbling in my heart. Sometimes I would see the "Apple Man," as I called him, sitting in the branches, his skin green and smooth, his smile broad; at other times I knew him to be the tree itself. These were my earliest days, where reality could shift and blur with ease without rationalising or analysing, just being in easy communion with nature and its spirits, as I believe we are all truly meant to be.

There was also another tree of great significance whom I called the "Wise Old Oak." The village cricket pitch was surrounded by a small woodland that opened on to a farmer's fields. To me, those woods were full of faeries and mysterious shadowed dells. Ivy and elder clothed nooks and crannies fit to hide a child from the sunny glare of the open playing field, and they called to my soul in a way I couldn't explain then. When other children sought to run and shout, I wanted to climb, scramble through the thicket to spin and dance in circles around the trees, and find secret places to sit quietly and listen to the wind sighing in the leaves. Out farther in the wilderness before the farmland stretched on forever was the huge oak tree. It stood proud, marking where the woodland turned to meadows with its broad crown and furrowed trunk, its great roots stretching out like serpents, diving in and out of the soil. It marked a place of change between the dark of the woods and the golden fields beyond.

In the dappled sunlight I once saw a fox dive deep between its roots and vanish as if into another world. This image had a profound effect on me, as if it came in a dream. I remember the air tingling with power, although I couldn't have described it like that at the time. I was used to seeing spirits and was lucky enough to have a family that accepted my experiences with equanimity as nothing unusual, but this was different. I had come across the veil between the worlds. I knew it in the core of my being. It was also probably a fox den, and I knew it to be that too, but my senses told me it was so much more.

Over the years these trees became deeply formative presences, as I grew seamlessly into the spiritual path I walk to this day. To me, trees have always held great magical and spiritual significance, and I have always considered them our green kin. They have so much to teach us if we could but listen. Training as a witch in my teens and later as a shaman and druid was a natural product of my communion with trees, and they have been my greatest teachers. I believe spiritual life is inseparable from nature, and the spirit world and our own merge and flow in and out of each other with the same ease the fox dives from the earth into the sunlight and back again. Here is where the gods (and indeed a whole host of gods and goddesses) can be found in infinite variation. Priestessing the earth is for me personally the only natural response to the awe and deep love this evokes in me. Learning from and working with the spirits of nature directly is our birthright, as the land is as much our mother as theirs. While we may learn a great deal from each other, especially from the traditional lore that each land holds, it is my belief that to enter into any spiritual relationship with the earth our practice must always stem from this key experience first, must rise up from beneath our feet. For this reason, I find greatest spiritual meaning in the magical and spiritual lore of my own lands—Britain and Ireland—and my ancestors, those elusive people known in popular culture as the Celts.

The Celts venerated certain trees all across Europe, Britain, and Ireland, and although they did not have a written language, a great deal of their knowledge has survived in folklore and common custom, as well as that mysterious set of sigils known as ogham (pronounced *oh-am*). My work with the ogham goes back well over twenty years. When I first discovered it, I was so thrilled and felt like I was re-remembering something lost and infinitely precious. Here at last was our ancestral magical tree lore preserved, albeit in a highly cryptic and disguised form. Picking the way through it can be much like making your way through the thicket: a step at a time, untangling from briars, and sweeping back the ivy to the core knowledge that lies beneath. Yet through it all, the path remains straight and true like the tree's trunk or the central "stem" of the ogham script itself. Studying the ogham and working with it both spiritually and magically is a lifelong road, but one I find deeply rewarding. Doing so renews my soul as surely as new leaves emerge in spring. Within its branches climbed one after another, we find the wisdom of the trees. Nothing to me more strongly represents the collected spiritual knowledge of these lands than can be found in the trees' heartwood—from roots to twig and leaf tip.

This book therefore holds as its primary concern trees from a Celtic perspective as recorded in the Irish ogham alphabet. As such, it provides an in-depth study of the main twenty original and earliest ogham trees, as well as an overview of the *forfeda* (pronounced *for-feya*), the later collection of an additional five trees (for completeness).

The Path Through the Trees

Celtic Tree Magic is first and foremost a book about Celtic tree lore and its uses. However, to really develop our understanding of this, we must place it in context. Therefore we will first take a look at the nature of Celtic pagan spirituality via an exploration of their sacred enclosures known as nemetons, and how both trees and related deities were honoured and represented in these spaces. In the next section, "Into the Forest," we will look at how to make this knowledge relevant to our practice today, how to relate to individual and groups of trees in nature, and how to work with them in sacred and magical ways via developing relations with their spirits and the powers of place within our own landscapes. We will also explore finding our own ogham guides and allies to work with in nature and in the otherworld via seership and inner vision, discovering how to find and work with our own "inner grove" and its resident guardian.

We will then turn our attention to the ogham trees themselves in greater detail. Each tree's practical and magical uses and healing attributes are included, as well as the spiritual lessons and energies they represent. In this way we can use this traditional lore to develop our own experiences and insights.

Our study of each of the trees is divided into the following sections in addition to its general botanical description.

Lore and legend covers the mythological, textual, and folkloric story of each tree and, by extension, its general energetic properties and significance.

Practical and magical uses discusses the particular trees' applications in crafts and spellwork, including traditional examples.

Healing covers the trees' medicinal and healing properties, be they herbal, chemical, or energetic in nature, again with traditional examples where relevant.

Ogham divination meaning is included to give the reader an insight into the meaning and relevance of the ogham sigil or tree in a divination spread or when found in Celtic shamanic journeying or inner vision.

Excerpts from my private magical journals are also included so you can see how I relate and work with these trees in my daily life, hopefully encouraging and inspiring you to seek similar experiences and build your own relationships with our green spirit kin in turn. After that, we will discuss each of the forfeda to add additional insight into the ogham lore. From there we will explore how to make ogham wands and staves based on our connection with the spirits of each tree, and how to perform ogham divination. We'll also explore how to use the ogham as magical sigils, both individually and in combination with each other for spells and other magical purposes. We will also look at the traditional layout known as Fionn's Window and its uses not only in divination but in creating sacred spaces with its own distinctive energetic atmosphere. Finally we will look at using ogham trees and plants for spells, charms, and potions, including vibrational essences and tinctures.

The forest teaches that everything is connected, from the smallest bacteria to the greatest of trees, and so it is with knowledge, each of us on our spiritual paths as well as our journeys through life. For this reason, whilst concentrating mainly on Celtic tradition, aspects of tree lore from other cultures around the globe are included where relevant for further elucidation and example. Nothing exists in a vacuum, and to fully understand and work with trees in a magical or spiritual context, we must consider the whole as much as the individual point of focus. The same remains true, in addition, about how we experience trees and tree lore. This is not a purely scholarly book, as we cannot fully comprehend the ogham from a purely intellectual perspective. We must approach the forest not as outside observers but as kin via relationship, interaction, and ultimately communion with the tree spirits themselves.

The Ogham Alphabet

The Celtic tree ogham is a mnemonic device and magical system whose origins are at least seventeen hundred years old. Ogham-inscribed stone monuments dating from the fourth century CE have been found all over Ireland, mostly in Kerry, Cork, and Waterford, as well as in Wales, Scotland, Orkney, the Isle of Man, and a small number in England.[1] However, some scholars believe the ogham to be perhaps centuries earlier in origin, with the scholar James Carney dating it to within the first century BCE.[2] Certainly its use on stone is sure to have vastly outlived any inscriptions that may have been on wood or other materials, which may or may not have been of an older date. One theory is that it developed, along with the Norse runes and within a similar time frame, in response to increased interaction with the Greeks and Romans, who unlike the Celts had a written script.

Ogham was used primarily to write in Primitive Irish as well as other Brythonic languages whose sounds were difficult to effectively transcribe

---

1   Damian McManus, *A Guide to Ogam* (Maytooth, IRL: An Sagart, 1991), 1.

2   James Carney, *The Invention of the Ogham Cipher* (Dublin, IRL: Royal Irish Academy, 1975), 57.

into Latin and Greek.[3] Another theory is that ogham was a deliberately cryptic alphabet used by druids as the religious and political leaders in Ireland in order to communicate without the knowledge of those writing in Latin and Greek in the politically sensitive era preceding and after the Roman invasion of Britain.[4]

Ogham is often called a "tree alphabet." Although this term has its merits, it can be misleading. In fact, the ogham is far more than a writing system. The ogham sigils are called *feda,* which means "trees," and sometimes *nin* "forking branches." The ogham as a whole is marked vertically upwards along a central stem and is described in the seventh-century CE *Auraicept na n-Éces* (*The Scholars' Primer,* the main text that survives today on the ogham) as a tree which is to be "climbed."[5] Furthermore, every letter or sigil has a tree or plant associated with it, referred to in the *Bríatharogaim* ("word ogham") texts which provide a *kenning* or short poetic description of the ogham's meaning. The Bríatharogaims reveal a clear relationship between each ogham sigil and its representative and companion tree or plant. Combined, these two form a relationship which becomes a mnemonic device for conveying a vast amount of knowledge and magical insight. In this way the ogham works on many levels simultaneously—as linguistic script, as a shorthand depository of ancient lore and insight, and finally as a magical and spiritual tool.

The word *ogham* itself is of uncertain origin. Irish mythology and the primary source for the ogham, *In Lebor Ogaim, The Ogham Tract* (as well as *The Scholars' Primer,* in which it is contained) tells us that the ogham script was created by the Irish god Ogma of the Tuatha Dé Danann, the primary gods of Ireland.[6] Ogma is likely to be the same or related to Ogmios, the Gaulish god of eloquence. Ogma has the epithet *grianainech*

---

3   McManus, *Guide to Ogam,* 4.

4   Carney, *Invention of the Ogham Cipher,* 62–63.

5   George Calder, ed. *Auraceipt na n-Éces, The Scholars' Primer* (Edinburgh, UK: Grant, 1917), 73.

6   Ibid., 273.

"sun face" attached to his name, and this may suggest that he is illuminated from within via embodying divine inspiration, known as *imbas* in the Irish or *awen* in the Welsh. Heroes and magicians throughout Celtic myth who are associated with attaining divine inspiration as a source for their magical power and prowess are often referred to as shining or luminescent in some way, such as the Welsh bard Taliesin, or "Shining Brow."

The Ogham Tract tells us that:

> *Ogma, a man well versed in speech and in poetry, invented the Ogham. The cause of its invention, as a proof of his ingenuity, and that this speech should belong to the learned apart, to the exclusion of rustics and herdsmen.*[7]

We are told that Ogma is the father of the ogham, and that the mother is the "hand or knife of Ogma" that inscribes it.[8] This is interesting, as it is not the scribe's quill that is referred to here, but the "hand or knife," suggesting its roots and purpose are not literary, but as we know it is inscribed with a knife onto wood or stone, or by the hand alone. We know that the Celts and druids did not use a linguistic script, and this suggests that the ogham's use was for far more mysterious purposes; it is a "speech"—a living thing for the conveying of information only used by the "learned," the druids, the magical and political lore keepers. Furthermore, as *The Ogham Tract* tells us, each ogham inscribed is performed by the hand of Ogma himself—thus every act concerning its use is performed according to the will of the god, with the practitioner by extension becoming the tool, the "hand or knife of Ogma" in turn. As such, it is a very magical and very powerful system indeed.

A further legendary origin for the ogham comes in the later eleventh-century *Lebor Gabála Érenn* (*The Book of the Taking of Ireland,* also known as *The Book of Invasions*). In this version, the ogham script is invented

---

7   Calder, *Scholars' Primer*, 273.

8   Ibid.

together with Gaelic by the legendary King Fenius Farsa at the fall of the tower of Babel, selecting the best details from the scattered languages that were found there.

Textual Sources

Ogham is mentioned in relatively few textual sources: medieval manuscripts which either duplicate or overlap each other, sometimes with notable variations and contradictions. The main source, *The Scholars' Primer* (*Auraicept na n-Éces*), is commonly believed to have been first recorded in the seventh century by a scholar named Longarad, but only later copies remain, the earliest being in the twelfth-century *Book of Leinster*, as well as the fourteenth-century *Book of Ballymote*. The other main source is *The Ogham Tract*, or *In Lebor Ogaim,* which is found preserved in numerous fragments in various fourteenth-century manuscripts, as well as a later sixteenth-century text, and is also included in part in *The Scholars' Primer*. *The Ogham Tract* includes a large number of ogham lists, not only relating to trees. For example, there is also bird ogham, dog ogham, hand ogham, and foot ogham, amongst others. Sadly, so little information survives about these that their use and meaning are incredibly obscure and almost unworkable. However, *The Ogham Tract* is also the main source for the Bríatharogaims, or "word oghams"—the poetic descriptions or kennings that elucidate the meanings of the main sigil-based ogham. Not every ogham letter or sigil name translates to the name of a tree or plant, but the Bríatharogaims successfully link each one to a tree or plant, hence its common description as a "tree alphabet."

The Bríatharogaims have three variant lists, each attributed to a different author. The first is by a character called Morainn mac Moín. Morainn (or Morann) was the chief judge and druid in Ulster during the mythical Irish Red Branch, or Ulster Cycle, which concerns the deeds of the hero Cuchulain, including the famous *Taín,* or "The Cattle Raid of Cooley." Although the main manuscript sources of the Red Branch cycle are mostly twelfth-century, scholars agree that it must have been transmitted orally for more than a thousand years, as it contains elements that describe faithful accounts of a remote Iron Age past in startling detail.[9] The second Bríatharogaims list is attributed to the god Oengus mac Óg, the Irish god of love. Both of these are contained within *The Ogham Tract*, whilst a third, attributed to the hero Cuchulain himself, is only preserved in later sixteenth- and seventeenth-century manuscripts, although this is no indication of it being of any less antiquity. Each of the Bríatharogaims is included in this book with each tree to assist the seeker with their own interpretations.

Mythological Sources

Ogham and its use is mentioned in many Celtic myths and folktales. According to *The Scholars' Primer*, the first message ever written in ogham was the sigil for birch, written seven times along a stave, to warn the god Lugh that his wife would be taken from him unless he watched over her.[10]

The use of ogham is mentioned numerous times in the Red Branch Cycle, mostly in the twelfth-century *Book of Leinster*, and the *Book of the Dun Cow* (also twelfth-century), but as already mentioned containing elements of an oral tradition going back as far as the Iron Age and potentially even earlier. These give tantalising implications for the antiquity of ogham that are sadly unlikely to ever be firmly proven. There are two instances of the ogham being used by the hero Cuchulain in the Táin. The first is when he took an oak sapling and twisted it into a hoop secured with a peg, upon which he carved ogham in order to warn the Ulstermen of the invading army of Connacht. He did this all this standing upon one leg and using only one hand and one eye, a posture used by many otherworldly being and druids in Celtic mythology—perhaps signifying that one half of him was in this world, while the other was in the spirit realm. The ogham reputedly said, "Come no further unless you have a man who

---

9   Peter Berresford Ellis, *A Dictionary of Irish Mythology*
     (London: Oxford Reference, 1991).

10   Calder, *Scholars' Primer*, 91.

can make a hoop like this with one hand out of one piece. I exclude my friend Fergus."[11] At a later part of the tale, Cuchulain also leaves ogham in the fork of a tree that he places in the middle of a river to hold back the army of Connacht; the message is emphasised by the four heads of Connacht warriors that he also hangs from the branches.

Ogham is also mentioned in the *Tochmarc Etain* (The Wooing of Etain) where a druid called Dalan uses ogham on four wands of yew for divination, each inscribed with three ogham sigils. This may be similar to a German technique of divination referred to by Tacitus in the first century CE. In the tale "Baile Mac Buain," a whole library of ogham is described on "rods of fili" (oracular poets) where whole sagas are recorded. Baile and his ill-fated lover die before their relationship is consummated, and upon their graves grow a yew and an apple tree that are later used to inscribe ogham stanzas.[12] In "The Voyage of Bran," we are told that Bran composed sixty quatrains of poetry in ogham on rods. These examples may perhaps refer to a now forgotten practice of using ogham to record important information in a condensed form. In the tale of Lomna in the Fenian Cycle, Lomna warns Fionn mac Cumhail of his wife's infidelity using the ogham.[13] At the funerals of heroes, ogham is inscribed upon rods of aspen to be buried alongside them.[14]

Ogham in mythology usually has magical uses (spells in particular), but like the surviving ogham stone inscriptions, it is also used to write messages and inscriptions of particular importance or for the use of leaders, gods, heroes, and magicians. The most notable are the *filid*, or oracular shaman poets who preserved much of the original Celtic oral tradition well into the Christian era. The Old Irish word *fili* (plural *filid*) is likely to come from the proto-Celtic word *widluios* meaning "seer." These were not purely

---

11   Thomas Kinsella, *The Táin* (London: Oxford University Press, 2002), 70.

12   Bernhard Maier, *Dictonary of Celtic Religion and Culture* (London: Athenaeum Press, 2000), 30.

13   Ellis, *Dictionary of Irish Mythology*, 188.

14   Ibid.

mythical characters but a historical elite class of Irish lore keepers, teachers, and healers, as well as oracular poets who took on much of the roles
of the earlier druids in their communities and were protected by law and
even given land. Their position was maintained in Ireland well into the
thirteenth century, and much of the Celtic lore that has survived is due to
their influence and work.

Nemeton: The Sacred Grove in Antiquity

Central to Celtic tree magic is the concept of the sacred grove. This was called a *nemeton* by the Gauls and Britons, and a *fidnemed* in Ireland from the proto-Celtic word *nemeto*, meaning "sacred place" or "sanctuary." The grove as a sacred enclosure was of prime importance to Celtic belief, venerated as the home and gathering place of powerful spirits as well as a meeting place of the three worlds, known in the Welsh tradition as Abred, Gwynfyd, and Ceugant. There is a wealth of archaeological, classical, and vernacular evidence for the use and presence of sacred groves across Europe, Britain, and Ireland. The Roman writers Tacitus, Pliny, and Lucan all write of shadowed groves with altars piled high with gruesome offerings. Lucan refers to a sacred grove near Marseille where the druids gave offerings of blood to the tree roots to appease the "barbaric gods."[15] Tacitus describes altars in the sacred grove at Anglesey that were covered in blood and entrails.[16] Cassius Dio refers to human sacrifice

---

15   Lucan, *The Pharsalia, Book III,* trans. H. T. Riley (London: H. G. Bohn, 1853), Kindle edition, 399–452.

16   Cornelius Tacitus, *The Annals, Book XIV*, trans. J. C. Yardley (London: Oxford University Press, 2008), 30.

at altars to the Icenian goddess of victory, Andraste, being ordered by the tribal queen Boudicca.[17] Yet these texts need to be taken into context; their viewpoint—of Roman conquerors writing home—is clearly biased. In fact, whilst there are many instances of unusual burial, there is relatively little clear evidence of human sacrifice within Celtic archaeology. Ideas about sacred groves are invariably tangled with other issues, ideas about politics, beliefs, and our modern perceptions of a warrior culture.

The Celts were headhunters, but the importance of heads in both ritual and warrior practice is often misunderstood. The severed head was prominent in Irish and British myth, and the heads of slain warriors of the tribe were used to protect sacred enclosures and to give wisdom and strength after the body had passed. The heads of enemies were also collected as totems of great power. In the Celto-Ligurian area of southern Gaul are several distinctive pre-Roman sanctuaries, the most important of which is a clifftop shrine north of Marseille at Roquepertuse dating to the sixth to fourth centuries BCE. This shrine had a portico housing the nailed-on skulls of young warriors who had died in battle.[18] In Britain, hill forts like the one at Bredon Hill in Worcestershire had severed heads mounted on poles at the gates as symbolic or magical protection.[19] Heads as the seat of the soul were the focal point of the person's spirit presence, and as such, of ancestral support and connection. This can be seen in the tale of Bran in the collection of Welsh legends known as the Mabinogion, where Bran's head entertained and brought luck to his companions for seven years before being placed on Tower Hill in London to watch over all Britain. The Irish hero Cuchulain also collected the heads of his enemies, which he placed upon stones both in honour and as a source of

---

17   Cassius Dio, *Rome, book LXII*, trans. Herbert Baldwin Foster, (New York: Parafets, 1905), 2.

18   Miranda Green, *Dictionary of Celtic Myth and Legend* (London: Thames & Hudson, 1997), 116.

19   Ibid.

power and pride for protection and the discouragement of his enemies.[20] These heads were supremely valuable and a sign of the deceased persons' worthiness (friend or foe), and their presence within a sacred grove must be seen in this context. As there is little physical evidence of widespread human sacrifice in Celtic custom, the few examples that have been found in groves and shrines are more likely to be the sacred heads of fallen warriors and leaders than the victims of unwilling sacrifice. Thus the grove housed the spirits of the ancestors and sometimes the trapped power of the tribe's enemies together with the powers of place, the spirits of tree, flower, soil, stone, and often water.

Sacred groves were often also places where there was a natural spring which was also venerated as sacred. This provided healing waters as well as another aspect of the liminal, where the worlds and the elements met and suffused one another, making magic and meaning from the numinous forces of nature. These sacred springs also received offerings and sacrifices, often coins and deliberately "killed" objects, such as freshly made broken swords and axes, as well as butter or produce. All sacrifices and offerings were objects of great value and importance.

Groves and other sanctuaries were usually enclosed or marked by circular or square trenches or post fences, and also contained votive items, often found in pits or ritual shafts. One example is the carved oak heartwood figures found, probably dedicated to the goddess Sequana, at Fontes Sequanae.[21] Other offerings, such as the bodies of humans and animals have also been found in such pits across Europe and Britain and are most likely to be efforts to contact and honour the spirits of the underworld, as well as the ancestors, and may indicate that the individuals concerned were being honoured in some way. These are also likely to be gifts to the "powers of place" resident in the very earth itself. Groves also have been found containing massive central trees or symbolic wooden posts. One such at

---

20   Ellis, *Dictionary of Irish Mythology*, 142.

21   Green, *Dictionary of Celtic Myth*, 164.

Goloring in Germany, dated as being in use during the sixth century BCE, had a colossal central post twelve meters high that was most likely a representative of the great World Tree itself.[22] Another at Libenice in Czechoslovakia, dated to the fourth century BCE, contained a huge post adorned with bronze torcs, symbols of power and prestige. These may well have embodied the guardian spirits of the tribe or location. Occasionally sites have been found with two central posts, perhaps suggesting they represented a divine and/or ancestral couple.

The Goddess Nemeton and the Divine Couple

The sacred grove was commonly presided over by the *genii loci*—resident gods and goddesses who granted blessings, healings, and justice—and guardian spirits who facilitated the people's connection with the divine in union with the priests/priestesses/druids, forming a line of connection. Often the goddess of the sacred grove was called *Nemetona*, literally meaning "goddess of the sacred grove." Evidence for the cult of Nemetona can be found across Europe and Britain, especially the Celto-Germanic tribe, the Nemetes.[23] Yet the name Nemetona is likely to be an overarching title, keeping the name of the resident goddess secret as a mystery teaching for her initiates. Nemetona was often worshiped together with Loucetius, the Romano-Celtic Mars, linked with not only war, but protection, healing, and agriculture. However, in Ireland, the most sacred trees were called *Bile*. Bile is the name of the Irish Celtic god of life and death, known as Bel and later Belinus in Britain.

Numerous Romano-Celtic inscriptions exist as dedications to Nemetona at several shrines across Europe and Britain. One in Bath reads: *"Peregrinus secundi fil civis trever Loucetio Marti et Nemetona vslm."* ("Peregrinus son of Secundus, citizen of the Treveri, for Loucetius Mars and Nemetona,

---

22   Green, *Dictionary of Celtic Myth*, 170.
23   Ibid., 160.

willingly and deservedly fulfilled his vow.")[24] Other inscriptions and altars to Nemetona also exist in Germany in the territories connected to the Treveri tribe, but it is known that she was venerated in Britain outside of Bath due to numerous place names being linked to her, such as Nemetostatio in Devon and Vernemeton in Nottinghamshire. Many Celtic religious practices show signs of Romanisation following the conquest of Britain in 43 CE and the earlier conquest of Gaul in 58–51 BCE. However, Roman customs and language often overlaid and merged with the indigenous beliefs and practices rather than destroying them. Despite Emperor Claudius outlawing druids in 54 CE, the practice continued in various forms far into the sixth century at least, in Ireland and Wales via the practices of the fili and the bards—oracular poets—although these were a sanitised and Christianised shadow of ancient practice.

Nemetona's presence in Celtic Europe is likely to have been widespread, as further inscriptions exist as do place names related to her and the sacred grove such as Nemetodorum in France and Nemetobriga in Spain, as well as the Celto-Germanic tribe the Nemetes and the Nemetatae mentioned by Ptolemy as living in northern Spain. She is often pictured in carvings as seated on a throne holding a sceptre of authority, so it is likely that she was also associated with the spiritual aspects of sovereignty and thus a goddess of the land, a role sometimes shared with male consort gods. This link with sovereignty can also be seen in the Irish god/hero Nemed, leader of the Nemedians who were the third mythical invaders of Ireland, and whose name also reflects the importance of the grove and its divinity. Nemed is the husband of the goddess Macha, another goddess of sovereignty as well as horses, thus suggesting the link to the sacred powers of the land once again.

A god frequently connected to Nemetona was Loucetius—"brilliance" or "lightning flash"—a Brythonic and Gaulish god of lightning who can be equated with the Welsh Lluch (*lluched*, "flashing light") or Llew, otherwise

---

24   Green, *Dictionary of Celtic Myth*, 160.

known as Llew Llaw Gyffes. Llew, the leader of a war party in the medieval poem attributed to Taliesin, the *Cad Goddeu* or "The Battle of the Trees" may be equated with the Irish Lugh, the god of light and skill, but Loucetius's link with lightning also links him with gods such as the Celtic Taranis, the thunderer. Gods of thunder and lightning were often connected to the sacred oak tree, and perhaps the Welsh Llew once had these associations as well. When an oak was struck by lightning, it became particularly sacred and powerful. Talismans and sacred objects were sometimes made of lightning-struck oak, as it was considered touched by the god, but such trees were also considered divine in their own right. At one point, gods of sun, light, and lightning were probably one and the same although they had different names attached to them. However, eventually they formed a cross-Celtic pantheon (and later a Romano-Celtic pantheon) with subtle changes over time and across regions. The god of lightning and the oak eventually became the oak king and the green man we know today, but his relationship to the goddess of the land is a continual tradition across the Celtic cultures from Europe to Ireland. Such gods had undoubted warrior aspects, but as already discussed they were also connected to protection, healing, and nature, developing into gods of agriculture as farming practices became increasingly sophisticated.

Nemetona's association with Loucetius/Llew equates her naturally to that romantic figure of Welsh myth, the flower goddess Bloddeuwedd.[25] Her tale can be found in the collection of Welsh myths contained in *The Mabinogion*, where it is said she was formed of flowers and sea foam by the Welsh wizards Gwydion and Math to be the bride of Llew llaw Gyffes. However, this is likely to be a patriarchal gloss over an earlier story, as Bloddeuwedd is said to attempt murdering Llew with her lover Gronw and is turned into an owl by Gwydion as punishment. This reveals Bloddeuwedd as a fierce and strong female character, a force of nature rather

---

25   Caitlín Matthews and John Matthews, *The Aquarian Guide to British and Irish Mythology* (London: Aquarian Press), 34.

than a passive creation of men. Her duality as flower maiden/owl woman shows her to be far more complex and probably a far more ancient goddess than the story suggests at first glance. There are several tales where a goddess is fought over by two male consorts who each have their divine roles, often related to summer and winter, or the world above and the underworld. This pattern can also be seen in the love triangle of King Arthur, Guinevere, and Lancelot, as well as in the tale of another goddess, Creiddylad, who is also associated with the land, spring, and flowers/fruit. She is due to wed the hero/god Gwythr ap Greidawl, but is abducted by the underworld hero/god Gwyn ap Nudd. The two heroes are set to fight every Beltane for the goddess's hand.

Nemetona was one of a far-reaching and long-lasting tradition of goddesses of the land with interchangeable names accompanied by interchangeable gods. This can be seen in the inscription found in Nettleham near Lincoln referring to Mars Rigonemetis ("Mars, King of the Sacred Grove").[26] As the public names of local secret deities, Nemetona and others represent overarching concepts of the goddess and god, in contrast to the experience of working with a specific sacred place, which formed the mystery teachings presented by the genii loci. These were carefully guarded as sources of power both for the tribe and the spiritual elite who served them. It is this experiential knowledge to which we will now turn.

---

26 Green, *Dictionary of Celtic Myth*, 144.

Into the Forest

Our knowledge of sacred groves in prehistory can be an enlightening force, showing us markers on the path to engaging these energies for ourselves. When we contact the spirits of the trees, we call in a whole set of related aspects: the spirits of earth and stone; the spirits of rain and wind, moonlight, sunlight; and the subtle presence of our magically adept ancestors whose consciousness can still be contacted in constant, timeless communion with the earth. We will also come into contact with the genii loci ("powers of place")—the guardian spirits of any or no spiritual race other than their own unique forms which guide and protect the environment and its spirit inhabitants (including the tree spirits), and help facilitate our work with them. These also act as "go-betweens" connecting us to even deeper energies, gods, and other beings. When we encounter these beings, we may receive visions, images, sounds, or symbols that act as energetic "keys" that unlock different realms. The genii loci also interact with our own energy field and ultimately with our souls; evolving, informing, and merging with our souls' purpose with far-reaching effects from this life into the next. These "keys" are well-worn paths trodden by mystics, seers, and those working with earth energies for millennia. It must be remembered that they are not aspects of our subconscious, and through they may be clothed with imagery from our minds, they exist regardless of our awareness. These energies interact with us as independent beings, and our awareness of the practices of our ancestors can inform our dialogue with them, educating us about the energetic language and forms this dialogue takes. Their experience of us is part of a continuous stream of interaction that has lasted for immense spans of time and adjusts only subtly over the years. In contrast to our fleeting impatient human consciousness, the spirits of nature, tree spirits, and related beings have a far wider and deeper awareness we need to slow into if our contact is to be fruitful.

We will now turn our attention towards working with trees and the wider forest in a way that is relevant to our spiritual practices today.

Exercise: Learning the Land

Naturally, to work with tree spirits requires regular practice out on the land itself; regular walks in woodlands are essential. Try to find a place that attracts you and can be visited regularly. Sitting still for an hour or calm and slow ambling gives you an opportunity to feel a resonance with a particular tree or group of trees. Allow your eyes to explore the environment in real detail, and look out for places which stand out to you—a group of birches lit by sudden sunlight, creaking branches overhead, or the shadowed boughs of an oak standing out in brooding darkness can all be markers to attract our interaction. Feel a resonance in your stomach, and be open to receiving guidance in whatever form it takes. Don't take it as a bad sign if you feel no guidance, as the ability to recognise spirit guidance fluctuates for everyone. Instead ask aloud to the powers of place to be led to a grove or tree that would welcome you. Let yourself wander to any tree that occurs to you.

Exercise: Aligning with an Individual Tree

When you have found a tree or group of trees to work with, approach slowly and allow the tree an opportunity to resist you. You may find you don't feel that comfortable there after all, and that's okay—move on. However, you may find that no sense of unease appears, and take that as a positive sign in itself. Take some time, gently touch the leaves, and speak to the tree announcing your desire to befriend it. Sometimes walking around the tree in a clockwise direction and spiralling inwards to the trunk is particularly effective at gently attracting the tree spirit's attention and harmonising with it, but this is not always possible due to other trees and bushes.

Approach the tree slowly, slowing your breathing and centering your awareness in your body. Make every step and movement conscious and sacred. Touch its bark, and spend some time standing against it. With every out breath, send your attention down into your feet and to the tree roots beneath and around you. Hold your awareness there. Then as you breathe in, send your awareness slowly up the trunk and into the branches. With full lungs, notice especially the rustling of the leaves in the canopy, any sounds—the wind, the birds, the swaying branches—or any silence and stillness there. Notice the light and shadow, the movements and patterns it makes, the forms the branches take, and the patterns the branches form as they cross each other from your point of view. Breathe out slowly again, sending your consciousness downwards. Don't look for meanings or verbal communication, just let your awareness totally absorb the scene around, above, and beneath you. Acknowledge the divinity present here, and send your care and respect to the consciousness of the tree spirit which you know to be standing before you. Whether you feel something clearly or not, this is an opportunity to *trust*, the first step in any real relationship. The rest will follow.

Repeat this process for a few minutes before settling down at the base of the trunk or somewhere suitably close and comfortable. Spend some more time just being physically present with the tree in easy companionship.

Invite the tree to be your ally and spirit companion, and ask it to communicate with you any needs it may have, and any way it would like to be communed with. Ask that it guide you in your understanding of trees, tree spirits, and other spirits of nature. Pay attention to any images you may receive in your mind's eye or inner vision in addition to other promptings and feelings—these may be communication from the tree spirit itself.

You may or may not get answers at this point, but it is important that you show the tree respect and a willingness to give it attention, support, and care just as you would like to give and receive from any friend. Develop this relationship consistently through weeks, months, and years, exploring different times of day and night. Over time, you may begin to notice differences.

Spirit Vision

To develop our awareness of tree spirits and other beings, it is essential that we develop our awareness of existence in their reality, and propagate an understanding of the unseen on its own terms. This requires exercise on two levels, the inner and outer. Our inner vision is strengthened by shamanic journeying, which allows us to alter our consciousness so that we can take spirit flight and encounter the spirit realms whilst our body remains in our awareness but no longer at the forefront of our minds. The other way of developing our awareness is to practice overlaying our usual consciousness and everyday vision with our spirit vision, a practice often called "seership." This is a gift that often runs in families as well as one that continues through reincarnations from one life to the next, as it forms a key part of the soul's evolution. However, it is also a skill that can be encouraged, as can shamanic flight or "journeying." Both these abilities alter our consciousness as well as affecting the body's subtle energies. Working together, they are a deep well of spiritual energy and support that allows us to move beyond the constraints of the mundane world. We can access the primal and divine energies of the planet and beyond.

Some people like to journey to recorded drumming made specifically for shamanic flight, and there are many recordings available. Others are lucky enough to have someone drum for them. Shamans also use bells and rattles for the same purpose. The simple repetitive beat mimics our heartbeat and gently aligns our pulse with its rhythm, which guides us to our destination and back. Percussive beats are not essential for shamanic journey, however, and it is good to experiment with and without to notice the differences and to be able to work effectively with a minimum of equipment and preparation. Slow, steady breathing has the same effects upon our consciousness and creates a slow rhythm of its own. In a sense, we are moving our spirits along the threads or currents of energy that connect all existence to our chosen destination. This is a perfectly natural thing to do, and is a skill we are born with; we are merely encouraging our natural ability, coaxing it from beneath layers of modern culture that lead us away from this deep knowing.

Exercise: Basic Shamanic Journey—
The Otherworld Forest and the Inner Tree Spirit Ally

Central to our magical work with trees is our connection to tree spirits. Fostering a connection with tree spirits on the inner planes, known in the Celtic tradition as the otherworld, is vital. Though very simple, it requires practice and patience to build these relationships over time, and if we are not experienced in journeying it is also essential to build this central skill and develop clear and effective inner vision. This exercise helps us make the first steps into these realms and initiate these relationships safely in a way that allows clear and sometimes even verbal communication.

This basic exercise can be performed within a circle or sacred space during ceremony or quite simply with minimum preparation. It is best repeated many times to build up relations with your primary tree ally before moving off the path or encountering other tree spirits in the otherworld forest. To begin, invocations may be made together with offerings given to assisting spirits, and attention given to stating the purpose of the journey beforehand. For example: "I call upon my guardians and allies to assist me to commune with my tree spirit ally" or "to encounter the spirits of the forest." A suitable offering for a tree spirit when at home would be a bowl of blessed spring water, but offerings are not always necessary, so draw upon your intuition and instinct. Don't feel you have to give offerings all the time or just to visit them, but offerings are good practice and help in building those relationships, as does giving thanks and respect.

Settle yourself preferably upon the floor, in a suitably comfortable position that you can maintain easily for up to twenty minutes. Some prefer to lie down when journeying but this can encourage sleep, and sitting up also assists in keeping the intention and focus of the journey clear. Also make sure you will be warm enough, and can be undisturbed for a suitable length of time.

With closed eyes, focus your attention on your breathing, feeling each breath in the pit of your stomach. With each breath, detach yourself from your inner chatter and daily concerns. Then as clearly as possible, visualise a simple oak door or gate with high hedges on either side. Spend time contemplating this gateway as the entrance to the great forest that exists in spirit, endlessly and eternally.

This great forest spans all lands and all ages. It moves and grows according to its own nature, like an infinitely huge collective being, roaming across the many layers of creation, expanding here, contracting there, but undiminished regardless of anything humans could ever do to its physical manifestations in the mortal world. The great forest is a spirit place in its own right, and while many beings and other destinations can be found via the paths and tracks across its vast wilderness, it is in itself perfect and may be an inexhaustible source of renewing and vitalising energies if we respect it. The beings encountered within the great forest are perfectly real and subject to their own customs and laws. We should always treat them with respect and use the same caution we would when encountering anyone we do not know. In time, allies of many kinds may be found within the forest and can assist in all manner of workings and practical as well as spiritual issues, but here at the gateway we must remember that we are exploring another realm of existence. We must move forward wisely, follow well-trodden paths, and adhere to the timeworn customs in order to draw the best from the experience. With that in mind, we announce our intention to discover our first tree ally, or indeed to visit it again. We ask that our steps be guided and blessed, and that the great forest supports our work. With that, we visualise ourselves stepping forward and opening the gate, passing through into the forest beyond.

On the other side of the gate, we see that we are standing upon a cleared path of pale stone that winds its way ahead through the trees. Notice if it is day or night, and what trees line the way. What season is it here? Pay attention to any sounds you may hear. Are there any birds? Does the wind blow through the branches? Are there other plants or animals here? Look down at your feet and try to feel the ground beneath them.Step forward and trust that this path will lead you through the forest to the tree and tree spirit that will be your primary tree spirit ally.

Try to take note of any details that appear in your journey, as they will form part of the forest's communication with you as well as being spirits in their own right that may guide or assist you. However, some beings may also challenge and even test you. Not all beings in the forest are friends of humans, and you must be aware that not everything is there for your benefit. If you stick to the path and maintain your focus, you will not encounter real difficulties, and by calling on your allies (even those you may not have consciously encountered yet), you will always receive the assistance you need.

Eventually, the path will lead you towards a specific tree that will stand out in your focus to a far greater degree than any other you have seen. If you doubt yourself and go past the tree, it will reappear in your vision no matter how much farther on you go. If you return from your journey without thinking you have found it, journey again and you will discover that you have seen the tree before in the previous journey; it will feel somehow familiar. Trust that your tree ally is waiting for you to approach. When you find it in your inner vision, greet it as a true friend and reach out to it, touch its leaves as with a physical tree, and approach its trunk. Take a few breaths merely being in the company of the tree, and ask for its spirit to reveal itself to you. It may take many forms, not necessarily human in shape or temperament. Be open to seeing the tree spirit as it wishes to present itself to you. Enter into simple dialogue with it—commune with this being and ask how you may contact it again. Perhaps it will have a symbol for you to visualise or a gift to give you that will call it to your mind when you wish its company. Give it the gift of your friendship. Ask if there are any ways that you can assist it and how it would like to commune with you. Spend some time exploring this new relationship. After some time has passed or when your accompanying drumming calls you back, you will feel as though the appropriate amount of time has passed and you can now return to the physical world. Thank the tree spirit for its assistance and friendship, and return along the path that led you to the gate in the high hedges.

Cross back through the gate, knowing as you do this you are returning fully to your body. Take a few breaths with your eyes shut, feeling yourself to be back in your body and in the present time and space. Clench and unclench your hands and feet. Open your eyes. The journey has now finished.

As with other workings, after shamanic journeying it is a good idea to write a record of what you have experienced. Writing may help ground the realisations and wisdom acquired into your daily life, as well as draw to mind details you may have forgotten but which reemerge in the writing. Always ground yourself after journeying into your body and the present moment. You can try eating, drinking, and moving your body about a little to reorient yourself in the everyday world.

The Inner Grove

Building a relationship with a tree spirit ally using inner vision develops a whole set of shamanic skills, and it is an important first step in working magically with trees in the outer world. It fine-tunes our senses and widens our perceptions to encompass these intelligences that operate beyond our everyday awareness. The natural next step is to widen the exercise further to encounter a magical grove—a collective of tree spirits and accompanying beings, a sacred space in the otherworld within its eternal forest. As already discussed, our druid ancestors and earlier Pagan nature worshippers held the grove as a place of great sanctity and connection, and many modern druids have begun to repopulate our landscape with consciously planted groves and reestablish working groves in woodlands already matured. These are all wonderful and essential ventures, restoring our long-held connection with tree spirits and nature with wide spread positive effects. However, spirit groves— found in numerous otherworld locations and traditions—remain as an eternal presence merely waiting for us to connect with their deep wisdom and healing energy. Many druid and other magical working groups have their own inner groves on the otherworldly planes, and it is a simple thing for individuals to do the same and find their own inner groves to work with in spirit, forming relationships and performing magical work in that primal divine place as well as within the everyday world.

Exercise: The Guardian and the Inner Grove

Begin this shamanic journey in the same way you would prepare to meet your tree spirit ally. Create a sacred space in a way that feels appropriate; set up a circle or sanctify your space in some other way, such as by lighting a candle, for example. Percussive accompaniment is not essential, but you can use drumming if it helps you. Before starting your journey, verbally announce your intention to discover your inner grove, your place of magic and sanctuary within the forest. This will be a place of connection and peace. You will develop relations with several tree spirits and the guardian of the grove. This guardian will instruct you, support your growth, and help connect you with other beings further from human consciousness. With time it is possible to build these relationships to a point where for short periods of time you may as a group become greater than the sum of your individual parts, forming a spirit alliance of incredible power and positive, healing, transforming potential.

Take several deep breaths. When you are ready, visualise the oak doorway or gateway to the great forest ahead of you. Take a few moments to acknowledge this place and moment as the beginning of your journey, and then pass through into the forest. See clearly before you a distinct shimmering path of pale stone winding its way through the trees ahead. This path will lead you to your tree spirit ally first and your sacred grove second. Call upon your allies and the great forest itself to assist you and guide your way. Follow the path.

You will be met by your primary tree spirit ally, who may or may not be with its accompanying tree. If you follow the path and your ally's instructions, you will find yourself approaching a special sacred place. There may be some kind of threshold, ditch and bank, gate, or path through two trees that facilitates passage into a deeper and more sacred part of the forest. Or the threshold may simply be a transition between a densely wooded area that opens up to a clearing. Each grove is unique, developing organically rather than following a set pattern. When you approach this threshold, greet the place itself, bow in acknowledgment, or give some other sign that you respect and honour this most sacred place. Take the guidance of your allies and your inner promptings.

You may now be approached by the guardian of the grove. Again, this is always a unique experience, and the guardian may appear in any form. You may also be challenged or asked questions before being granted admittance. The guardian may have a gift for you or words of advice. Respond honestly and openly, allowing whatever response rises out from you. Sometimes this first interaction may take the form of an ancient and ritualised sequence that has little to do with logical thought, so don't think too much about your response. That said, make sure you record it later for further consideration. Sometimes guardians don't appear at first, and this is okay—just enter respectfully. You will meet the guardian somewhere within the grove at a point specifically suitable for you. Just ask to meet the guardian and consciously explore the grove with this end in mind.

Accompanied by your allies and the guardian if they choose to come with you, enter into the grove and begin to explore it, beginning by walking clockwise around the area and spiralling gradually inwards unless you are directed otherwise. Try to greet every single tree, and make a point of trying to acknowledge every being in the area. Other beings may take the forms of trees, other plants, stones, springs, and spirit beings of every conceivable description. Some part of the grove will hold something, someone, or be a place of particular sanctity. This element will form a key part of the work to be done there, for it is the grove's secret; discovering it or being led to it may take several visits. Again, the experience will be unique to every person and grove, and the process cannot be rushed or explained in logical or linear terms.

After spending some time exploring, seat yourself upon the earth in the grove, and just "be" with the experience. Allow space for spirit to unfold or occur, and allow your energy to harmonise with this sacred place. After a while, thank your allies and the grove, paying particular mind to thanking the guardian. Return to the everyday world following the path the way you came. Remember to ground yourself afterwards by eating and drinking, and make sure you record the details of your journey in your journal.

This journey should be repeated frequently. With repeated visits, you will be establishing your otherworldly relationships, enabling more focused work when these relationships are strong and your ability to focus and dwell in the otherworldly grove has developed sufficiently for more specific work to take place there. Advanced magical and healing work within the grove may occur spontaneously when these skills have developed to an appropriate degree, and every visit will build upon the previous in an organic pattern of growth.

Energy Raising

Tree magic relies on positioning ourselves within the natural order, on communion and cooperation rather than domination of any kind. By seeing ourselves as part of a natural whole, we may draw upon the energy and intention of a collective of harmonious intelligences working together. To that end, we energise ourselves in the same way as our allies and move our consciousness into ever greater harmony with the earth. Thus we draw upon earth energy to empower and heal us, and use it to energise our magical and healing work. In this way we access the energy of "the Source"—the ever-powerful creative impulse—as manifesting in the earth itself, the Source as Earth Goddess. Ever nurturing and life-giving, the earth as goddess gives forth and supports all life that we know. This in turn forms a partnership with solar and lunar energy, but these are secondary in energetic terms. To explore energy raising with regard to tree spirits, it is essential our connection to the earth energy is primary in our focus and given the utmost respect. Disconnection from earth energy has led to humans regarding the earth as merely a resource to use in order to facilitate unsustainable lifestyles and greed-driven ambition. The earth becomes merely our dumping ground, and our relationship to the earth and all nature spirits is damaged as well as our environment. To align ourselves once again with the Earth Goddess is to restore this relationship and return to harmony and reverence for the divinity that is our home and birthright.

Figure 1: Tree Spirit Alignment

Drawing upon earth energy is as simple for us as it is for the trees. It is ever-present and offered to us freely, just like a mother's love for her children. When we draw in this energetic nourishment, we effect positive changes in our energy and physical bodies, healing and rebalancing, restoring our place in the natural energetic web of life.

Exercise: Earth Energy Raising

This type of exercise is popular in many traditions, and it can be fine-tuned to take into consideration your own inner promptings and experience, but the core skills are perfectly simple and widely used. This is particularly good to know when learning, because you are performing a time-worn magical exercise. The accompanying energies support you throughout your practice.

Position yourself standing comfortably upon the earth, feet approximately hip width apart, and take several deep breaths. Feel your feet firmly upon the ground, and then send your attention farther beneath them, deep into the earth. Sense or imagine a deep well of inexhaustible energy in the earth, impossibly far beneath you, and spend some time contemplating this as the vast beating heart of the goddess. It is immensely powerful and tirelessly compassionate to all living things. Give your heartfelt thanks to the Earth Goddess, and visualise a channel of this energy drawn from the goddess welling up through the earth towards you.

See yourself as having energetic "roots," extensions of your own energy field burrowing through the earth towards this energy, and find that the two connect very swiftly and easily, merging into one. These roots draw up the energy from the goddess into your body just as a tree draws in water. Feel this energy rising into your feet, warm and golden. Then let this energy fill farther up your body, rising up through your legs, and surging up your spine, activating all your energy centres. Feel it rise up your waist and into your chest where it meets your heart—the energy naturally increases. Then let the energy flow into your arms and shoulders, into your hands, and up your face till it tingles in your hair. In your inner vision you can see yourself as a glowing golden being, linked by an energetic umbilical to the heart of the goddess, an extension of her and the earth itself. Continue to breathe deeply and remain bathed in the energy for a while, letting it heal and energise you.

This exercise will have many subtle effects on your energy field and soul progress, but it can also have positive effects upon the physical body and your state of mind. It has deep healing power that should not be underestimated. Regular use has profound effects and is an essential core practice before directing this energy for further work.

This exercise can be performed indoors, even in upper stories of buildings, as the energy itself rises with equal ease through structures as through rock and soil, although allowing extra time for your perceptions to be able to sense it without your mind getting in the way can help. Practice and patience are the keys.

Exercise: Drawing Energy from Above

The next skill to develop is drawing energy from above—the sun, moon, and stars. Individual perceptions differ when calling in energy from above, but intention, as well as the condition of the sky above you, are important factors to what energy is drawn down. Sunlit days are easiest to connect with solar energy, although it is ever-present. Full moons naturally encourage "drawing down the moon" and inviting the moon goddess to descend and send her energy into the body. Clear starlit nights encourage star connection, but any or all of these can be called upon as general "universal" or nonterrestrial energy.

This exercise can be performed without any earth connection, but doing so can lead to some very spaced-out and inflated perceptions, as the "universal" energy is drawn down without any context to position it within a mortal human body. Instead it is better to copy the trees, and hold both earth and sky energy in balance, mirroring the tree's roots, trunk, and branches.

Therefore this exercise is performed *in addition* to raising earth energy as a natural extension of that practice. First, draw the energy from the heart of the earth, and feel it filling your whole being. The energy rises up your spine and radiates across your chest and arms before rising farther to the top of your head. As this occurs, gently raise your arms and send your attention above you into the sky. Although you may feel some muscular tension, keep your arms raised, as this helps to prevent the energy from dissipating into the universe. Focus on feeling the sun or moonlight upon you and call it into your body, to merge with the earth energy within you. When earth energy has been raised, energy from above is naturally attracted to meet it, and at this point visions or sensations may occur, as these two distinct vibrations and divine intelligences merge within you. Feel the energy from above pour into your body, merging with the earth energy in your heart, where it naturally increases and shines out like a star. Gently lower your arms to chest level and hold them there for as long as possible. Further energy pours down through your body, blending harmoniously with the earth energy, both being held within you.

Hold this position and energetic state in your consciousness for as long as possible, breathing deeply and slowly into your belly. Feel it energise and empower you. Feel it nurturing your soul and your connection to the universe, aligning you with your soul's path and your original divine state of perfect health and awareness. The star in your heart is your divine spark, the conception point between earth and sky, which reminds your whole body, mind, emotions, and energy field of your soul's potential and natural divinity. This place is the core of your connectedness to all creation, the source of your power. Remember this, and hold this knowing in your body—calmly, gently, and confidently. After a while, slowly lower your arms, thanking both earth and sky for their blessing and energy. Imagine the connection from above gently retreating and the energy from below in the earth gently easing, but the energy in your body remaining. See yourself as full and whole.

Complete this exercise by grounding back into normal life—eat and drink, and record any experiences or sensations in your journal. If earthing feels difficult, spend an additional few minutes with your hands as well as your feet in contact with the ground, letting your energy settle.

As with raising earth energy, regular practice has powerful and entirely beneficial effects upon your energy field and subtle effects upon your body, such as greater vitality. This exercise is particularly powerful when performed in a high place, such as a hilltop. When performing indoors, as with earth energy raising, simply allow that the energy is not blocked by the building, flowing with equal ease above and below.

Offerings

The tradition of giving offerings to tree spirits goes back millennia, as a form of ritualised exchange which is invaluable when building a relationship with these venerable beings. As already discussed, there is some evidence to suggest that the blood of enemies was once poured onto the roots of sacred trees. In the West Country of Britain is a tradition, going back many hundreds of years at least, of offering *clooties* (Scots for "cloth")—strips of ribbon or cloth—to a tree, tying them onto the branches with a prayer. This is particularly common at trees near holy wells, and the practice was once part of a magical healing technique where the cloth was soaked in holy spring water and used to lave the body of the sick or disturbed.

These days it is always important to consider our environmental impact, and sadly many such sacred trees have become sites of excessive rubbish and non-biodegradable clooties, such as candy wrappers being given as offerings. For this reason, we must rethink our traditions, and today there is no better offering than clearing a site of rubbish, being careful to leave the energy of any offerings with the tree should you take the physical matter away for disposal. This can be done by verbally asking the tree and cutting the energetic threads binding the offering with a knife using your inner vision so that the tree retains the prayers' intentions without the physical object. Alternatively, offerings of water or sacred dance or song are excellent choices. When it comes to offerings, always try to sense the will of the tree spirit itself and heed your intuition. Remember to be practical and environmentally conscious. In this way we build a relationship with special trees, and do no harm.

The Ogham Trees

We will now turn to each of the twenty original ogham trees in turn. They are traditionally grouped into four *aicmes* or tribes, each named after the first tree in their group.

We therefore have the aicme of *beith*, or birch; the aicme of *huath*, or hawthorn; the aicme of *muin*, or blackberry; and the aicme of *ailm*, or pine. For each tree we will be covering their kennings (word oghams)—poetic clues to their meanings and significance, their botanical description, lore and legend of each tree, practical and magical uses, a tree's uses in healing, and its divinatory meaning. We should remember that each tree is a distinct being, and each type of tree will have its own general attributes with variations present in each individual plant of its genus. While practical, magical, and herbal attributes remain constant for each type of ogham tree, every tree spirit we encounter will in addition have its own personality and unique qualities. Let this guide to the ogham trees be just that—a guide to help you in understanding and elucidating your own experiences with the trees themselves.

The Aicme of Beith

Birch/Beith (*Betula alba/Betula pendula*)

⊢

....
Other names:
Beth, berke
....

Word ogham of:
Morainn: *Féochos foltchaín*
"Withered foot with fine (fair) hair"

Cuchulain: *Mais malach.i.creccad*
"Browed beauty, worthy of pursuit"

Oengus: *Glaisem cnis* "Greyest/most silver of skin"[27]

---

27   McManus, *Guide to Ogam*, 43.

Description

Birch is a fast-growing deciduous tree that grows up to thirty metres. The branches, angled upwards, tend to bow at the tips, lending graceful curves to its shape. Its triangular double-toothed leaves grow on alternate sides of the stem. The slender female green catkins form on the same tree as the male yellow-brown ones, and both form in the months of April and May, and fall in September. The silver birch has distinctive, beautiful bark. Starting as reddish brown when very young, it turns pinkish or white with grey horizontal markings and darker scales. It has deep fissures at the base of the tree—hence Morainn's poetic kenning for the tree as "withered foot with fine hair." Birch grows in a wide variety of environments, from open woodland, fens, bogs, heaths, and wastelands to mountainous regions (although this is rare and numbers are often limited in other areas due to competition with other trees). A pioneer tree, it was one of the first trees to populate an area after the receding Ice Age. Birch is relatively short-lived, providing nutrients for other slower growing trees which usually colonise an area after it has prepared the soil. Its pioneering, self-sacrificing qualities are a clue to its magical nature. Birch is hardy against frost even when young, one of the first trees to flower in spring, and has long been associated with beginnings and fresh starts. Silver birch grows widely in continental Europe, Ireland, the UK, and Scandinavia, as well as southwest Asia and the US.

Lore and Legend

One of the seven peasant trees according to the Brehon law, birch nonetheless occupies a special position in the Celtic tradition. According to legend, the first ogham ever written was beith, written seven times to create a warning and magically protective talisman on a sliver of birch, by the god Ogma to warn the god Lugh that his wife was taken away by the *sidhe* (the Irish for faeries).[28] For this reason the birch is always considered to be full of the god

---

28   Calder, *Scholars' Primer*, 273.

Lugh's light, bringing clarity and chasing away stagnant energy and shadows within and without. Birch is often associated with light, particularly moon- and starlight, reflected in its silver bark. Birch twigs are also used as witches' besoms (brooms) which are used for ritually cleansing a space and are also used for "flying" in the pursuit of shamanic vision, due to the magical light that is believed to be in the wood. The use of brooms, clearing the old to make way for the new, reveals a key quality of the birch: preparing for and supporting newly emergent growth and circumstances. Its connection to beginnings is so strong due to the fact that the tree itself is self-sowing, creating its own groves. The Siberian Yakut people also connected the birch with light, believing that the creator of light, Ai Toyon, dwelt in a birch with eight branches which supported nests filled with children.[29]

Traditionally the birch is used for purification and the cleansing of negative spirits, sometimes in the practice of "birching" or flagellation to remove negative energy from the body as well as toxins, and also to force out negative entities and correct "misdeeds."

It is said that birch was used to beat Christ, and Roman soldiers carried *fasces* in advance of important officials, which were made of birch stalks enclosing an axe. These symbolised the power to punish by flogging with the birch sticks as well as to execute by the axe. As such, the birch can be associated with the concepts of law and punishment as well as healing and renewal. Birch was also used to "beat the bounds" where the boundaries of an area were ritually beaten with birch to enforce and clear the parish or village boundaries. Beating the bounds was considered a purifying behavior that removed negative influences and created a fresh start for the community within. Sometimes boys would be beaten at the boundaries to enforce the cleansing, and in some parishes,

---

29   Gary Varner, *The Mythic Forest, The Green Man and the Spirit of Nature* (New York: Algora, 2006), 57.

council officials would be carried to a hole and dipped headfirst at the boundary line, both an echo of earlier Pagan sacrificial rites.[30]

Birch is known as the "white tree," and it lends purity and renewed vitality wherever it grows or is used with magical intent. The English poet Coleridge called birch "the lady of the wood," and it is usually believed to be a very feminine tree. Considered to be under the rulership of the planet and goddess Venus, birch has a gentle, fresh energy that may seem at odds with its use in chastising and banishing qualities.[31] Although it is often connected with autumn and the festival of Samhain, the Celtic new year, it also has strong associations with spring, and Samhain's sister festival, Beltane, on May 1. Birch was the chosen tree for the maypole in Wales, as well as the fuel for the Beltane fires, which were jumped for blessing, cleansing, and fertility. Cattle were led between the Beltane fires to bless and protect them for the rest of the year. Wreaths of birch were also used as tokens for romance and initiating courtship. Basque witches used birch oil (birch bud, *Betula alba*) for love spells, and it was traditional in Basque country to offer a birch twig in order to initiate courtship; this lends a further clue to its uses—it attracts fresh, fertile energy and shows the links between the Celtic traditions of the Basque and those of the insular Celts in Britain and Ireland.

Despite its gentleness and the delicate atmosphere it creates, the birch has immense vitality that is a powerful initiator for change. It is unstoppable in its gradual forward movement; it pushes stagnant energy away, disintegrating it within its path. This tree restores the flow of life force and encourages flexibility of mind, body, and spirit, which makes future stagnation less likely to recur. Sacred to Norse goddesses Frigga and Freya, it is also associated with Bloddeuwedd, the Welsh goddess of flowers and springtime, whose other side is the owl huntress, illustrating the birch's dual

---

30   Alan Cleaver and Leslie Park, "Beating the Bounds," *Strange Britain* (http://www .strangebritain.co.uk/traditions/bounds.html).

31   Nicholas Culpeper, *Culpeper's Complete Herbal* (London: Fousham, 1939), 50.

nature. These goddesses can be wild and fierce as well as gentle and loving, and the same can be said of the birch. It assists change gently and mercifully, but when resistance is encountered it has a fierce strength which will see that change occurs regardless. The spirit of the birch is a boundary guardian which both constrains and initiates, just as new beginnings require appropriate work and preparation. Cuchulain calling the birch "browed beauty, worthy of pursuit" suggests the serious but worthwhile and attractive challenge of creating a genuine fresh start.

Birch's association with the boundaries between realms or states can be seen in the Scottish border ballad "The Wife of Ushers Well," in which spirits of the dead wear birch twigs to protect them from being blown away by the world's wind—that is, the energy of the living denying them presence in the physical world.[32] Faeries and the faery realm are also connected to birch trees, growing in the areas where many worlds meet, a place on the cusp of things.

Across the Northern Hemisphere, birch was considered as the World Tree in the earliest cultures, and was used as ridgepoles in various structures, symbolising the sky-supporting cosmic pole around which the world turned. The Siberian Buryat people call it *Udesi Burkhan*—"the guardian of the door" which opens the way to the sky realms for the shaman.[33] Before such astral journeys are undertaken, a young birch is placed inside their yurt to represent the cosmic axis. Nine notches are cut in the birch's side to represent the nine celestial planes, and it is decorated with red and blue ribbons that connected it to other birch poles outside. Tartar shamans also believed a birch tree stood at the centre of the world, and it has been suggested by scholars that the Eurasian Birch was the original Tree of Life as it appeared in India and the Near East. In all these cultures, the birch has a relationship with the hallucinogenic fly agaric mushroom, which has

32   Francis James Child, *The English and Scottish Popular Ballads, Volume 1* (Mineola, NY: Dover, 2003), 238.

33   Mike Williams, *The Shaman's Spirit: Discovering the Wisdom of Nature, Power Animals, Sacred Places and Rituals* (London: Watkins, 2013), 81.

been used by shamans and witches for centuries, believed to be both a central ingredient in the famous "flying ointment" of British and European witches, and the much-earlier appearing sacred drink, the legendary Soma, which is praised in the *Rig Veda* for giving visions to both humans and gods alike. Although fly agaric is now relatively rare, it was once common across the north of Asia, America, and Europe. It usually grows at the foot of birch (and sometimes pine) trees, but shows itself above the surface soil as startling faerytale red mushrooms with white spots, for just two weeks or so in autumn. It is this that may have linked the birches magical significance with the festival of Samhain, when the mushroom could have been used to aid in the shamanic travel the birch facilitated.

Birch trees have long been used for purification and removing bad luck. In Russia, birch trees had a dual nature; deep in the forests, they were the dwelling places of the *leshy*, fearsome faery folk who lived in their branches. Yet these beings also removed curses, and for this purpose birch trees were dressed as women and fed from a feast which was held at its feet at Whitsun.[34] The tree was then cut down, carried home, and treated as an honoured guest until thrown in the river, having drawn away negative influences from the home and community. The tree was also used by Dutch farmers, who decorated the tree with red and white ribbons to protect the farm from evil influences and protect the crops and livestock.

The Chippewa revered the birch as sacred to their mythical hero Wenebojo, who formed their culture and taught them how to live. It is said that Wenebojo was once pursued by thunderbirds and he took refuge in a hollow fallen birch, which the birds could not touch. Because of Wenebojo's blessings, it is said that the birch is never struck by lightning and the patterns on its bark are pictures of the thunderbirds created by Wenebojo himself. This connection with thunder and lightning is echoed in Norse mythology where the birch is sacred to the thunder god Thor.

---

34   James George Frazer, "The Relics of Tree Worship in Modern Europe," chapter 10 in *The Golden Bough* (http://www.sacred-texts.com/pag/frazer/gb01000.htm.)

Practical and Magical Uses

Birch wood is very tough and flexible. It is good for carpentry and has been used to make tools, furniture, cradles, and of course, besom brooms. Birch has also been used to make charcoal that produces a high heat which can be used in metalworking. The bark makes good kindling, and is also invaluable for traditional tanning.

The Chippewa make use of birch bark for all manner of storage containers and wrappings, and they used hollowed-out birches as canoes; the bark is very flexible and waterproof. Harvesting the bark and wood was only ever done after making prayers to the spirit of the birch, with offerings of tobacco to each of the cardinal directions.

Birch bark was used for similar purposes across Scandinavia, and the Finnish hero Vainamoinen was said to have a magical harp, the *kantele*, which was also made of birch.

Birch bark can be burnt for energetic auric and physical purification, a practice long used by the Dakota Sioux.

Birch is an excellent choice for carving runes or ogham sigils, and its bark is perfect for parchment for domestic, artistic, or magical use. The oil is excellent for love spells, and it can be used to anoint candles or diluted to wear as a magical perfume. Burning birch bark or dried leaves make a good incense for love spells as well as cleansing and purification.

Offerings of birch wreaths can be made to water spirits to ask that storms or excessive rain be delayed or averted, and birch wands may be used when invoking Freya or Thor.

Due to its associations with springtime and fertility, birch can be used to decorate the sacred space at Beltane and the spring equinox, and it can be called upon to help invoke other gods and goddesses of fertility and light such as Eostre, Bel, Oengus, and the Dagdha. It is also a supreme tree to assist in calling Lugh, and to invoke protection against and the banishment of darkness.

Healing

Birch is considered to be one of the most healing trees—its suppleness, its ability to draw large amounts of water, and its white bark symbolising purity all allude to its healing properties. It is astringent and diuretic, good for skin problems, sore throats, and chest congestion when used via steam inhalation. It is an effective germicide, and water bored from the trunk was a traditional tonic to break up kidney stones and heal bladder problems. The buds can be eaten for stomach problems and it aids digestion.[35] It is useful as an insect repellent and is sometimes used in perfumery. The oil has a leathery aroma and has much the same uses. Leaves should be gathered in spring, and the sap is best tapped in April. One of its modern believers was Rudolph Steiner, who actively promoted its use in holistic medicine. It is said to demineralise the tissues and promote suppleness, and anthroposophic physicians now recommend taking birch elixir as a tonic in spring.

As a vibrational essence, birch helps bring hope and innovative thinking, sometimes encouraging purification before a breakthrough. It encourages a pioneering attitude and the courage to move on from ossified circumstances. It helps the introverted to step out of the crowd. It brings renewal and springtime to the spirit. It aids in clear thinking and clarity of purpose whilst providing the energy and confidence to embark on new adventures.

Ogham Divination Meaning

As an ogham, beith counsels proper preparation and support of new emergent energies by making way and clearing out the old or negative influences. Its renewing energy must be respected by a phase of recognition of its position—the now in between the past and the future. It encourages self discipline and inner authority. Birch asks you to check your motivations and purpose, insisting that you clear away old, stuck patterns and energies if a new start is to be achieved.

---

35   Maud Grieve, *A Modern Herbal* (Surrey, UK: Merchant, 1973), 104.

Journal Entry: The Birches of the Honister Pass, Cumbria

The birch tree is always a light bringer. The silver birches here stand out as beacons in the shadows of the mountains. Their palest fresh green leaves just unfurling on their black branches are a promise that spring is really here at last, even if the cold winds still blow. There is one birch tree that stands alone, and the light about it seems to shimmer with life and magic. Sitting at the base of the tree, I can feel the green fire of spring rising up from the earth. Sitting in peace and silence, eyes closed, the light rises up through the trees all around me, and up my spine, filling me with its vibrancy. It is as if the birch has breathed in all the sunlight over winter, and breathes it all out now, exhaling new life upon the land… There cannot be darkness where the birch tree stands, and as my senses tingle, I can feel the spirits of the wild places gathering in its branches, as I would sit by my hearth fire at home. They are warmed by its presence. It stands like one of the shining ones, one of the sidhe—gentle and luminescent, and no darkness can endure.

With its permission, I gather some birch twigs. Sitting at its roots, I bind them with red thread to make a small handheld ritual broom to beat the bounds of a home I know which has had troubles over the winter. The birch will send the bad luck and spirits away and give the family a fresh start.

Rowan/Luis *(Sorbus aucuparia)*

....

Other names:
The quicken tree, the enchantress of the woods

....

Word ogham of:
Morainn: *Lí súla* "Delight of the eye"

Cuchulain: *Lúth cethrae.i.leam*
"Strength (or friend) of cattle"

Oengus: *arae ceathrae* "Friend
(or sustenance) of cattle"[36]

Description
The rowan, or mountain ash, is like the apple and hawthorn a member of the rose family. A deciduous tree, it can grow up to twenty metres with a loose crown, and it can often have many stems. Rowans can live up to two hundred years, and may retain their shape throughout. Tolerating poor soil, it likes higher altitudes and grows well up mountains, especially in the Scottish Highlands. Rowan, like the birch, is excellent for breaking in new ground and provides good conditions for other trees to grow which will later overshadow it. Its ability to grow up to 2,500 feet gives it one of its common names, "lady of the mountain." Rowan's smooth, grey, shiny bark features horizontal lenticels and is quite distinctive, as are its clusters of scarlet berries that appear from August to October and its frothy white blossoms that show in May–June. The leaves of the rowan are ten to twenty centimetres long, and appear as elliptical "leaflets" that

---

36   McManus, *Guide to Ogam*, 43, with additions by Calder, *Scholars' Primer*, 91.

spring alternately along a stem, giving rise to its association with the ash (which is in fact of a different species altogether).

Lore and Legend

In Brehon law, rowan is one of the seven peasant trees and is known as Caerthann.

Luis can mean "flame" and "herb" as well as "swarm" or "great many." Traditionally rowans were an assembly point for warriors as told in *The Lays of Fionn,* especially the tales called "The Rowan Tree of Clonfert" and "The Wry Rowan."[37, 38] The name "rowan" comes from the Gaelic *rudha-an* "the red one," and also the Norse *run,* from which the word "rune" comes, meaning "secret, spell, or charm." The rowan is usually considered a magical tree more so than a practical one.

Rowan is ruled by the sun, and is, like the birch, connected to Lugh the sun god, who slew his grandfather, the evil Balor, with a spear of rowan through his cursing evil eye. In this and in other stories, the rowan spear is more of a magical weapon than a physical one. The collection of Irish tales relating to place names, known as the *Dindsenchas* ("The History of the Names of Places") mentions a female druid called Dreco, the granddaughter of Cartan or Caerthann, which means "rowan."[39] Dreco also carried a spear of rowan.

Rowan is sacred to the Celtic goddess Brighid, again revealing its fiery and solar energies. She is said to have three fiery arrows made of rowan. Brighid is always associated with threes, and her name drawn from *Breo-Saighead* is translated as "fiery arrow" as well as "the bright or high one." It is said that a tower of flame shot up to heaven from her head when she was born, and this alludes to her having the gift of divine

37   Eoin MacNeill, ed., *Duanaire Finn: The Book of the Lays of Fionn, Part 1* (London: David Nutt, 1908), 102.

38   Ibid., 196.

39   Edward Gwynn, trans. *The Metrical Dindsenchas* (1905) (http://www.ucc.ie/celt/online/T106500D.html).

inspiration, what the poet W. B. Yeats called "the fire in the head," the "shining brow" of Taliesin. Brighid, and thus the gifts of the rowan, can be seen as channels for divine knowledge and energy, magical and spiritual insight, prophecy and vision, but also the fiery passionate energy to create change, to work magic, not just understand it. Brighid's three arrows relate to her various triple aspects such as healing, smithwork, and poetry; or poetry, prophecy, and inspiration—gifts and abilities drawn straight from the otherworld. The three combined are sometimes thought to be what is represented in the awen symbol, three downwards rays used by many druids today. The goddess Brigantia, who is almost identical and may be the original British name for Brighid, is also said to have three arrows of rowan. For both Brighid and Brigantia, the arrows form three streams of knowledge sent out into the world from the otherworldly source. It is these streams that the rowan represents and embodies. A final connection between Brighid and the rowan tree is its popularity for divining, using a forked branch. Brighid is the goddess of smith craft, and the rowan has long been thought to be particularly effective in divining for metals.

In Ireland the rowan was known as "the druids' tree," and in the tale of Diarmuid and Grainne, we meet a rowan tree protected by a lord of the animals, the fearsome one-eyed giant Searbhan Lochlannach (the Viking of Lochlannach). Searbhan is an archetypal character, the otherworldly Wild Man of the woods, whose one eye reveals him to be between two worlds (Lochlannach, or Scandinavia, is another name for the otherworld in many Celtic myths). His bed is a mighty rowan tree in which the lovers shelter. This teaches us about the two sides of nature, the fierce and the bountiful, as he grants the lovers protection until by misdeeds Diarmuid slays him, and they lose the protection of the forest. This tree was the first rowan tree in Ireland whose otherworldly seed was dropped by a faery bard from the Land of the Ever Living, and which grew into the mightiest tree in the wood of Dubhros. This tree, the first druid tree, had special magic.

*There was virtue in its berries, and no sickness or disease would
ever come on any person that would eat them, and those that
would eat them would feel the liveliness of wine and the satisfac-
tion of mead in them, and any old person of a hundred years
that would eat them would go back to be young again, and any
young girl that would eat them would grow to be a flower of
beauty.*[40]

Rowan is also connected to other wild men and the lords of the Hunt—
Cernunnos, Herne, and the Dagdha. All are connected with the animal
world, hence rowan's titles as "friend and strength of cattle." Rowan bark
shavings were used in Scandinavia as well as Scotland to add to cattle fodder for protection and nutrition, again alluding to the rowan's poetic titles.

The rowan's ability to convey otherworldly or magical knowledge (as
well as protection) can be seen when Fionn and his warriors, in pursuit of
Diarmuid and Grainne, camp at the foot of this tree. Fionn plays a game
of *fidchell* or "wood knowledge" (similar to chess) beneath its boughs, but
his opponent manages to outwit him, with the help of Diarmuid who is
hiding above, who drops rowan berries on to the squares he should play.[41]
Magically speaking, it is the rowan which lends the knowledge and ability
to win against the odds. In another version of the tale, Diarmuid is sitting
in a yew tree above Fionn's game, suggesting his assistance comes direct
from Spirit or Source.[42]

Ancient druids used to burn rowan wood in order to receive shamanic
messages of warning and danger, especially before battle. Its red berries are
considered the blood of the gods. Morainn calls the rowan *lí súla*, which
is usually translated as "delight of the eye," as *sula/suil* in modern Gaelic
means "eye" and also "vision." Furthermore, *lí* taken here as "delight," can

---

40   Lady Gregory, *Irish Myths and Legends* (Philadelphia: Running Press, 1998), 342.

41   Ibid.

42   Gerard Murphy, trans., *Duanaire Finn: The Book of the Lays of Fionn, Part II*
      (London: David Nutt, 1908), 402.

also mean colour; so *lí súla* may also be understood as meaning the "colour of vision" hinting at its visionary properties, its aid in psychic vision, seership, or scrying for knowledge. Druids made platforms of woven rowan known as the "wattles of knowledge," used as a bed during a ritual known as *tarbh fheis,* seeking a trance state to gain hidden magical knowledge. While little is known of the ritual today, the wattles of knowledge may have been used as a visionary power plant as well as a practical resource.

Another aspect of the rowan's magical reputation is the tiny pentagram or five-pointed star which can be found on the berry. The pentagram, originally referring to the five-stage passage of Venus around the sun, has been a protective symbol for millennia, reinforcing the rowan's position as a protective force.

In both Irish and Scandinavian myth, the first woman was born from a rowan tree, and it is considered to have strong female energies. Its protective attributes have been used for millennia, and a slip of rowan clearly intended for ritual use was even found in a Bronze Age burial mound in Denmark. The rowan is also said to have saved the god Thor when he fell into a river by bending low and catching him.[43] Furthermore, rowan was the chosen wood upon which Norse rune staves were carved; due its magical abilities, the spirit of the wood was able to speak the spells or messages written upon it. It is also excellent for carving ogham. Rowan trees growing in inaccessible places such as the cleft in a rock face or within another tree are thought to be especially magically powerful, and are said to be "flying trees."[44]

The Finnish also place great importance upon the rowan, where it too has a link with the god of thunder. The goddess Rauni gave birth to all the plants of the world whilst in the form of a rowan tree after making love with the god of thunder, Ukko.

---

43   Kveldulf Gundarsson, *Elves, Wights, and Trolls* (Bloomington, IN: iUniverse, 2007), 9.

44   Ibid.

In the Scottish Highlands, the rowan was once known as *fuinnseach coille* or "the enchantress of the woods," and it was considered auspicious to have one growing near the house, as its spirit would lend those near it protection. Often, pins of rowan were used to magically seal the front door to prevent bad luck, ill will, or wicked spirits entering the house. The combination of rowan wood tied with red thread in whatever form goes back a very long time, with the thread sealing the magic, the act of tying enforcing the person's will upon the charm. Hence the old Scottish saying:

> *Rowan tree and red thread*
> *puts witches tae their speed.*[45]

The rowan has special significance in the Highlands, and it was taboo there to cut its wood unless for ritual or magical purposes. Kings were sometimes crowned beneath their boughs, and many place names still refer to its importance. In modern Scots Gaelic the rowan is known as *caorunn;* locations such as Beinn Caorunn in Inverness-shire obviously refer to it.

Another name for the rowan is the "quicken tree," and an old tale from Herefordshire tells of how there were two barrels of gold hidden in a secret vault at Penyard Castle protected by a magical guardian in the form of a jackdaw. The vault was also hidden behind huge iron doors. One day, a farmer with the help of twenty steers found the vault and proceeded to try and pry the iron doors open. Within, he could just catch a glimpse of the golden treasure, when the doors slammed shut and a voice cried out:

> *Had it not been*
> *for your quicken tree goad,*
> *and your yew tree pin,*
> *you and your cattle*

---

45 Robert Chambers, *Popular Rhymes of Scotland* (London: W & R Chambers, 1870), 328.

had all been drawn in![46]

Instead of retrieving the treasure, the farmer and his cattle would likely have been the victims of evil magic and never escaped but for the magic of the rowan and the yew which he unwittingly carried with him.

Rowan trees are especially useful at helping maintain healthy boundaries, especially with faeries. Rowan crosses over doors and children's cribs were used as powerful protection against unfriendly faeries, and rowan was also used in milk churns, as stealing milk was a popular faery pastime. Rowan is traditionally sewn into clothing and into hats to prevent the wearer being "faery led," that is, being led astray and getting lost or tricked by will o' the wisps. Walking sticks and cattle switches were also made of rowan for the same purpose. Rowan walking sticks are mentioned in several folktales as allowing both access to and safe passage from the faery realm itself. In this way, it helps establish good psychic boundaries, negotiating beneficial and respectful relationships between the mortal realm and the otherworld.

Another old name for the rowan is the "wicken" or "witches' tree." While it has the reputation for protecting against witches, rowan has in fact been used by magical practitioners of all sorts for millennia. The "witches" it protects against are negative influences, whether from mortal or magical sources, rather than witches as we know them today.

Practical and Magical Uses

The rowan is a powerful ally for the magical practitioner. Protective as well as instructive, it grants access to divine and otherworldly knowledge, "quickening" the life force of those who come into contact with it to make shamanic or visionary work possible. Today it is the witch's friend and a

---

46   Jennifer Westwood and Jacquelline Simpson, *The Lore of the Land: A Guide to England's Legends, from Spring-heeled Jack to the Witch of the Warboys* (New York: Penguin, 2005), 328.

popular magical wood. It is a reliable spirit that can lend us assistance and protection as we undertake greater magical and spiritual challenges.

Rowan is a strong, flexible wood sometimes used as a substitute for yew in the making of longbows and tool handles. It was also once used to make spindles and spinning wheels, also giving it a reputation as being a wood of the Fates.

Druids once used the bark and berries to dye cloth black for ceremonial robes, a practice that can be reproduced today quite effectively.

Equal-armed crosses (also called sun wheels) of rowan tied with red thread are an ancient protection charm hung over doorposts in the home, in the barn to protect cattle, as well as over babies' cribs to lend their protection from wicked faeries and other spirits.

Working shamanically to befriend the rowan spirit can help us achieve a greater level of insight as well as gain a powerful protector, who will help us see challenges before they reach us. It is a valuable ally for household magic, as it is the best protection for children and the safety of the hearth, but it also assists those who work with the edges of the spirit world as faery friends, guarding our boundaries and helping us negotiate relations with otherworldly contacts that are respectful to both parties.

Healing

Warning: Rowan seeds are poisonous to children.

Rowan is astringent, diuretic and anti-inflammatory. Its berries are very high in vitamin C and used to be taken to prevent scurvy. The juice of the berries is used as a laxative, and gargled to relieve sore throats. Rowan berry jam is usually made with apples and is said to help ease diarrhoea. Rowan jelly is good with meat and cheese, as well as being medicinal. Rowan berry wine is delicious and is an old remedy for cheering the spirits.

As a vibrational essence, Rowan teaches the skill of discernment and gives psychic protection, as well as aiding insight. It encourages good judgment and hones instincts.

Ogham Divination Meaning

As an ogham, rowan warns of danger but also suggests that you are suitably protected so long as you do not act foolishly, and remain aware. It fosters courage, greater vision, and imagination to overcome difficulties.

Rowan reminds you to keep your wits about you, look deeper, and see what surrounds you with clearer vision. The need to stay grounded and to use common sense is highlighted, as well as the journey into greater spiritual awareness and magical ability. Progress always means new challenges as well as rewards, and the rowan counsels you to seek the knowledge and protection you need to move forward successfully and in balance.

Journal Entry: The Rowan Trees of Loch Lochy, Highlands

Today is the autumn equinox; day and night are equal forces across the land. The shores of the loch are green and golden as the leaves turn and the ferns wither… The water is a silver mirror beneath a grey sky. But the rowan trees are aflame with berries, their leaves still green as summer. Their life force is tangibly strong still, and this far north their limbs are wrapped in silver lichen. The rowan stands at the liminal places, at the shoreline, and upon the dense forest edges that shroud the foothills of the mountains. They stand at the boundaries between the worlds. As dusk gathers and light and dark are equal for a while, I sit by the waters and make rowan charms—their bright spirits dancing around me in the breeze. May those who may need protection in the gathering winter, as Samhain opens the way between the living and the dead, be kept safe from all harm. May the flame of the rowan light their way through the darkness to come.

Alder/Fearn *(Alnus glutinosa)*

....
Other names:
Owler tree
....

Word Ogham of:

Morainn: *Airenech fíann* "Vanguard/
shield of hunting/warrior bands"

Cuchulain: *Dín cride.i.sciath*
"Protection of the heart"; "shield"

Oengus: *Comét lachta* "Guarding
of milk/milk container"[47]

Description

Alder is a deciduous tree that grows up to twenty metres tall, although
as a popular hedge tree in the British Isles it is often kept much shorter.
It has a straight trunk or multiple trunks with smooth grey-brown bark,
becoming darker and more ridged with age. It has alternate rounded
leaves which are slightly concave at the tip. The sticky buds are brownish
violet, and the flowers are small reddish brown catkins in the female, and
longer drooping catkins in the male, which can be seen from March to
April. In September to October, it has small narrow-winged "nutlets," in
oval woody cones. Growing as far south as North Africa and as far north
as Siberia, and it prefers rich soil by river banks and damp deciduous
woodland. Alders grow in symbiosis with a bacteria called *Actinomycetes,*
which absorbs nitrogen from the air, fixing it into the soil and improving
fertility. This, together with the alder's fibrous root structures, result in

---

47   McManus, *Guide to Ogam*, 43, with additions by Calder, *Scholars' Primer*, 285.

it binding the soil together on river banks and generally improving the conditions for other trees and plants.

Lore and legend

In Brehon law, the alder is one of the seven peasant trees.

Like hazel and birch, the alder likes to grow at the edges of forests, but the alder's most significant position is by the riverbank. Alder is an excellent material for making bridges and posts for trackways over boggy or fen land. As such, it has a reputation for reclaiming the land from water, colonising and moving forward confidently and creating human-made environments out of the wilderness. It does the same thing energetically and magically, being especially useful for breaking new ground.

Fearn is Old Irish for the alder, being cognate with the Welsh *gwern*, "alder tree."[48] The name "alder" may come from the Old German *elawer* which means "reddish." When cut, the white wood inside turns red, considered the colour of sanctity in the Celtic tradition. It is the colour of fire, the sun, and blood, thus the colour of life. It was therefore thought that when cut, the alder bleeds. It was for this reason that alder was the favoured wood for making shields for Celtic warriors; the alder spirit magically bled in their stead, thus conferring magical protection as a kind of spiritual exchange. In Irish mythology, these shields were often given names and believed to have magical powers in their own right. They were so important that in the famous Irish tale *The Táin* ("The Cattle Raid of Cooley") is a special room in the palace of King Conchobhar especially set aside to house the shields of the warriors when they were not at war. This was a place of honour.[49]

In Irish myth, the first man was born from an alder tree, as the rowan birthed the first woman, again referring to this link between the tree and the mortal life. In Celtic culture, the alder was used to make palisades to keep prisoners confined and to protect from invasion. Often these alder walls were topped with the heads of slain enemies.[50] Ferocity and exceptional

---

48   McManus, *Guide to Ogam*, 36.

49   Kinsella, *The Táin*, 5.

50   Green, *Dictionary of Irish Mythology*, 117.

defensive ability are attributes of the alder, both of which aid in moving boldly forward spiritually as well as physically, whilst maintaining good protection.

The alder tree is always associated with the Celtic god, the giant Bran the Blessed, whose name means "raven"—the bird most associated with prophecy and fate. His sister Branwen ("white raven") has a son with the king of Ireland, Matholwch, who is called Gwern, Brythonic for "alder." Matholwch mistreats Branwen, and she is rescued by Bran and his men invading Ireland. The invasion is disastrous but successful—none but seven men return, and Bran is fatally wounded. He instructs his men to decapitate him, and his severed head continues to utter prophecy and song long after his death. Bran and his men sojourn in the otherworld in this way, entertained by "the singing head" before returning to Britain, where they install his head at Tower Hill in London as a protector of the land, where it looked out towards France before being removed by King Arthur. Bran's totems, the ravens, are still kept at the Tower of London to this day, and a prophecy tells that the land will fail should they leave.[51]

This is the most famous example of the old Celtic cult of the head. Many heads feature in Celtic myths as voices of the otherworld, or the ancestors, and many gods were represented by large stone heads in temple complexes known as nemetons. As the seat of power and the soul, the heads of enemies were also positioned in prominent places such as in wall niches, in the case of honoured warriors, or impaled upon alder palisades, as mentioned earlier. Iron Age warriors collected "brain balls"—the shrunken brains of their enemies hardened with lime—for similar purposes. In this way, they held the power and skills of the fallen as well as their own.[52]

Thanks to its usage in the Celtic cult of the head, we can see the alder holding a position as a tree of prophecy and sacrifice, intimately connected with warriorhood. This is practical mysticism, the spiritual lessons of life

---

51   Green, *Dictionary of Irish Mythology*, 42.

52   Ibid., 117.

and death, of mortality—instructed by the otherworld, and yet applied here in the mortal realm. The greatest shield of the warrior is accumulated knowledge or skill.

Bran is closely connected with the concepts of time and fate, as are ravens. The wedding gifts he gives to Matholwch at his wedding to Branwen are a gold disc, a silver rod (both markers of the sun and moon respectively), and horses (which are associated with the passage of time, the seasons, and the journey of the sun across the sky). Here we see the alder also being associated with the idea of forward motion in life as well as the progression of the year, hence its reference in the *Cad Goddeu*: "the alder trees in the front line, began the affray."[53]

Bran's "singing head" utters prophecy and recounts lore to entertain and soothe his men after their travails in Ireland, and thus they are healed of their sorrows. The prophecy and lore referred to here are not fortune-telling—they are utterances from the otherworld or underworld; from the Source, the heart of the earth. These utterances can be seen as tales and songs, but can also be understood as currents of energy, life force, divine vivification, threads of the great web upon which we all travel from womb to tomb. And like the alder tree, we rise from the birth waters to reach out boldly into the world.

Bran's "singing head" is reminiscent of another from Greek mythology—that of Orpheus the bard, who is also associated with alder trees. Orpheus is also associated with the underworld, which he travelled into in an attempt to win back his wife, Euridice, who had died of a snake bite. Like the alder tree, Orpheus is associated with the sun; his father is the sun god Apollo. Eventually, Orpheus was killed by the Maenads, worshippers of the god Dionysus, but his severed head continued to sing and prophesy. It was placed in a cave by the Muses until Apollo ordered it to be silent. Like Bran, Orpheus makes divine utterances from the underworld

---

53   Robert Graves, *The White Goddess* (London: Faber and Faber, 1990), 46.

to the world above, representing a stream of energy or vivification from Source into manifestation.

In an englyn (traditional short poem) connected to the Welsh *Cad Goddeu,* the magician Gwydion clinches victory by magically uncovering the secret name of the god Bran, thus gaining power over his otherworldly foe by identifying him with the alder tree:

> *Sure-hoofed is my steed impelled by the spur;*
> *The high springs of alder on thy shield;*
> *Bran thou art called, of the glittering branches.*
>
> *Sure-hoofed is my steed in the day of battle:*
> *The high sprigs of alder are in thy hand:*
> *Bran thou art, by the branch thou bearest.*[54]

This positions the alder and the god Bran firmly in the otherworld reaching into the mortal realm, from the water to the earth. In the *Cad Goddeu,* the god Bran is an ally of Arawn, the god of the underworld (called Annwn). Annwn is not a place to fear, but a land of rest and renewal, a place of transformation in the womb of the goddess. The magician god Gwydion then wins magical knowledge direct from the Source. He receives the gift of prophecy or divine insight from Bran the raven, who is also the alder tree, and so civilisation rises out into manifestation. The soul's journey progresses from the silent warmth of the womb into consciousness.

As the third of the first nine trees of the ogham, alder is considered one of the nine sacred woods in modern Wicca, and it is used to build "need fires" at each of the eight seasonal festivals. Smoke from these fires (made of the other eight woods as well) can be used for divination, as can the movement of the flames. However, the alder has an older association with divination, drawn from the movement of the top branches

---

54   Charles Squire, *Celtic Myth and Legend* (London: Gresham Publishing, 1905), 308. https://www.archive.org/stream/celticmythlegend00squi#page/n0 /mode/2up.

of the trees in the wind and the sound of its rustling leaves, which like the head of Bran will utter prophecy for those able to hear it. In finding silence and listening to the wind in the trees, we can hear whispered wisdom and good advice, especially when we are calm and centred and thus able to perceive their communication. Alder's position by the river is another link to its association with divination, as ancient druids would seek prophecy by sleeping next to rivers in order to hear the words of the spirits in their murmuring during the quiet of the night. Ritual flutes and whistles were made of alder wood for similar purpose.

In this way, alder can be seen magically as a tree of confident progress. It is a wise adviser that assists in bravely facing obstacles or issues that need attention. It aids in developing stability and solidity, which come from the firm foundations that alder creates. It converts psychic land from bog and marsh and primordial chaos, allowing us to move from emotional storms and tough environments into clarity and safe, steady ground.

Practical and Magical Uses

Alder was used to build Celtic lake houses, especially those found in Scotland, Orkney, and Ireland. These houses were known as *crannogs,* and they required long-lasting timbers buried deep under water. It was also used to build bridges and trackways over marshy ground. The alder imbues these structures with its defensive energy, and it is also practically advantageous as it is highly resistant to water damage. We have another clue to alder's nature as being able to defend and ensure safety on all levels, above and below the surface of reality—wise for those on spiritual or magical journeys. The word ogham of Oengus, *comét lachta* or "guarding of milk" refers to another of alder's uses as the favoured wood to make milk churns, again due to the wood's water resistance.

We also see it in the shamanic use of alder in making spirit shields, which keep the shaman's journey clear and on track, allowing effective progression. As a wood for shield making, alder brings to mind the balance that must be maintained by any warrior—when to use the sword, and when to use the shield. Alder teaches the wisdom and appropriateness of timely defence. To defend oneself or one's territory is not about bravery or cowardliness; neither is it about retreat, but rather effective protection and *preservation*—another good word when we think of the alder. This is about empowerment and assertiveness as well as the end result of physical and practical acts. To not defend ourselves when our territory or boundaries are invaded is to give away our power… thus we are defeated before we even begin. A wise warrior, spiritual or otherwise, knows the importance of maintaining an empowered attitude where we are able to consider all angles and keep all options open when considering our response.

It is possible to work with the alder magically in a great many ways, but all work must begin with relating to the alder spirit first and attaining its assistance as an ally. A collective endeavour is far more effective, as the alder's wisdom will be added to (not overrun by) your own. Alder is particularly effective when starting new projects or when defending yourself becomes necessary. It also helps overcome periods of inaction, weakness, lack of direction, and victimhood, and when you feel stuck in a rut. Alder will lend strength, endurance (especially to cope with sorrow or grief), and help you find a way forward you had not envisioned before.

Seeking inspiration or divination beneath alder trees is particularly effective. Traditionally held to be under the rulership of the planet Venus, it also has uses in becoming eloquent, charming, and in supporting stable relationships. An alder leaf placed against the heart will help shield you from emotional harm, and it will attract loving relations.

Alder wood is very durable, but burns badly. However, it makes good charcoal, and is useful for smithing and metalwork. It can also be used to make a wide variety of dyes—its flowers make green dye, red can be made from the bark, the twigs make brown, and the bark together with the young shoots and added copper make yellow.

Healing

Alder has good anti-inflammatory properties and has been used in a whole host of way for diseases like rheumatism. Alder leaves used to be placed on the soles of the feet or in shoes to ease weary aching feet. Beds of alder leaves used to be made to ease aches and pains. A similar effect today may be had by stuffing a cushion or duvet cover with fresh leaves. The fresh rubbed leaves also make a good insect repellent.

Culpeper recommends a decoction of alder bark for burns and inflammations and it can also be used as a gargle for sore throats.[55] The inner bark may be boiled to make a wound wash, and it may once have been drunk to help heal internal injuries.

As a vibrational essence, alder lends a steadying influence and helps to ground and process overly strong emotions. It helps in moving forward, and encourages strength and endurance and the ability to clear the way ahead if necessary.

Ogham Divination Meaning

Fearn, the alder, encourages you to move ahead with confidence and courage. It tells you to get grounded and practical, ensuring your own safety in physical realms but also aiding in psychic protection where a grounded and present attitude ensures you remain self-possessed and empowered. It is an excellent ally in aiding and teaching you how to defend yourself emotionally, physically, mentally, and spiritually. As a tree closely associated with warriorhood, it encourages you to seek honourable conduct and the right use of power, in addition to discrimination and discernment—when to use the shield and when to use the sword forged in its slow-burning flame.

---

55   Culpeper, *Complete Herbal*, 34.

Journal Entry: Alders of the Avalon Marshes, Glastonbury

Here the land and the water are always dancing to and fro. This land is never one or the other for long. It is in truth the Summerland; the waters claim it in autumn and will not let it go until Beltane and the blossoms are on the hawthorn. The edges are guarded by the alder often hidden amongst the willows. It endures and shields us from the worst of the storms and the wild things that come in the darkness... for not all the spirits here care for humans and our ways. This was not meant to be a place for people, but somewhere set aside for them and the old gods. I went this evening to sit by the rare, lone standing alder beside the lake. No matter how high the waters, it endures. This tree has been my guardian on many a dark night as I weave my magic at the water's edge, in honour of the Lady, the Tor a shadow ahead of me, the wind whispering and hissing in the reeds. Alder teaches endurance. I gather alder cones to add to protection spells and for charms to give people courage to move forward bravely. He twines a fallen leaf in my hair, and I place it against my chest as a shield. Alder's spirit encircles me, guardian and ally, as I walk through the wild night, homeward bound.

Willow/Saille *(Salix caprea)*

....

Other names:
Osier, saille, sally tree, saugh tree, withe, withy tree

....

Word Ogham of:
Morainn: *Lí ambí* "Pallor of the lifeless"

Cuchulain: *Tosach mela.i.sail*
"Beginning of honey"; "loss"

Oengus: *Lúth bech* "Sustenance of bees"[56]

Description

The willow used in the ogham alphabet is not the famous weeping willow, but the pussy willow *(Salix caprea)*, although they have similar uses and energies.

Pussy willow is a small deciduous tree which reaches to about twelve metres. It has alternate elliptical leaves about four to ten centimetres long and about five centimetres broad. The leaves are shiny green on top and somewhat hairy and silvery blue-green underneath. The male has yellow catkins and the female green; both emerge before the leaves in March to April. Its smooth grey bark becomes ridged with diamond-shaped warts with age.

Willows can be found throughout Britain and Europe, as far north as Siberia, and extending to Turkey and South Asia and America. They prefer rich, damp soil but can tolerate poor, raw soil, from lowlands right up into the mountains. In the Alps, they grow at 2,000 metres.

---

56   McManus, *Guide to Ogam*, 43, with additions by Calder, *Scholars' Primer*, 279.

Lore and Legend

Willow is one of the seven noble trees according to Brehon law.

Willow trees are usually associated with water and the moon. All willow varieties thrive near water and their position by riverbanks naturally connects them to the alder. The alder was called the king of the waters, and the willow was the queen. Its connection to water lends it a whole host of associations with the otherworld in the Celtic mind, be it Faery, the underworld of the ancestors, or the realm of the gods. The word ogham of Morainn, *lí ambí* relating to the willow—"pallor of the lifeless"—refers to the willow's connection with those of the otherworld, including the dead, and much of its teaching has to do with crossing the boundaries between different states of existence, particularly around issues related to mortality. It also perhaps alludes to moonlight, when everything appears to be subtly altered.

Sacred to the moon, the "feminine" qualities of flexibility and flow, and the mysterious wisdom of the instincts and emotions are all present in the willow tree's energy.[57] Its position, so often near water yet actually preserving the dry land, illustrates its lesson of holding these qualities in balance with the demands of our often more solar daily lives.

The moon has long-held associations not only with the feminine cycle, but with intuition, imagination, and instinct, that hidden thread of knowing that defies logic and the rational mind. The moon is the unseen and indefinable, the yet to be, the *becoming*. To see by the light of the moon is literally to see things in a "new light," where some details attain greater significance, while others are obscured. The moon has been worshipped as a goddess for millennia, and the willow is a special tree to help understand her ways, her wisdom.

The willow is sacred to the Welsh goddess Ceridwen for this reason, who rules over the moon. Her cauldron of transformation bestows poetic vision, otherwise known as psychic ability or prophecy. It is also sacred to gods of eloquence—perhaps because of this ability to restore the flow of

---

57   Culpeper, *Complete Herbal*, 390.

emotions and ideas. Apollo, Orpheus, and Bellinus all received their eloquence from the willow tree.

Psychic vision, often known as "seership" in the Celtic lands, was a gift that was highly respected and valued by people of all walks of life. Seers were able to glimpse through the veil into the heart of events, perceive the spirit world, and give prophecy and advice. The willow has always been associated with such people, with divination, clairvoyance, and magic, as well as emotional sensitivity and empathy. Like the willow at the water's edge, it supports people who stand between two realms, the mortal world and that of Spirit.

The moon and psychic abilities also have strong connections with dreams and dreaming, whether as a vehicle for granting access to the otherworld or as a healing resource. Several ancient druid practices used dreaming as an oracular tool, either by sleeping by a river bank, close to willow trees, or by sleeping in a special hut after making offerings and remaining there until they received a vision, a practice known as *imbas forosnai*.[58] An altar has been found to the Gaulish god Esus depicting a priest cutting slips of willow while three cranes fly overhead, illustrating the willow's use in shamanic flight and divination.[59] Willows were often used by the Celts for the making of baskets, fences, and coracles; there are many tales of travellers, shamans, and transgressors being sent "over the ninth wave" on vessels made of willow—to travel to shores unknown. This type of voyage can still be the basis for magical journeys today, in vision.

A thirteenth-century poem, "The Song of the Forest Trees" states, "The noble willow burn not"—it is a tree sacred to poems, and willows are indeed often associated with poetry and bardic gifts.[60] As a result of the ability to cross into other realms that the willow enables, the bard may

---

58   John O'Donovan, trans., *Cormac's Glossary* (Calcutta: Irish Archaeological and Celtic Society, 1868), 94.

59   Green, *Dictionary of Celtic Myth*, 93.

60   (no author) "The Tragic death of Fergus mac Leide" (www.ancienttexts.org /library/celtic/texts/fergusmacleide.html).

have access to imbas (Irish) or awen (Welsh), that is, divine inspiration and poetic or shamanic vision, a glimpse of the infinite.

In the Celtic tradition there is strong crossover between bardic and shamanic skills, both functioning as walkers between the worlds and voicing utterances from beyond the veil. Thus the willow is connected with bees as messengers between the mortal world and the gods and honey (referred to by Cuchulain and Oengus), which was often used to describe the gift of prophecy upon the tongue.[61] The bards of old were powerful magical practitioners, able to weave spells and transformations with their poetry and song—or inflict terrible curses upon those they satirised. The willow was a powerful ally to bards, and harps were traditionally made of willow not only because it was excellent for their construction, but because the spirit of the willow would magically support their work, increasing the flow to and from the otherworld. The famous and beautiful harp of Brian Boru, made in the fourteenth century, is made entirely of willow. The highest grade of poet was called a fili, and they were said to have attained a "tongue that cannot lie"—that is, they had gained the ability to utter prophecy and be a direct voice of the gods. Thus again we can see the willow's links with prophecy and the otherworld.

The willow is often magically paired with the alder, as it has compatible uses and energies; both are concerned with the journey to and from the otherworld. Like the alder, the willow has a connection to the Greek poet Orpheus, whose lyre was made of willow. That lyre played magical music that enchanted the god Hades as Orpheus attempted to rescue his wife, Euridice, from the underworld.

The willow often appears in mythologies around the world as the site of a god or goddess's first appearance, as if they are birthed into the tale from the otherworld beneath its boughs. The coffin of the Egyptian god Osiris was found amongst willows, while his soul in the form of a phoenix sat it its

---

61   Giraldus Cambrensis, *Description of Wales (1195)*, ed. Ernest Rhys (London: J. M. Dent and Co, 1908), 179.

branches. Willows were also sacred to the goddess Hathor. An inscription on the wall in her temple at Denderah says:

> O divine spirits, come in joy playing the tambourine continu-
> ously, the women are delighted, the inhabitants of Denderah are
> joyful, the goddesses are adorned with crowns of willow.[62]

Crowns of strung willow leaves were also worn by mummies for the deceased to wear upon entering the afterlife, notably Ahmose I, Amenhotep I, and Tutankhamen. These were known as "Crowns of Justification" to identify the wearer to Osiris.[63]

The Greek goddess Artemis was associated with the willow, especially due to its connections with the moon, and it was said that she was discovered amongst willow trees. The goddess Hera is also associated with willow trees.

Another goddess associated with the willow is Hecate, who may have originated in Anatolia but later was worshipped as part of the Greek pantheon.[64] Hecate is usually depicted carrying a torch, and whilst today she is usually considered a crone goddess, originally she had three faces of equal age. She is considered to have rulership over earth, sea, and sky, and she is a light bringer—a saviour and mother of the world soul. However, her tripartite nature also connects her with the three phases of the moon, hence her connections to all plants under its rulership, especially the willow. In Thrace, Hecate ruled over all liminal places, especially gateways and the wilderness. Again we see the connection with willow as a tree linking the waters of the otherworld with the land and mortal realm.

Although Hecate shared some attributes with Artemis, the former was also associated with ghosts, demons, and the dead. She was closely related

---

62   André Dollinger, "Ancient Egyptian Plants: The Willow" (http://reshafim.org.il /ad/egypt/botany/willow.htm).

63   Ibid.

64   *Larousse Encyclopaedia of Mythology* (London: Batchworth Press, 1959), 190.

to witchcraft and sorcery, and offerings at three-way crossroads were made at the full moon to seek her protection from evil spirits. She was also said to be able to create or hold back storms and rain.

This connection with weather magic can also be seen with the Celtic goddess Brighid, who is said to bring the spring after defeating (or having transformed from) the Cailleach, or Old Woman of Winter. At Brighid's special festival, Imbolc, on February 2, she is said to carry a white willow wand tipped with an acorn she uses to control the weather. We see again the willow functioning as a mediator and moderator of liminal spaces—in this instance the boundaries between winter and spring, another clue to the willow's energy and magic. It is one of the few trees which can regenerate and make a new tree should a single branch or twig be placed in the soil—it has such strong life force that such branches can grow several metres in one season. This vigorous growth matches the rapid change that occurs during springtime, when life and land is reclaimed from the winter and the often damp, flooded landscape returns to rich fertility.

The willow also has another facet—the comforter. The chemical salicin, present in all willow species in varying degrees, has great pain-killing properties which have been used since ancient times and are still used in modern medicine today. The energy of the willow assists in easing the difficult feelings that arise from periods of change and the sense of loss that often follows. It can be seen as having an affinity with motherly and crone energies for this reason, soothing the pain of sacrifice and the bitterness of letting go—surrendering to the wheel of mortal lives.

The willow has a reputation for being intimately associated with grief, sadness, and the healing of sorrow, again related to its connections with water and emotions. It can help ease these sorrows by coming to terms with their ebb and flow, and making peace with the emotional, intuitive, and subconscious sides of life.

Practical and Magical Uses

The willow is used in basket making, as well as for constructing hurdles and fences. It also used to be used to make coracles, and it was the favoured wood for harps.

Magically its uses in divination are many. Willow rods used for divination are mentioned in the tales of Manannan mac Lir, "…a man of them to take nine straight willow rods, and to throw them up to the rafters of the house, and to catch them again as they came down, and he standing on one leg…"[65]

Willow wands can be used for protection and guidance for otherworld and underworld journeys, and as a tool to help anchor someone with psychological or emotional distress. It also has uses in weather magic, healing and fertility spells. Tipped with an acorn, it becomes the phallic life-giving wand impregnating all it touches with new life and vigour.

Willow is good for all sorts of moon magic, and willow whips or cord are good for binding spells. It is a traditional material for practical binding tasks, especially in making brooms, witches' brooms included. Willow talismans are good for love and healing spells, and for aligning oneself closer to the lunar goddesses.

Healing

In herbal medicine, willow has of course pain-killing uses, as well as being good for catarrh, and lowering fevers. It is a good styptic—stopping bleeding quickly—another clue to its magical nature. It helps with sore throats, and as a disinfectant willow tea has been used to soak bandages. The leaves can be chewed to help with mouth ulcers.

Culpeper says of the willow, "the moon owns it," and it is really helpful in a variety of ways.[66] It can assist in magically healing emotional distress, and as a vibrational essence it heals all forms of emotional bitterness and

65   Gregory, *Irish Myths and Legends*, 130.
66   Culpeper, *Complete Herbal*, 390.

resentment, dissolving areas where we have become ossified or deadened. Willow helps restore flow and harmony within ourselves and in the world around us. It also it helps come to terms with intuition and repressed feminine aspects in both sexes.

Ogham Divination Meaning

The ogham *saille* suggests harmony and balance, being in tune with feeling and wisdom that comes from otherworld sources and dreams. It encourages flexibility, especially emotionally and practically, to help expand awareness and knowledge of the otherworld as well as altered states of consciousness. It encourages healing and a gentle, forgiving attitude. It also encourages remembering the healing virtues of tears and increased compassion. It gently asks you to tune in to your heart and move forward aligned with the heart's wisdom. You can access otherworldly magic and insights. There is more to see and to understand than mortal knowing can contain, and this is a blessing; the otherworld is not a place of sorrow but of ease and refreshment. The willow encourages you and nurtures you to return to this gentle divine state.

Journal Entry: Lake Village Willows, Avalon Marshes, Glastonbury

Tonight the moon is full, and I sit by the willows at the edge of the river and see her silver reflection upon the water. The night is still and quiet, and the river is slow, almost sleepy, murmuring secrets as she ambles through the marshes. I reach out to touch the willow leaves, eyes closed, listening to the tales saille and the waters share with me this night, following the moon's silver road across the waters. Around me are the low grassy mounds of the lake village. Here, many moons ago, my Neolithic ancestors lived in houses built upon the water surrounded by the willows at the foot of Glastonbury Tor. A gentle mist rises and wreaths me in silver and the willows sigh; their ancestors also stood upon this place. Together they wove the wattle walls to keep out the night; they made baskets to hold bread and babies, they made coracles so that we could set sail upon the womb waters of Avalon—to fish, to hide, to seek healing and vision on the sacred hill before me. Fishermen, poets, and shaman women who knew the secrets of this hidden land sailed across the waters to the otherworld and came back changed, eyes bright and hearts on fire with the vision of the gods. I gather slips of willow wood for healing spells to ease those in pain, and to make talismans that help those seeking vision easily cross the waters to the otherworld.

Ash/Nuin *(Fraxinus excelsior)*

....

Other names:

Hoop ash

....

Word Ogham of:

Morainn: *Costud síde* "Establishing of peace"; "A check on peace"

Cuchulain: *Bág maisi.i.garman* "Boast of beauty, a weaver's beam"

Oengus: *Bág ban* "The boast of women"[67]

Description

Ash trees can grow to up to forty metres tall, and are rounded or oval in shape. Ash has narrow elliptical leaflets with finely toothed margins, positioned opposite one another along the stem. Its hermaphrodite greenish yellow flowers can be seen in April to May, before the leaves open. They are arranged in many-flowered panicles, which droop over time. Its bark is pale grey and smooth, becoming ridged with age. Its seeds, the famous "ash keys," each two to four centimetres long, ripen from green to brown and hang in bunches, remaining upon the tree for many months if not longer.

Ash prefer to live in mixed deciduous woodlands, in lowlands, but are happy up to 1,300 metres. They often grow along rivers or streams. However, they also tolerate drier, more shallow soils and are commonly planted along roads or in parks. Ash grows all over Europe, Scandinavia, and in the US.

---

67   McManus, *Guide to Ogam*, 43, with additions by Calder, *Scholars' Primer*, 91.

Lore and Legend

In Brehon law, ash is one of the seven chieftain trees known then as *Iundius*.

The ash has been a tree of spiritual importance all over Europe for millennia. In Scandinavian myth, the World Tree Yggdrasil was a giant ash tree connecting all the realms of existence. For this reason it is also sacred to Odin, who hung himself upon an ash tree in search of wisdom.

> *Nine whole nights on a wind rocked tree, wounded with a spear.*
> *I was offered to Odin, myself to myself, on that tree that none*
> *may ever know what root beneath it runs.*[68]

Yggdrasil is an example of the *axis mundi,* the centre of the world around which all life turns and upon which all life is dependent. Not only a tree, it is also the steed of the god Odin, or Woden, on which he travels to all realms— that is, Yggdrasil is the structure and substance of the universe and the tool to traverse it. As such, both the tree and Odin are essentially shamanic spirit beings: they are givers of knowledge, the vehicle, and the receiver. Yggdrasil's connection to shamanism also ties the ash to the concepts of microcosm and macrocosm—universal patterns that reflect each other from the very small to the very large, repeating through the seeming chaos of creation. It was this chaos Odin pierced in order to understand the workings of the universe, in turn manifesting into creation as the runes.

Yggdrasil was protected by the mysterious Norns, the three goddesses who were the keepers of destiny.[69] These were known as Urdr ("fate"), Verdandi ("being"), and Skuld ("necessity"). These three maidens attended the tree by watering it and covering its bark with clay to protect and preserve it. They were also associated with childbirth, as they took the fruit of the tree and burnt it before giving it to women in labour. The Norns and their function as the Fates are similar to the Greek goddess Nemesis.[70]

---

68   Saemund Sigfusson, *The Elder Eddas,* Benjamin Thorpe, trans., (London: Norroena Society, 1906), 44.

69   R. I. Page, *Norse Myths* (Austin, TX: University of Texas Press, 1990), 58.

70   *Larousse Encyclopedia,* 187.

Nemesis carried an ash branch to symbolise her role as a divine instrument of justice, another function of the Fates or Furies that ensured that happiness and good fortune as well as justice were dispensed fairly for all people. Nemesis would take all good fortune from those who used their riches for selfish ends. She is also associated with another Greek goddess, Adrasteia, the daughter of Oceanus, who brought rain and fertility to crops. Adrasteia was known as "nemesis of the rain-making ash tree" and her symbols were a wheel, a scourge, and an ash branch.[71] There is some argument that suggests the Celtic goddess of victory, Andraste, could be the same or a related deity in a Celtic form.

Adrasteia was an ash nymph who was the foster nurse of Zeus. As Nemesis, she was Zeus's lover. In Greek mythology, ash nymphs (known as Meliae), were born from drops of blood spilled when Kronos, the titan/god of time castrated his father, the sky god Ouranos. This connects the ash to the lightning god and the oak tree, another "world pillar." Poseidon is also associated with the ash tree, as is the hero Achilles. Achilles's father Peleus was given an ash spear when he wedded the goddess Thetis; the spear was cut from a tree on Mount Pelion, polished by Athene (the goddess of battle and wisdom), and the spearhead was forged by the smith god Hephaestus. Ash was also sacred to Ares, the Greek god of war, due again to its usefulness for spears. It is also said that in ancient Greece, an ash was planted for each baby's birth.

The ash is often associated with lightning, as its height appears to attract it with startling regularity, hence the old saying "avoid an ash, for it courts a flash!" Lightning is magically significant the world over, as the touch of divinity, and wood that has been struck by lightning is always considered to be especially powerful. Another god of lightning, Thor, had a spear of ash, again strengthening this connection.

The name for the ash in Old English, *aesc*, as well as its Latin name, *fraxinus*, both mean "spear," and ash was the favourite choice of the Celts

---

71   Robert Graves, *The Greek Myths, Part 1* (London: Pelican Books, 1975), 42.

for making spear shafts—a primary weapon before the Iron Age due to the branches' strength and straightness. These spears were often carefully engraved, and many were named, considered treasures handed down through generations. Spears traditionally were considered female objects, hence Oengus's description of ash as "the boast of women," alluding to the prowess of spears in battle. Cuchulain also refers to this, using the kenning for the spear—a poetic title "the weaver's beam" as it is referred to in the battle of Moytura. Morainn's reference to it as "the establishing (or checking) of peace" testifies to its status as a primary weapon. Ash is usually held as sacred to the god Lugh for its masculine, solar energy, as well as its associations with justice, as Lugh was also considered to be a god of law and order in addition to his solar qualities.

The ash had especial significance in Ireland, perhaps due to its connections with Vikings via their successive invasions. There were five sacred, special living trees in Ireland that, like Yggdrasil, were probably understood and maybe even functioned ceremonially as World Trees. Three of these were ash trees: the *Bile Tortan* (the sacred tree of Tortiu), the *Bile Usneg* (the sacred tree of Usnech), and the *Craeb Dathi* (the bushy tree of Dathi). These trees were felled as Christianity swept over Ireland, taken as symbols of victory over Pagan druids.

Ash is also useful for making magical staves and walking sticks. A druid staff found in Anglesey was made of ash with spiralled copper ribbon around it that would have caught the light beautifully.[72] Here we see the ash's importance as a wood of power, but also its significance as a central pole of the world, and the cyclical nature of existence around it. In the Celtic tradition as already discussed, ash is usually associated with spears and is valued for its strength and straightness. Its additional use as the staff of a spiritual leader here is especially significant.

---

72   Cyril Fox, *A Find of the Early Iron Age from Llyn Cerrig Bach, Anglesey* (Cardiff, UK: National Museum of Wales, 1945), 35.

Practical and Magical Uses

On a magical level, the spear can be seen as an alternative to the magician's wand—a tool to direct energy. The many tales of magical spears remind us of the power of direct and focused intention; like the rays of the sun, the spear's solar and fierce qualities are formidable. The spear symbolises the direction and application of power and skill, and it can be used magically to break all forms of inertia as well to reach an intended target. The focus here is on its skillful use in order to become effective rather than blindly stumbling forward. Its sacredness and connection to the many-skilled god Lugh are testament to this.

In Pagan Europe, the ash was the traditional wood for the making of witches' broomhandles, as well as being the wood of the maypole, reminiscent of its position as the World Tree and its attributes of magical flight. Here we see the shamanic uses of the ash as World Tree, which the witch is able to ride at will to travel to other worlds or to view the mortal world through spirit vision. It may also refer to the ash representing phallic energy, alluding to the witch gaining vision of the otherworld via sexual ecstasy.

Ash is also used for divination fires, again because of its associations with flight (of the spear, the witch, the shaman) and its connection with destiny and magical power. Ash "keys" are effective fertility and love charms that lend their power of direction to open up opportunities. Carry some that have been charged and blessed in a green or gold pouch, remembering to always gather with the tree's permission. You can also place some under your pillow before sleeping.

As it relates to magic, the ash teaches important lessons about the right use of strength, and the gaining of skill to make the strength effective. It encourages self-control, courage, respect, and durability. Old folk songs refer to the oak, ash, and thorn as a sacred trio; the oak is masculine energy representing the god, the thorn (the hawthorn) is feminine energy representing the goddess, and the ash as the World Tree and druid's staff is the phallic link between the two—the transmitter of the energy as well as the product of the interchange. As "magical children" of the gods, druids and witches sometimes carve figures out of ash wood for use in healing. These "poppets" or "fith faths" represent the person to be healed and act as a focus and transmitter for the energy. Equal-armed crosses of ash were carried by sailors as protection at sea, perhaps from a lingering memory of its sacredness to Poseidon. The seafaring Vikings used oak for their ships and ash to kit them out with magical protection. In a modern twist, ash wood or leaves are sometimes used by witches and druids today in their cars to afford the same protection in transit.

The ash as a conveyor of magical knowledge is also used in dream spells, where placing some ash leaves under the pillow—especially if they have been gathered at the full moon, and with the permission of the tree—will lend the dreamer magical and prophetic dreams. Ash leaves may also be scattered about the magical circle to assist in invocations. This is especially useful in the south, for the sun and fire, and the west, for the element of water. Ash leaves all around the circle will also help to balance all four elements within a working as well as within the practitioner.

Ash burns well as firewood and gives off a huge amount of heat compared to other trees. Due to this and its magical uses—especially its connection with the sun—it was the favourite wood to use as the Yule log at the winter solstice. The log (sometimes a large root), was decorated with ribbons and given libations of wine or mead before being burnt upon the fire, signifying the returning sun. The last of the log would be used as kindling for the solstice fire the following year, and the ash of the burnt wood was used as a magical talisman to protect against lightning strikes.

Healing

Culpeper places the ash under the rulership of the sun and suggests that there was lore referring to the ash tree and serpents that recommended young ash leaves as good antivenom for snake bites, but of course that would not be recommended today.[73] Culpeper attributes the antivenom properties to previous recorders of herbal lore, citing Gerard and Pliny, who suggested that it was once believed snakes recoiled from ash trees. This may be an old memory of the world serpent coiled around Yggdrasil.

Tender ash tips and leaves were used for rheumatism, gout, and jaundice. After being dried, they were turned into powder. An infusion was made from the powder that was to be drunk or applied topically. Dried ash leaves were also imbibed in infusions for longevity. The leaves were also taken in this way as laxatives and diuretics.

Ash bark can be steeped in hot water and cooled to apply to the scalp to treat itching and infestations. It can be taken to ease fevers, and it is considered more potent when cut in the spring as the sap rises. Ash roots can be used as a tonic and stimulant, especially for liver problems, again most likely due to its diuretic effects.

Ash keys were once considered to be highly aphrodisiac, and decaying ash wood was an ingredient for aphrodisiac powders and spells. Ash keys will keep all year if gathered when ripe.

Energetically or as a vibrational essence, ash encourages strength and endurance, helping us endure the harshest circumstances. It lends the strength to protect land, family, and all that is important in a person's life. It helps them operate from a sense of rootedness and inner balance. Ash also stresses the importance of inner resources, feelings, and motivation. It encourages good connections with tribe, family, or community.

Ogham Divination Meaning

Ash's ogham, *nuin*, suggests strength, uprightness, and correct focus. It is a symbol of the newly matured, hardened warrior at the height of his or her prowess. It refers to the direct application, the pursuit of wisdom, and the value of getting to the heart of a matter. It encourages the solar qualities of courage and determination, as well as exuberance and vitality. It shows the value and pleasure of being fully alive and being yourself,

---

73   Culpeper, *Complete Herbal*, 34.

even in difficult circumstances. As the World Tree (and the connection between earth and sky, male and female), it helps balance the concepts of "being" and "doing" as well as giving and receiving energy and resources in equal measure. It therefore encourages the rebalancing of any excess in behaviour, and it helps your coming into greater balance with the world around you. Ash may be understood as being akin to the lightning flash, the point of union between the mortals and the gods. Prepare for the touch of fate, the spirit world, or magical insight to descend upon you!

Journal Entry: The Barrow Ash— Compton Dundon Iron Age Hill Fort, Somerset

I sit atop the mound as the sun goes down. The ash tree, tall and straight and strong behind me, its branches reaching into the wide sky, its roots burrowing deep into the underworld, must twine around the Bronze Age warrior who lies here. Does his spear lie beside him still? Or is it only in my vision? Has he long since crumbled to earth? Long ago, they built the mound over him, an act of honour, of respect, to mark his place of rest as sacred. He who dwells in the mound is a guardian and guide, looking out across the wide plain. All who come here are under his gaze. I have spoken with him on this wild wide hill in the gathering dusk, but I will not pass on his secrets here. He sits in the distant past and saw the Iron Age Celts arrive and build their fort around him, eager for his protection. I am in his vision also, as are the ravens that cry out in the gloaming. The branches of the ash tree sway in the breeze that goes by far above me, the ash keys dancing in the sky. I gather these sometimes to grant strength and to increase the power of spells, drawing warrior strength into my magic. Most, however, fly off with the birds or on the wind, seeding new life on the hillside. I'm sure he watches those seeds turn to trees, as he has a hundred more, and those in future days who shall sit by his side in far-off times, a million sunrises and sunsets and all that goes between.

The Aicme of Huath

Hawthorn/Huath *(Crataegus monogyna)*

⊣

....

Other names:
Whitethorn, mayflower, may
tree, hawberry, thornapple

....

Word ogham of:
Morainn: *Condál cúan* "Pack
of wolves"; "pack of hounds"

Cuchulain: *Ansam aidche.i.huath*
"Most difficult night, hawthorn"

Oengus: *Bánad gnúisi* "Whitening
or blanching of the face"[74]

---

74   McManus, *Guide to Ogam*, 43, with additions by Calder, *Scholars' Primer*, 279.

Description

Hawthorn, a member of the rose family, is a pioneer tree and can grow in some of the most difficult habitats. It began to spread largely as a result of the Neolithic tree clearances, as it is often one of the first trees to repopulate an area, being able to grow on steep hillsides as well as in moist or dry environments. It can grow up to ten meters, and live for up to 400 years, although it is usually much younger than this, and simply looks very old due to its gnarly shape. Its low branches and many thorns may give rise to Morainn's name for the hawthorn, the "pack of wolves" or "pack of hounds" that call to mind a mass of sharp teeth. It is sharp and dangerous on every side. Its leaves are broadly oval, three to six centimetres long, with three to seven deep, pointed lobes. The hawthorn flowers from May to June in white or sometimes pinkish upright clusters, with each flower head consisting of five petals. The individual flowers are hermaphrodite so it can pollinate itself and other trees easily, creating hybrids with ease. Its red berries are edible, and each contain a single stone. Berries appear from September to October. Hawthorns can be found throughout Europe, North Africa, Turkey and the Caucasus, and across North America.

Lore and Legend

Hawthorn is one of the peasant trees according to Brehon law.

Hawthorns are always connected to the faeries, and are considered highly sacred in many communities across Britain and Ireland.[75] One of the most famous tales involving the hawthorn is that of Thomas the Rhymer, who met the Queen of Elfland beneath a hawthorn tree.[76] Because of its connection with faeries, severe penalties are thought to be imposed on anyone who violates the tree in any way, and it is often associated with periods of testing and challenge. Its dual nature, of flowers

---

75   Lewis Spence, *The Fairy Tradition in Britain* (Whitefish, MT: Kessinger, 1995), 181.

76   James A. H. Murray, ed., *The Romance and Prophecies of Thomas of Ercledoune* (Somerset, UK: Llanerch, 1991), xlix, liii.

and sharp thorns, relates it to traditions of the triple goddess who is seen as both beautiful and kind, as well as cruel and harsh. For this reason a solitary hawthorn has often been considered a trysting place. Hawthorns are also often guardians of sacred springs and wells, demanding the very best behaviour from all mortals who are in their presence. Hawthorn's guardianship is the reason for the tree's association with the festival of Beltane (May 1) as it flowers during this season and is traditionally used as the crown of the May Queen, the personification of the goddess.

The hawthorn teaches that the Queen of the May is not easily won, and can only ever wed the Oak King. This ancient mystery teaching concerns the attainment of inner sovereignty and worthiness—union with the goddess. The hawthorn demands only the very best in all things. To win her as your beautiful bride entails successful completion of many tasks and the surmounting of seemingly impossible challenges. The prize is the goddess herself, the sacredness of the land, and the highest possible achievement and honour.

Ultimately, the triumph over difficulty is the mortal's eternal quest for the grail, for the soul. This quest is undertaken under the eye of the Crone, and she periodically sets harsh tasks through all our lives. This is why Cuchulain called the hawthorn "most difficult night." It is a time of fears and storm, but at the end of it comes the dawn. Oengus's words "whitening of the face" also refer to the difficulties she sets. Challenges of worthiness do not come when we are strong and at ease; they are unexpected, and strike when energy is down and we are disempowered. The challenge is always to retrieve that power, despite "the whitening of the face," when we literally blanch at what is before us.

The hawthorn's berries (its least famous feature) are good for all things related to the heart, reflecting that the Great Mother as well as the Maiden bride and the Crone are symbolised here. Despite the challenges that the hawthorn represents, it is also highly protective—of the small animals that shelter in its thicket, as well as all people suffering vulnerability of any kind. It is sacred not only to brides and virgins, but women in childbirth as well, who are all protected by its fierce thorns, physically or magically. The hawthorn in the green world is a living example of the *temenos*—sacred enclosure—the ultimate sacred enclosure being within a woman's body. Only the good and truly worthy may enter.

In the Arthurian sagas is a story about Sir Gawain marrying a hag called Dame Ragnell. He must answer the ancient riddle "what does a woman truly want?" The answer is "sovereignty over herself." When Gawain accepts his bride's right to her own self-determination, she changes into a beautiful maiden.[77] This is the teaching of the hawthorn; the law of sacredness demands respect. The hawthorn also has many connections with the heart, and it is this knowing one's own heart that is the key to its mystery—allowing the beloved to be true to their heart, and being true to your own as well. In the tale of Culhwch and Olwen, Culhwch's worthiness of his future bride Olwen is tested by her father, the terrible giant Yspaddaden Pencawr—whose name means "giant hawthorn."[78] In passing Yspaddaden's tests, he proves his respect for his bride-to-be.

Hawthorns are sacred to the Roman goddess Cardea, who, symbolised by the hawthorn itself, is the goddess of doorways and weddings. It is said that Cardea will not bless a marriage if the groom has not made sufficient sacrifices or passed sufficient challenges to be worthy of his bride. She is also the goddess of doorways because to pass the tests of the hawthorn is to pass through into another phase of life, the lessons of the oak, whose name *duir* also means "door."

The hawthorn is also connected to notions of erotic desire, and is a great energiser that raises the life force. Its association with the May Day festivals illustrates its very powerful fertility magic. Unlike today, Beltane was not considered an auspicious time to wed to the Celts—the goddess weds anew each year and her consort is interchangeable. In fact, this time

77   Matthews, *Aquarian Guide*, 140.
78   Ibid., 56.

was traditionally when divorces were made. If you could make your marriage pass the tests of May, and the hawthorn, then it was a worthy match indeed.

Hawthorn has another role in her Crone aspect, as her great energy has also been traditionally used to clear negative energy. It used to be traditional to plant hawthorns near to where an accident or death had occurred, to remove the negative influence on the land. Sacred to Macha, an Irish Crone goddess, the water used to wash a dead body was also sometimes taken and poured at the roots of hawthorn trees. Perhaps this also in the hope that the regenerative energy from Crone to Maiden would support and regenerate the spirits of the dead.

The name *huath* is likely to have originally have been *uath*—which in Old Irish means "frightful" or "horrible," perhaps due to the hawthorn's considerable Pagan importance.[79] Its associations with the Crone, as well as its connections with passionate love, eroticism, and emotional commitment, are sadly still considered frightful to some repressed modern and orthodox Christian psyches. Perhaps this is why the *Cad Goddeu* refers to it being "unbeloved," as so few rise to its challenges.[80] The ability to handle the surges of energy, wildness and passion the hawthorn embodies is a sign of maturity and spiritual development—not by abstinence, but by integrating these qualities. Wholeness and inner sovereignty can then be achieved.

Practical and Magical Uses

Hawthorn flowers are always associated with Beltane, the May Day celebrations, and as such with marriages and betrothals. They are therefore very useful in love spells where the seeker intends to attract a suitable life partner. It is also useful for assisting connection with the goddess, especially goddesses of the spring such as Bloddeuwedd and Creiddylad. This goddess connection also helps a woman improve her self-image and self-esteem; for

---

79   McManus, *Guide to Ogam*, 37.

80   Graves, *White Goddess*, 47.

men the connection gives courage in love. An old country charm was for young women to break a twig of the newly flowered hawthorn but leave it hanging, and overnight she would dream of her future husband. If the twig was found the next day, it could then be used in a love spell to draw him near.

Crowns or circlets of hawthorn blossom are worn at Beltane festivities and ceremonies, and it was once popular especially in Ireland to leave out such crowns as gifts to the faeries. Another gift to the faeries, sometimes known as a "faery house," was popular in farmsteads, where relationships with the local faeries and spirits were encouraged to ensure good crops and safety for the animals. These agricultural faeries, often known as "brownies," were thought to lend both their protection and assistance around the farm. To thank them, a globe of woven hawthorn twigs was hung in the kitchen near the hearth. However, a great many other folkloric tales say that hawthorn should never be brought into the home at all. Certainly it should never be worked with without its express permission.

In Ireland and some parts of Scotland, "faery thorns" as they are known are so sacred to the local inhabitants that roads or other building plans have been diverted to avoid their disturbance. One such is the faery tree of Dromoland that caused the diversion of the motorway between Limerick and Galway in 2000, after public pressure demanded it be left alone.[81]

Hawthorns are intimately associated with healing, and are often found growing next to holy wells, such as the one at Madron in Cornwall, named after Madron/Modron a Celtic mother goddess.[82] These hawthorns are dressed with clooties (Scots for "cloth") as they are known in the West County—strips of cloth used as prayers of thanks. Sometimes these cloths are dipped in the healing waters and used to lave the sick or those in need of a blessing, before the cloth is hung upon the tree. Today,

---

81   "The Heritage Tree Database: Hawthorn," Co. Clare, Ireland (http://www
      .treecouncil.ie/heritagetrees/395.htm).

82   "Madron Well and Baptistry," Pendeen, Cornwall, UK (http://cornishancientsites
      .com/Madron%Well%20%26%20Baptistry.pdf).

this tradition has become confused: many nonbiodegradable ribbons and other ties are left at sacred places as so-called offerings that can actually harm the tree as they do not break down and restrict the tree's growth, not to mention the littering. If you would continue this tradition today, think carefully about what you leave behind you, and take some rubbish with you when you leave, remembering that these are sacred places and should be honoured appropriately and thoughtfully.

Hawthorn trees were ritually decorated with flowers and (biodegradable) red ribbons at the summer solstice, a practice known as "bawming the thorn." The tradition continues to this day in the small Cheshire town of Appleton.[83] After dressing the tree, the children dance around it, mimicking the faeries. This is probably a very old custom, dating back to when the trees were properly revered by our Celtic ancestors as part of a ritual temple site (a nemeton).

As sacred faery sites, hawthorn trees near wells or natural springs are places where the veil between the worlds is thin and interchange between the mortal and the spirit world is possible. They are also places of great earth energy, where the soul of the earth herself rises to the surface with the water. As such, they are excellent places to perform divination, healing magic, or to develop a relationship with the *genius loci* (spirit of place). Such places usually have powerful spirit guardians, and whilst sitting in quiet meditation, or embarking on a shamanic journey, it is possible to learn much from these beings. An old technique is to just sit quietly beneath the hawthorn's branches and rest your eyes upon the water. In time you may feel a presence or get a flash in your mind's eye as the tree or the local guardian (sometimes this is one and the same being) makes contact with you. Tread slowly if you wish to do this kind of work. Always thank the spirit and show great respect to it and its sacred domain.

---

83   "Bawming the Thorn," Cheshire, UK (http://www.appletonthorn.org.uk /bawming-day).

Hawthorn trees, a hawthorn twig (fallen, *never* broken or cut) or a chain of hawthorn berries make excellent protection for animals and the beds of children and pregnant women. When magically charged, it eases fears and anxieties and helps heal broken hearts. In Pagan times, sick children were often taken to hawthorn trees, especially if they were near a well, and prayers were made that the hawthorn would take the sickness away and leave the child strong and healthy.

The hawthorn's protective qualities are said to help shelter and protect from lightning, as opposed to the oak and ash, which attract it. It is also said to protect sailors at sea, and was hung in the rafters of barns and houses to protect from storms, fire, ghosts, and evil influences.

Hawthorn burns very hot and makes excellent charcoal. While it is useful on the fire, it seldom grows into large logs. Even green it makes good kindling, and it helps get a fire started, similar to its magical uses. Its wood is useful for small things, and is often used for the handles of magical knives and daggers. Hawthorn root has a beautiful fine grain, and was once used to make combs and trinket boxes.

Hawthorn bark makes a good black dye, and the berries are a useful and delicious foodstuff. They are often made into jellies and chutneys that are usually eaten with cheese or meats.

In Cornwall, a clod of earth and a sprig of hawthorn used to be placed upon each boundary stone as protection and to magically guard the territory. Hawthorn hedges work in a similar way, being practically as well as magically protective. Sprigs of hawthorn can be placed around your home or at the boundaries of your land to draw on this protective energy, and hawthorn trees can be grown and their spirits befriended for the same purpose. The hawthorn makes excellent hedging, as it is durable, hardy, and quick growing, and because it supports a vast array of life, providing food and shelter to numerous animals and insects.

Healing

Herbally, hawthorn is excellent for all nervous disorders and heart-related issues, both physically and emotionally. Culpeper places it under the ruler-ship of Mars, which is interesting when we consider its life force-enhancing qualities, as well its ability to test the seeker and draw him or her into contact with the heart's wisdom (which may sometimes be hard to bear).[84] Haw-thorn berries, leaves, and bark are sedative, anti-spasmodic, and diuretic, and are quite safe to use. (The same cannot be said about the seeds, which are poisonous.) Hawthorn is an excellent tree for regulating heart condi-tions such as arterial blood pressure. It is sometimes known as the "valerian of the heart" as it is so gentle and soothing in its action, giving a greater sense of vitality and well-being all over. It is excellent for help recuperating from long illness or from life traumas. It eases palpitations and anxiety and increases circulation. It is also useful during menopause.

Hawthorn berry tincture can be made in the autumn. Place the ber-ries in a glass jar or bottle, and cover just barely with alcohol, preferably one that is 80 percent proof. Cover tightly and leave in a darkened place for about two weeks before straining and rebottling in a sterilised glass container. Take two to three teaspoons a day.

Dried and crushed hawthorn berries made into a tea or decoction with added honey makes a good gargle for sore throats and infections, and it eases kidney inflammation or diarrhoea.

Hawthorn flowers are used to heal facial blemishes and can improve one's sense of worth and inner beauty. With magical intent, washing in hawthorn flowers steeped in water improves your self-image. Practical and magical steps taken together can be particularly useful for those with low self-esteem, or teenagers who may feel awkward or unattract-ive as they move through puberty. To make hawthorn flower tea, take one teaspoon of the dried flowers in a cup of boiled water and steep for

---

84   Culpeper, *Complete Herbal*, 178.

fifteen minutes. Use as a facial wash, or pour a little onto cotton wool and dab over blemishes.

As a vibrational essence, the hawthorn lends courage through difficulties, and creates movement through stuck emotions or repressed desires, instilling fresh emotional energy. It opens the heart to pleasure and intimacy, and it helps individuals lose fears of commitment. It lends energy to become grounded and more present, manifesting primal life force.

Ogham Divination Meaning

As an ogham, the hawthorn suggests challenge in both positive and/or difficult ways. It also suggests a surge in energy to rise to the test. It questions your worthiness, and even if you fail, you will be nearer your goal than before. Hawthorn leaves you changed, transformed into something more real, honourable, and capable than before. It shows you the truth of your heart. That truth may not always be pleasant but it is always worthwhile. You are encouraged to consider your boundaries and remember to respect the boundaries of others in equal measure. It can signify love, union, and connection with the goddess if your heart is ready.

Journal Entry: The Hawthorn of Madron's Well, Cornwall

To me, hawthorns are sacred to the Great Goddess in all her forms and names; it is no coincidence that they so often grow beside holy wells where the Earth Mother rises up and gives life-giving water to the land. Such places were always revered by my Celtic ancestors. Here in Madron, the spring and well are hidden deep in a thicket of hawthorn trees. A lengthy shadowed lane between overhanging branches leads us forward as if on the ancient green road to Faery.

The sound of water merges with the whisper of the leaves and the gentle shush of rain upon the hillside. The hawthorn is richly decorated with clooties and prayers, each one a heartfelt plea or gift of thanks. Coloured ribbons sway over the waters in the breeze and dance in their reflection.

Sitting here in silence, I feel the goddess of the waters approach, ancient and ever-flowing in her compassion, and it is both humbling and inspiring. I feel her deep eyes upon me, searching into my heart. She allows me to gather hawthorn berries for tinctures and a few for a charm to help a friend heal a broken heart. As I return from her sacred enclosure, I feel my heart beating slow and strong within me, and I know that the magic of the goddess has enfolded me for a while in her green mantle.

Oak/Duir *(Quercus robur)*

....
Other names:
Royal oak, druid's oak, druid's tree
....

Word ogham of:
Morainn: *Ardam dosae* "Most
exalted tree"; "sheltering defence"

Cuchulain: *Slechtain soíre.i.niama sairte*
"Most carved of craftsmanship/kneeling
work"; "bright and shining work"

Oengus: *Grés soír* "Craft work"; "carpenter's work"[85]

Description

Oak trees are actually a part of the beech family, and can grow up to fifty metres. An oak has a very large root system firmly anchoring it into the soil the same size and extent as the branches above. It has an irregular-shaped spreading crown, and its branches usually begin fairly low down its trunk, which has craggy grey-green bark. Its alternate leaves are five to fifteen centimetres long, each with three to six lobes on each side. The oak flowers in May with male and female catkins appearing on the same tree. Its seeds, known as acorns, appear from September to October, and are about three centimetres long in groups of up to five, with the scaly caps reaching to a third of their length. Green at first, acorns ripen to brown as autumn gathers pace. The oak prefers to grow in mixed broadleaved woodland, as it likes to have plenty of light. It can cope with moist or even poor soils quite well. Oak interbreeds well with other types of oak,

---

85   McManus, *Guide to Ogam*, 43, with additions by Calder, *Scholars' Primer*, 285.

particularly the sessile oak and the downy oak, which are similar. Oaks can be found across Europe and the British Isles, and similar oaks grow all over the world, particularly in North America.

Lore and Legend

In Brehon law, duir, the oak, was the primary chieftain tree, held above all others.

The oak is an exceptionally strong wood, and as the most famous of trees they have long been considered a symbol of Britain, drawn from the days of their special significance to the druids and their use in the making of ships for the Elizabethan navy. In fact, so many oaks were felled for the navy it almost became extinct until it became the first tree species to be protected by legislation, thus planting a very small acorn in the British consciousness towards the future growth of environmental conservation. It is the wise guardian of the green world.

Famous ancient English oaks include Herne's Oak in Windsor Great Park, from which Herne is said to ride out with the Wild Hunt every Samhain (October 31); the Major Oak of Sherwood Forest where the green man outlaw Robin Hood took refuge; and the twin oaks, Gog and Magog in Glastonbury, which bear the name of two ancient British giants.[86, 87, 88] The district of Gospel Oak in London is named after an ancient oak under which King Edward the Confessor pledged to keep and defend the laws of England. In the word ogham of Oengus, the oak is called "craft work," which implies the development and application of skill—and by extension responsibility and maturity—and refers to its considerable practical applications.

The name for oak in Irish, *dara*, or in the ogham, *duir*, share the root for the word *druid*, which means "one with the wisdom of the oak."

---

86   Westwood and Simpson, *Lore of the Land*, 29.

87   Ibid., 583.

88   Ibid., 62.

Traditionally the druids' grove was amongst oak trees, or it focussed upon a single oak. In fact, there are many oaks in the UK locally known as "the druid's oak," a lingering trace of this practice. The druids' close association with oak trees shows its significance as an access point to spirit and even deity, a signifier of the values they held dear. There is so much to suggest that the druids held the oak tree as a being of supreme importance in its own right that it is sometimes argued that druids worshipped the trees themselves. It is certainly very likely they were highly revered as representatives of the gods and served as manifestation points and centres of focus for magic and spiritual practice, so much so that later Romano-Celtic "Jupiter columns" were deliberately decorated with carved oak leaves and acorns.[89]

The oak tree is also inseparable from the ancient tradition of the oak king, a symbol of male sovereignty and the fertility god of the green world. From the lessons drawn from the hawthorn comes the purpose for energy, development, and the right use of the power earned from rising to the challenge of the goddess. The primary purpose of kingship is to protect and provide for the people, via the responsible use of power and energy. Sovereignty in the individual runs along the same lines. *Duir* means "door" as well as "oak tree," and oak groves are places where the otherworld, the sky world, and the world of earth meet. Thus oak trees are guardian spirits extraordinaire, providing the ability of shamanic flight between worlds and encouraging spiritual development. At the same time, they provide stability and strength for the people. They are father figures and guardians of the soul's journey.

Being the god of fertility, the oak king is also the king of summer. This correlation probably harks back to the oak representing the god of the sun in early or pre-druidic tradition where the sun god gradually fell through the seasons, rising again at the winter solstice. As such, the oak king is one half of the god's dual nature, the other half being the holly king—the hunter god of winter and the underworld. Thus we find a correlation in

---

89   Green, *Dictionary of Celtic Myth*, 164.

Morainn's words that the oak is a "sheltering defence" and Cuchulain's that the oak is "kneeling work" (work that requires humility and care to serve others or taking responsibility for the collective). Yet he also calls it "bright and shining work"—kingship is work worthy of honour, and at the same time a path that leads to enlightenment and the growth of the soul. This is also rightly a great source of pride.

Duir also means "rutting deer," its root word *deru* developing into meaning "oak," "door," and "stag." There are also connections between the oak, stags, various Celtic gods such as Cernunnos and Llew Llaw Gyffes, as well as several mysterious antlered goddesses (figurines of which have been found across Europe and England).[90] This connection can also be seen in the oak's sacredness to the Dagdha, the Irish "good god" who is also connected to the image of rutting deer and is famous for his great strength, his cauldron of plenty which provided for the people and protected them, and his great earthy physicality. There are other examples round the world, such as the Sumerian god Enki who was also known as *Dara Mah*—"the great stag."[91] With the oak we have a symbol of kingship at the height of power and ability. That power is gained by holding and correctly wielding the life force, the vitality—not by denying it.

Oaks are also sacred to Taranis, the Celtic god of storms and lightning as well as the Celtic Jupiter, marking where energy from the otherworld meets our physical earth.[92, 93] Elsewhere the oak is sacred to Zeus, Jupiter, and Thor, also gods of lightning. Oak trees which have been hit with lightning are especially magical and of the greatest druidic significance. However, oaks are also sacred to the goddess Brighid, whose sanctuary at Kildare in Ireland was originally an oak grove. It gets its name from *cill*

---

90   Green, *Dictionary of Celtic Myth*, 164.

91   Bobula Ida, *The Great Stag: A Sumerian Divinity* (1953), reprint from *The Yearbook of Ancient and Medieval History*. (http://www.stavacademy.co.uk/mimir/greatstag.htm.)

92   Green, *Dictionary of Celtic Myth*, 205.

93   Ibid., 164.

dara, "the church of the oak tree," as Brighid became Christianised into a Celtic saint.

In Greece the rustling of oak leaves was used as a divinatory tool, as was the movement of birds in its branches, and it is likely that they were used by druids in similar ways. In fact, timber circles or "woodhenges" of the Neolithic and early Bronze Age were made of oak, and at Seahenge in Norfolk in the east of the UK is a circular enclosure of oak posts enclosing an inverted oak stump which was clearly of ritual significance.[94] These give testimony to the oak's great importance as *axis mundi* or World Trees—the central point upon which all existence turns. Perhaps the "henge" structures even functioned as representations of the gods themselves to both the Celts and their earlier Bronze Age and Neolithic ancestors.

Practical and Magical Uses

Among the most magical parts of the oak tree are the acorns. Phallic in shape, they have been used in love and fertility magic for millennia as well as being used as a focus of power at the tip of wands and staves by many ancient Pagan cults. Lovers used to place acorns in a bowl of water to see if they would stay together; if the acorns drifted apart, so would the couple in due time. A spell from the fourteenth century to prevent unfaithfulness in wives was to place two halves of an acorn under the woman's pillow. Acorn necklaces are often worn during magical working to contact the oak's great strength and sovereignty, as are an oak's leaves. They are useful for contacting the hunter gods and goddesses, and those connected to lightning, such as Thor, Taranis, Zeus, as well as Andraste, Brighid, Danu, and Athene. In fact, acorns are useful for contacting any ruler-type god, as the oak occupies such a central pivotal position in all tree magic. As both the door and guardian between realms, oak can be seen as a magical passport, offering access and protection to all realms.

---

94   "Seahenge," Lynn Museum, Norfolk, UK (http://www.museums.norfolk.gov.uk
      /view/NCC095944.)

Acorns can be used as charms to attract love, good luck, fertility, wealth, or security. After magically charging them (with the tree's permission), they can be carried in a pouch or upon a cord around the neck. Carefully inscribe them with what you want to attract, and leave them to do their work. Bury them after a while, and they will continue to work as the tree grows or the acorn returns to the soil.

Acorns, oak leaves, and bark can all be burnt as incense alone or in a blend for empowerment, divination, healing, or journeying, or for love and money magic. These are always more powerful if they are charged by the tree and the tree spirit works with you.

Talismans of oak inscribed with the name Taranis can help protect against storms and lightning.

Oak galls, which are made as the tree's reaction to parasites, also have a great many magical uses. One ancient method of divination concerned using a gall to predict the fate and welfare of the nation as a whole, so great is the oak's reputation as a tree of sovereignty. The gall was broken into at special times of the year (most likely Beltane and Samhain), and its contents foretold what was to come for the following season. An ant inside foretold a good harvest; a spider meant pestilence; a maggot meant sickness; a worm, famine; a flying insect, war.

Galls were also used to divine whether children were bewitched. A gall was placed in a bowl of water and set beneath the child's bed. If the gall floated, the child was well; if it sank, the child was afflicted and more steps needed to be taken.

Oaks are magically connected to the mysteries of the mistletoe, which Pliny recorded as being ritually cut from the tree at the winter solstice with a golden (probably bronze) sickle.[95] The mistletoe as the semen of the sun god/oak king was both sacrificed and reborn to bring fertility back to the

95   H. Jones Rackham, W. H. S. Jones, and D. E. Eichholz, trans., book 16, chapter 95 in *Pliny's Natural History* (Cambridge, MA: Harvard University Press, 1938).

land with the distant spring.[96] Lightning, also held so sacred and significant when striking the oak, perhaps signified the god's divine inception upon the earth, as well as the strike of divine ignition upon our souls.

Mistletoe was called *Druid-lus* (the druid's herb) as well as "all heal" due to its many healing and magical properties. These are thought to vary depending on what tree the mistletoe grows upon; mistletoe growing on the oak has different properties from mistletoe growing on any of the other trees it colonises, such as the apple. The combination of oak and mistletoe in magical workings lends extra power and manifestation potential, as well as extreme fertility and fecundity. Traditionally mistletoe is hung over beds for fertility and to ensure healthy pregnancy. The addition of oak will help with becoming a good parent and provider.

Oak is an extremely durable and close-grained wood. After the first hundred years of growth, it grows very slowly, making it strong and long-lasting. Traditionally it was used to make bridges and water breaks as well as houses. Neolithic trackways made of oak across wetlands and marshes have been found in the UK, still well preserved after thousands of years. Oak was also central to shipbuilding, from Viking longboats to those used by the navy of Elizabeth I used in the war against the Spanish armada. The very earliest boats found in Britain were made from single oak trunks. Oak was also used for coffins, one famous example being the supposed coffins of King Arthur and Queen Guinevere discovered at Glastonbury Abbey.

Oak bark was a valuable resource for dyes, and an infusion of oak bark and copper was used by Scottish highlanders for a beautiful purple dye.

A decoction of oak bark is used by gardeners to enrich the soil, although it can also encourage fungi.

Oak leaves are used to make wine; acorns are edible and were a staple diet for our Neolithic ancestors as well as still being consumed in acorn

---

96   Philip Carr-Gomm and Stephanie Carr-Gomm, *The Druid Plant Oracle* (New York: St. Martin's Press, 2007), 80.

coffee to this day. They are also used for animal feed. Romans used to roast acorns for feasts and made acorn bread.

Healing

One method still useful today is to use oak galls for healing. First, you must befriend and honour the tree the galls come from so that the oak gall will work for you. As an alternative, an oak ball can be made by binding tightly strips of bark into a bundle, asking the oak for its assistance as you tie it, perhaps also intoning the word duir ("dooiirr"). Ask the tree to help you with the healing, whether for yourself or another, and tell it what you need to happen. Ask for its advice as well as its magical assistance. Allow plenty of time for quiet so that you may hear its messages. The ball may then be charged in sunlight and worn by those in need of the healing. The ball can also be rolled over the body to convey its healing energies and extract the illness. When the work is done, the ball or gall should be laid upon the earth or buried so the illness can be earthed and transformed.

Herbally, the oak is very antiseptic as well as anti-inflammatory, being useful for sore throats, skin inflammation, minor wounds, and fevers. Oak bark can be dried and made into a decoction by taking 100 grams of bark and boiling it for ten minutes in a litre of water. This can be gargled for sore throats and sinusitis, and it will staunch bleeding gums. It can also be put into hot baths for chilblains. This decoction can be taken as a good women's tonic combined with nettle and yarrow.

Bruised oak leaves ease inflammations and can be applied to bruises and sprains. This application is especially good when combined with comfrey leaves. A foot wash made of oak leaf tea soothes weary feet and also helps one to find the right path through life.

Culpeper mentions using the water found in hollow bowls upon the oak tree to heal sores and skin infections.[97] His recommendation can be attributed to the oak's antiseptic and anti-inflammatory properties, which

---

97   Culpeper, *Complete Herbal*, 254.

will seep into the water.[98] Water found in the trunk's nooks and crannies is also especially magical and would be understood as a vibrational essence today. Such naturally occurring magic potions are created by the interaction of the tree spirit and the water spirits of the rain alone. While they are especially powerful, they may not be safe to drink. Instead, they can be carried on the body, applied to the skin, or stored in a witch bottle. They can be preserved with alcohol or glycerine, although the best will stay fresh on its own for some time.

Magically and as a vibrational essence, oak is a great empowerer, useful for finding the energy to fight against great difficulties without loss of hope or draining of energy. Magically it applauds courage and can also instil it in those who are trying hard to endure. It helps you discover your inner sovereignty by holding and developing your inner authority and mastery, leading to a greater ability for kindness and responsibility. It is also a very powerful spirit ally that protects your connection across the worlds and keeps you grounded and present in the process.

Ogham Divination Meaning

As an ogham, duir implies and teaches strength, security, and the ability to sustain growth over lengths of time, through varied circumstances. It helps and encourages you to open the doors of your perception and enter into initiatory experiences that allow you to do and be more than you were before, in addition to assimilating this new way of being. It is a symbol of growth in all ways—materially, intellectually, emotionally, and spiritually via the connection in yourself between earth and sky, divinity and matter. As the ogham of sovereignty, it encourages right action and being fully present and conscious of your actions, embodying wholeness and nobility.

---

98   Culpeper, *Complete Herbal*, 254.

Journal Entry: Gog and Magog,
The Old Oaks of Avalon, Glastonbury, Somerset

The most sacred oaks in Britain to me are Gog and Magog, who sit together through the centuries, guarding the ceremonial entrance to the Isle of Avalon. Once they were part of a mighty avenue of oaks, making their way up to the feet of Glastonbury Tor. Each oak is a guardian and a marker of the way between the worlds, and how much more so must this whole avenue have been … Now these two are all that remains, but they hold all the power of the others within them, all their memories and sacred hidden knowledge. Gog no longer puts forth leaves, and sitting with him one can feel he is more than halfway to the otherworld. Magog is still strong, however, and she scatters her acorns far and wide. A small forest grows at her feet. At this most sacred and ancient place, I travel in spirit to the misty isle while she guards the way. And when I return, she allows me the gift of an acorn myself, that I may hold a little of her knowledge. I keep it as a talisman, aligning me to her ancient ways, granting me a little of her strength.

Holly/Tinne *(Ilex aquifolium)*

....
Other names:
Christ's thorn, holy tree, hulm tree
....

Word ogham of:
Morainn: *Trian roith* "Third of a wheel"

Cuchulain: *Trian n airm.i.tinne*
"A third of weapons, an iron bar"

Oengus: *Smiur gúaile* "Fires of coal";
"marrow of charcoal"[99]

Description

Holly is a small evergreen shrub or small tree that grows up to ten metres in many different environments from woodlands to gardens. It is native to the British Isles as well as much of Europe. It can grow in the Alps up to 1,800 metres. Often forming a valuable undergrowth in deciduous woodlands, the holly has smooth grey bark and alternate leaves that are stiff and leathery and often have sharp spines. The leaves are dark green and shiny above and paler beneath. It flowers from May to June, with small, frothy pale flowers gathered about the stem, with the female flowers showing prominent green ovaries. The red round berries form from September to October, and are seven to ten millimetres across, containing four or five seeds. These berries will sometimes stay on the tree throughout the whole winter, providing food for numerous birds, particularly thrushes who seem to love them.

---

99 McManus, *Guide to Ogam*, 43, with additions by Calder, *Scholars' Primer*, 91.

Lore and Legend

According to Brehon law, the holly was one of the seven chieftain trees, called *cuileann*.

The word *tinne* means "ingot" or "molten metal." It is related to the Old Irish *tend* meaning "strong," and the Irish and Scots Gaelic word for fire, *teine*, as well as the modern Irish *tine*.[100] Holly was used by the druids, especially for solstice fires. It burns amongst the hottest of all trees and also makes particularly good charcoal. It was the preferred fuel for blacksmiths' fires when burned for the forging of swords, another clue to its fierce nature and Oengus's description as "fires of coal." Holly's fire is metaphysical as well, being fuel for the life force and leading to the illumination of the soul.

The holly's use in smith craft links it with the Celtic smith god Govannon (Welsh)/Goibniu (Irish), who possessed the mead or ale of eternal life, as well as the Saxon smith god Weyland.[101] These are gods associated with strength, endurance and the attainment of skill. Goibniu's eternal-life-granting mead may also be a reference to his great life force and vitality, the golden mead being akin to Soma and the risen kundalini or life force that gives rise to both enlightenment or "the shining brow" of poetic vision and shamanic inspiration. These are all within the distinct energies of the holly, which sees fertility and life force continue through the barren winter. The holly's importance to smith craft is highlighted in Cuchulain's words on the holly—"a third of weapons, an iron bar."

Holly is of course synonymous with the holly king, an ancient figure popular in medieval times, also reminiscent of the much earlier gods of the hunt—antlered gods such as Cernunnos—and the lords of the underworld, the gods of winter. The holly king is the shadowy counterpart to the oak king, who has dominion over the other half of the year. These two are in an eternal symbolic struggle, ritually enacted in many Beltane traditions—when the oak king wins and brings fertility to the land—and at

---

100   McManus, *Guide to Ogam*, 37.
101   Ellis, *Dictionary of Irish Mythology*, 137.

Samhain, when the holly king has victory, bringing the winter months. The struggle hints at two sides of a singular now-forgotten god of the sun. The cyclical struggle between these two halves is recorded in many ancient tales, including the sacrificial decapitation/initiation tale of "Gawain and the Green Knight," where Gawain is given a rod of oak and the Green Knight wears a crown of holly.

The holly king is primarily a sacrificial king. As a winter counterpart for the oak king, he ensures the safety and provision for the tribes under his protection. *Tinne* also means "link," referring to its linking, pivotal position between the worlds (like the oak), where the king oversees the safety of all who traverse those ways via its ability to raise the life force. Where the holly king can be seen as an element of the antlered gods like Cernunnos, we can see the horns as reflecting this rise in power and potency. The great rise in energy the holly facilitates allows great things to be achieved. It is a shattering of inertia that may come on the magical path when internal winter strikes; it happens in preparation for working and living in a new way and taking things to a new level. As the lord of the underworld, the holly king is also connected to issues surrounding the shadow self, when fears and stuck patterns can threaten to overwhelm and destroy spiritual progress and magical development. Yet holly also lends the courage to persevere and face these issues head-on.

With the assimilation of the oak's lessons comes the ability to handle responsibility. With the holly this responsibility is seen to continue through a span of time, which brings new problems and matters of endurance through the inevitable lean times that always appear periodically, as well as the reaping of the consequences of your actions, some of which may not be desirable. The holly's fierceness and energy enables the seeker to find solutions and track down new possibilities and resources, even when the winter of the soul is at its bleakest. Its fire lends itself to illumination and the rekindling of the life force, raising it to a blaze that melts the harshest of blockages and most barren of circumstances.

In Ireland especially, holly is considered particularly sacred and a great initiator and spiritual catalyst, as can be seen in the figure of the Green Knight. The holly has the ability to withstand the harshest of weather, and its spiked evergreen leaves are testimony to its great life force and responsive and defensive capabilities. Morainn's words—"third of a wheel"—refer to its use in the making of chariot wheels, a role it shared with the oak. The final third of the wheel's construction was the combination of both oak and holly, the whole thus becoming greater than the sum of its constituents. The use of the two woods makes an excellent metaphor for the spiritual journey. Its spirit encourages individuals to stand in their own power. Its fiery transformative energy burns away the dross in an almost alchemical way, transmuting our limitations into spiritual gold via the challenges and ordeals of the spiritual winter that is its herald.

Holly is also associated with lightning, which it is said to protect against, and it is also sacred to the Celtic god of thunder, Taranis (from the Celtic root *taran* "thunderer"), whose symbol is the wheel.[102] Taranis is also thought to be a god of war, linked to the holly via the prized technology of chariot wheels, as well as the forging of weapons in its super-heated flames. Spear shafts were also sometimes made of holly, as the wood could be tempered and made stronger by heat. In addition, it conveyed its magical properties to the warrior who held it.

Holly is also sacred to the Scandinavian gods Odin and Thor. Odin's spear Gugnir was made of holly, and was said to never miss its target. Holly is also sacred to his son, the thunder god (like Taranis) Thor, who was especially important to Viking warriors.

Holly wreaths were also used during the Roman festival of Saturnalia to honour the god Saturn, known in Greek as Kronos. Saturn, like the holly king, was an agricultural god but was also associated with old age, and is known as "old Father Time." This is the god in the underworld again, the god of the hearth fire, rather than the fields under the summer sun.

---

102   Green, *Dictionary of Celtic Myth*, 205.

Saturnalia took place originally on December 17, but was later extended to the 23rd, covering the winter solstice. It was a major precursor to the Christian festival of Christmas; revels, gift-giving, and feasting were its central features. Saturn and Kronos, as gods of the winter solstice, are of course akin to the holly king himself, the old men of winter, holding fort until the spring.

Practical and Magical Uses

Holly's ability to endure through the winter and raise the life force reveals it is also a tree of passion, useful for love and long-term commitment spells. A holly charm to bring a husband or wife is made by placing nine holly leaves, collected at midnight with clear intent and permission, in a square of white cloth. Make a libation to the holly tree and observe complete silence during collection and wrapping, and keep them under the pillow for at least a month.

Men carrying holly leaves were said to be irresistible to women, perhaps because they were carrying the energy of the holly king or the antlered gods with their robust and dark sexuality.

Holly is magically very protective, particularly during the winter months when the appearance of its red berries shows its heightened life force— enough to last through the cold barren season. This is why it is traditional to place holly wreaths at the front door at the winter solstice—to lend its great fiery and fertile energy to the house. However, it should never be cut without asking its permission first, as its fierce spirit may turn against you. Sacred to the sun, many cultures have used it for protection and blessing during winter months.

The Roman writer and naturalist Pliny the Elder records that holly leaves are said to calm wild animals when thrown at them, compelling an animal to lie down and be still. Pliny also records that when planted near a home, holly guards against lightning and witchcraft.[103]

---

103   Grieve, *A Modern Herbal*, 405.

A tincture of holly or holly-infused water was sometimes sprinkled over newborn babies for protection as well as to ensure good health, keeping the baby's life force strong.

Holly is also used in sleep magic, to induce good dreams and cure insomnia. Place a holly leaf or some holly wood under your pillow for prophetic dreams and to gain wisdom. However, you may find yourself encountering aspects of the underworld or your own deep subconscious, so be prepared for what that may reveal.

Holly wands are good for protection and in spells for legal success or things concerning competition, as they can encourage a swift resolution or sudden manifestation. Burning holly leaves as an incense is also useful for legal spells, protection, courage, endurance, and to attract success into any project.

Holly is also useful for sexual magic, especially between already established partners between whom it may help rekindle desires. Hung over the bedpost or burnt as an incense, it will help raise the life force and libido. This is especially the case for men, as its masculine, fiery energy will increase appetite and vigour.

Dreaming of holly is said to reveal the source of your problems and to encourage you to deal with your darker and more difficult emotions, again via its connection to the underworld.

Holly is a dense, white wood used for all sorts of poles and fine work, from billiard cues to chess pieces to fine inlay details. It was also once used for the hammers on harpsichords. Due to its white colour, it was useful for staining and holding other colours and was often a substitute for ebony. It was also used as a substitute (unstained) for ivory and was a popular wood for attractive knife handles. Holly was also used for walking sticks and coachman's whips.

Holly bark and leaves are a popular food for rabbits, and it will increase their appetites. Holly leaves placed around pea seedlings will deter mice, as they will prefer to eat the holly, and the prickly leaves also deter slugs and snails.

Holly was once used to make birdlime, a horrible toxic substance used to catch birds by sticking them to branches, and also as an insecticide.

Healing

Caution: Holly berries are mildly poisonous and dangerous to small children.

Herbally, holly leaf tea in very small proportions can induce sweating, ridding the body of toxins and fevers. It was sometimes used as a tea substitute in Europe for coughs and colds as well as bladder complaints, rheumatism, and arthritis. The berries are very purgative, yet when dried are very good for soothing stomach disorders and heavy menstruation.

Weak holly tea is also said to help calm the emotions, particularly anger and jealousy.

Culpeper writes that the holly is under the governance of Saturn, and recommends using a poultice of holly bark and leaves for broken bones and dislocations.[104]

A vibrational essence of holly is good for relieving feelings of jealousy, envy, anger, and revenge, and all challenges of the shadow self. In short, it addresses the prickly parts of people's natures. It helps overcome these difficulties and the feelings of fear and inadequacy or insecurity that can accompany them by raising and freeing up the emotional energy. Once you have released difficult feelings or internal turmoil, healing and a more positive outlook can eventually be achieved.

Ogham Divination Meaning

As an ogham, tinne invites the raising of internal energy to endure through difficulties and melt through the snows of winter in the soul's life. Everyone undergoes occasional periods of hardship physically, emotionally, or spiritually. The holly encourages us to raise our life force, and it ensures

---

104   Culpeper, *Complete Herbal*, 197.

we will have the energy to make it through and bring illumination to our darkness, raising the kundalini to new heights. This is a robust and passionate energy, akin to the hunter gods and the guardians of the underworld. The holly spirit lends its seasoned and experienced qualities to aid all souls in making it through to the spring.

Journal Entry: The Holly Tree of Glastonbury Tor, Somerset

The holly stands out as a being of great power and vitality, its rich green leaves, robust and full of life, its rich red berries providing a feast for the birds that gather and call in its branches. Standing here at the foot of the Tor, the holly king is proud and resplendent, honouring the lords of winter and the sun's descent into the underworld. From Samhain to winter solstice I gather sprigs for the altar to honour Gwyn ap Nudd and the underworld. When winter storms are due, I place a piece at the doors, gates, and each window for protection. Spears made from holly wood tempered by fire are especially strong, and this has a lesson for us. Sometimes I give some to people who come to me with difficulties, that they may know their shadows and discover what holds them back from finding their place in the world—to help them break negative habits, or patterns of disempowerment. Holly knows how to endure the winter of the soul, how to grow stronger by walking through the fire, and he guides them through, igniting courage in their hearts.

Hazel/Coll *(Corylus avellana)*

....

Other names :
Coll, the poet's tree

....

Word ogham of:

Morainn: *Caíniu fedaib* "Fairest of trees"

Cuchulain: *Milsem fedo.i.cno* "Sweetest of trees, a nut"

Oengus: *Cara blóesc* "Friend of nutshells"; "friend of cracking"[105]

Description

Hazels are deciduous shrubs or small trees growing to about six metres, found in many environments due to their shallow roots. It takes nine years for a hazel tree to bear fruit, those distinctive edible hazelnuts, which it does from August to October. Its male flowers, catkins, are visible from May. It has smooth grey-brown bark, and small rounded heart-shaped leaves which come to a point, and have jagged, serrated edges. The leaves are usually six to thirteen centimetres long, but may be longer on sucker shoots. The hazel prefers moist, deep, loamy soils but grows readily in many environments. It is found from lowlands to mountainous regions. Various types of hazel can be found across Europe, Asia, and North America. The tree's delicate beauty earns Morainn's name for it as "the fairest of trees."

Lore and Legend

According to Brehon law, hazel was known as a chieftain tree, named *coll* there also. To fell it unlawfully incurred the death penalty.

105　McManus, *Guide to Ogam*, 43, with additions by Calder, *Scholars' Primer*, 287.

Hazels are synonymous with the pursuit of poetic and druidic wisdom in the Celtic tradition. This kind of poetry is not only concerned with writing stanzas and preserving Celtic lore, but with the attainment of divine knowledge which is quite shamanic in nature—an awareness of all things. The Irish oracular poets, the fili, were renowned magical practitioners and seers. The hazel is said to hold all wisdom—awen or imbas—within its nuts. These were consumed in legend by the sacred salmon of wisdom, the oldest and wisest of animal spirits, who dwelled in Connla's well, near Tipperary in Ireland as recorded in the *Dindsenchas*.[106] (The well is also known as Nechtan's well and the Well of Segais—the mythical source of all the rivers of Ireland.) The salmon ate only nuts from the nine sacred hazel trees that surrounded the pool, relating hazel again to the number nine, it being the ninth ogham letter. The salmon swam out to sea and back again, transmitting this knowledge from spirit (the sea) to generation after generation via this magical process. Eating the salmon of wisdom lent knowledge of all arts and sciences, and this was the fate of the hero Fionn mac Cumhail ("Fionn, son of the warrior god Cumhail"), who is also connected to the hazel, as mythology tells us that the best Celtic warriors were educated in druidic wisdom. Another such divine druid warrior was Cuchulain, who stressed the wonder of this wisdom, calling it "the sweetest of woods." Fionn also had a famous magical shield named "the dripping ancient hazel" because it was cut from the hazel tree upon which the head of the god Balor of the evil eye had hung for fifty years, dripping poison.

Hazels are sacred to Oengus mac Óg, the god of love and eloquence who carried a hazel wand. Ancient Irish heralds also carried hazel wands as tokens of being under his dominion and protection. Oengus's words, "friend of cracking," suggest the hazel's willingness to aid mortals in the cracking or dismantling of mental/spiritual programming to become able to flow in and out of all things, thus gaining divine wisdom. Another

---

106   Whitley Stokes, "The Edinburgh Dinnsenchas" in *Folklore 4* (1893), 457 (http://www.ucd.ie./tlh/trans/ws.fl.4.001.t.text.html).

translation of the word ogham for the hazel, "friend of nutshells," also refers to this gaining of divine wisdom—even today the term "in a nutshell" means someone's understanding of a subject being complete and simple in its summation. Hazel is a tree that shows us the wisdom found in the micro- and macrocosm, a single point of focus reflecting the whole of creation within it.

The Irish triads tell us that the hazel and the apple were two trees that incurred the death penalty to those who felled them illegally, a sign of their deep spiritual and practical importance. The apple and the hazel are also placed together in association with the oak in the Great Tree of Mugna, one of the five most sacred trees in all Ireland.[107] This great tree was said to embody the qualities of all three, and its roots supposedly drank from the waters of Connla's well alongside the sacred hazels, descending deep into the otherworld. In some sources the tree of Mugna is an oak; in others, a yew.

Similar to the Irish legends, the Scottish lore also tells us of a sacred well guarded by hazel trees in which two magical salmon lived. It was said that these salmon were so holy that to eat them would induce punishment by the gods, as the wisdom and power the fish held was for them alone.

In British folklore, particularly in the southwest, silver snakes are said to surround hazel roots. This is its vibrant lifeforce, its awen, the ability to be connected and understand all things as swift as thought. It is said to be under the rulership of Mercury, and there are many connections between the hazel and the god Mercury/Hermes, who oversees matters of communication and knowledge.[108] Both these messenger gods carry a staff of hazel, sometimes depicted with ribbons or silver snakes wrapped around it. These silver snakes became the caduceus.

Hazel is also sacred to Brighid, the fire goddess of poetry and the home, and through her with death rites and "keening," ritualised mourning.

---

107   Stokes, "Edinburgh Dinnsenchas," 485.
108   Culpeper, *Complete Herbal*, 179.

Keening features in the tale of the battle of Moytura, where Brighid keened for the death of her son—here the hazel aided communication between life and death. The old Irish Gaelic name for hazel is *calltuinn*, "the loss of something." Hazels have a friendly, helpful, and clever attitude to poets and spiritual seekers, being much easier to contact shamanically or in meditation than some other trees.

Practical and Magical Uses

The hazel's link to wisdom and inspiration has led to the practice of using it for divinatory and magic wands. The "wishing wands" of Teutonic legend were also made of hazel.[109] Hazel is also the traditional choice for dowsing rods. A dowsing rod is usually a forked hazel, the two forks representing the snakes or dual forces of life and death so often associated with the hazel. Dowsing rods can help detect lines of earth energy that snake across the planet much like veins. These are sometimes known as dragon currents or ley lines, and they can bring health or illness, and attract many spirit presences. Places where these lines cross are often locations of sacred sites.

Dowsing rods should only ever be made with the tree's permission. When used, they are gripped gently; the wand dips towards the earth at the source of water or another feature. Cornish dowsers used to dowse for minerals as well as water with a hazel rod. Until the seventeenth century, dowsing was used to discover the whereabouts of lost objects and treasure, as well as sometimes finding thieves and murderers. Dowsing rods can be used to follow dragon currents; they detect a line's location in addition to its width and length.

A spell for invisibility can be found in the fifteenth-century *Book of Saint Albans*, which instructs the magician to get a hazel rod a fathom and a half long (nine feet) and to insert into it a green hazel twig.[110] Hazel wands

---

109   Jacob Grimm, *Teutonic Mythology, Vol. 4* (London: J. S. London, 1888), 1598.
110   Juliana Bernes, *The Book of Saint Albans* (1486) (London: Elliott Stock, 1881).

were very popular in much medieval magic and great store was put by cutting them appropriately.

As hazels are sacred to Oengus, the Irish god of love (who as already discussed carried a hazel rod), they are used in many love and fertility spells. There is an old traditional folk spell of observing the movement of hazelnuts in water or in flames to predict the success or failure of relationships. Another spell involves wrapping hazel flowers (catkins) in green or pink cloth, carrying them close to the heart before reciting an incantation to your love, and then burning the package in the hearth or over a pink or green candle.

Hazel was traditionally sewn into Welsh sleeping caps to induce good and inspired dreams, as well as to make "thinking caps" of woven hazel twigs. Hazel twig hats were also sometimes worn by sailors for protection against storms. The hazel's protection from storms is also accessed by placing hazel twigs on windowsills and through window fixtures. Sometimes hazel was placed inside the walls for this purpose. Three pins of hazel driven into the doorpost are also said to protect from fire, especially if the tree has given its permission; it can then alert those in the house to any danger.

Hazelnut necklaces are thought to bring good luck into the house, and have been found in prehistoric tombs, probably serving as amulets as well as decoration. In the bardic ritual *Diechetel do Chenaib* ("cracking the nuts of wisdom)," hazelnuts may have been chewed to induce poetic and magical inspiration and insight, again perhaps giving insight into Oengus's words that the hazel is "friend of nutshells."[111]

Hazel is extremely useful in crafts of many kinds, especially coppicing (cutting slender, straight poles that hazel naturally provides) and the making of fences, providing small timber, poles and rods, wattles in the ancient wattle and daub houses, and hedge stakes. The practice of coppicing goes back millennia and is highly sustainable. A coppiced hazel will continue

---

111   John Matthews, *The Celtic Shaman* (London: Rider, 2001), 163.

to grow and yield new strong shoots every year. These are very strong and pliable.

Since the earliest times, hazel has been used with willow whips, cow hides, and pine resin to make the small one-man boats known as coracles. While it was thought coracle building was a practice limited to Wales and Ireland, others have now been found in the Near East.

Hazel poles are also used in the construction of "benders"—small structures of bent hazel poles tied into dome shapes and stuck into the earth. These are ancient structures that were originally covered with hides or furs, and they are still used today for a whole host of activities, though usually with waterproof tarpaulin. Benders make excellent semipermanent structures and may have been used for Iron Age druid ceremonies, especially those where the fili or poet went into a darkened "hut" covered with bulls' hide to seek inspiration. These days they are often made into wonderful permanent homes by those seeking a low-impact ecological way of living close to the earth.

Healing

Hazel is not used herbally, but the nuts are thought to be a great source of nutrition, as they are rich in healthy fatty acids, vitamins E and B, and numerous minerals. Hazelnuts are used to make butter and milk, both of which are delicious. The nuts are also often cooked with salmon. Hazel was an important food during hunter-gatherer times, and is often found in Mesolithic midden piles as well as Neolithic hearths and tombs, where they often show signs of having been roasted.

Crosses made of hazel wood were once thought to draw poison from snake bites and to help cure toothache.

Ground hazelnuts were used to help fever and excessive menstrual flow, as well as diarrhoea, although it's unclear if this was efficacious. Ground hazels are still used boiled in mead or honey to ease stubborn coughs, sometimes with added pepper.

Hazelwood necklaces are sometimes used for mouth ailments, from a baby's teething time to mouth ulcers, eczema, and acid reflux. However, care must taken to ensure children do not choke and that the thread binding them is fine enough to break if caught on anything. Sometimes hazelwood necklaces available on the market have breakable clasps for safety and to ensure the wooden beads do not come free and become hazardous in this way.

In homoeopathic remedies, hazel buds are used for draining excess fluids from the body and to restore elasticity in lung tissues. They are also used to treat some liver and kidney conditions, pulmonary fibrosis, and emphysema.

Energetically and magically, the hazel's swift and clever nature is essential in the pursuit of wisdom in the Celtic tradition. Its connection to the bardic mysteries obscures its excellent assistance in the creation and writing of effective magical spells. It is a pathway for shamans and druids to contact the awen, the sacred inspiration that is the source of all knowledge—spiritually, artistically, and scientifically. It teaches the way for mortals to eventually achieve divinity via the primal and perfect wisdom of the soul.

As a vibrational essence, hazel assists in breaking free of old patterns. It allows you to seek inspiration, new ways of behaving, and a new path through life. Hazel will help you unleash potential and assist those who are rigid in their thinking to go with the flow. It is useful to support those undertaking a course of study and the development of skill. It brings stability, banishes confusion, and eases clear communication.

Ogham Divination Meaning

As an ogham, coll suggests the time of divine inspiration is at hand. Challenges have been endured, and now radiant light breaks through the clouds, illuminating everything with meaning and beauty. This is the purpose and source of poetry—written upon all existence to reveal the divine spark in all our souls. By living in connection with our own souls, our inner and outer lives become gradually aligned. We become able to see our place in infinity—a beautiful and awe-inspiring experience. Yet like the hazelnut, all this potential is held in a single point, the individual, until such a time when it can become manifest in the world. Thus we find a balance between the self and all creation. We are able to draw upon the whole as we choose. Often the result is a joyful surrender to the greater All That Is—illumination. Ultimately this signifies both the pursuit and purpose of wisdom. Your evolution is at hand.

Journal Entry: The Hazels of the Avalon Marches

Hazel grows abundantly on the low hills that rise above the marshes, as they do all over Avalon. Sacred to poets and bards (and writers!), I usually find hazel spirits are silvery beings, fast and light in their movements and speech, which often comes to me in a fleeting array of images. Sometimes as a result, it makes my heart beat faster. However I have also met hazels that are deep and ponderous, reminding me of the hazel's love of the salmon of wisdom and the deep sacred pool that is its otherworld home. Sitting with the hazels can be hard, and I often feel called to dance and sing around them, spiriting songs and rhythms, chants and mantras taking to the air like flocks of silver birds. Sometimes I write down these words; others come to me again in ceremony, healing, or spellwork like fleeting jewels. I gather hazelnuts to eat when working in the wild land to help me attune to the spirit of a place as well as to keep me strong on a long day's walk and visionary work. I make charms out of them for love, fertility, and creative success, and chains of hazelnut for wearing when working with faeries or the deep spirits of the earth. Forked hazel rods are easy to find, and when cut with permission, are excellent for divining water and tracking ley and dragon lines and faery roads. The hazel is the perfect mediator or messenger spirit, guiding energy and wisdom from the Source to the outer world and back again in a continuous flow, two serpents on the caduceus or the red and white dragons of British myth. When you walk with the hazel, you learn the earth is full of magic.

Apple/Quert *(Malvus sylvestris)*

....

Other names:
Fruit of the gods, the silver bough

....

Word ogham of:
Morainn: *Clithar baiscill* "Shelter
of lunatics"; "shelter of hinds"

Cuchulain: *Dígu fethail.i.cumdaigh* "Dregs of clothing"

Oengus: *Bríg anduini* "Substance
of an insignificant person"[112]

Description

The apple referred to in the tree ogham is the uncultivated crab apple, which is the originator of the cultivated species. It is a deciduous tree which grows up to ten metres with a dense, rounded crown. Unlike its cultivated descendants, it retains its short thorns on the twigs. The bark is grey-brown, cracking into plates. The crab apple has alternate, broadly elliptical (often oval) toothed leaves between three and eight centimetres long. The leaves are hairy at first, becoming smooth over time. The tree flowers at the ends of the shoots from April to May in small clusters of white blossoms with pink tips. Each flower is made of five petals, each one to two centimetres long with yellow anthers. The small rounded fruit appear from September to October and are usually between two and three cm across, yellowy green, with red flushes when ripe. Crab apples are usually very sour and dry to the taste.

---

112   McManus, *Guide to Ogam*, 43, with additions by Calder, *Scholars' Primer*, 279.

Crab apples are found all across Europe and western Asia, preferring lowlands and the edges of rich deciduous woodlands, river valleys, and hedgerows. A very similar species, sweet crab apple (*Malus coronaria*), grows in North America.

Lore and Legend

According to the Brehon law, apple was one of the seven chieftain trees.

The letter Q, for *quert*, is nonexistent in Old Irish, however *quert* has been interpreted as referring to the Old Irish word *ceirt* or "rag" as a reference to wandering lunatics, a recurring motif in Celtic myth.[113] Alternatively, *quert* has been taken to refer to *cu* meaning "wolf" or "hound"—synonyms for the warrior. Both of these in this context refer to the individual's ability to face death (physically or via psychological disintegration) and gain entry to the otherworld or altered states of consciousness before returning as a fully able being with new insight. This connects the apple with the Cailleach—the old veiled one, the goddess as Crone in whose hands the human soul is taken from the mortal world to return again renewed. One of her symbols is the five-pointed star, the pentagram, which can be seen in the apple when halved widthways and is a testimony to the apple's profound magical nature.

The word ogham of Morainn calls the apple "shelter of lunatics." Lunatics, like cow- and swineherds in Celtic literature and oral tradition, occupy a mystical position, as they are often shapechangers and beings of power, responsible for the protection of a tribe's wealth. The battling swineherds Friuch and Rucht argued and changed into many animals during their fight—birds, stags, phantoms, and dragons, finally settling as the famed brown and white bulls mentioned in the famous tale *The Táin* ("The Cattle Raid of Cooley").[114] This links them to the shamanic divine "lunacy" that led individuals to live alone in the forest, tuning into

---

113   McManus, *Guide to Ogam*, 37.

114   Kinsella, *The Táin*, 46.

the energies of the green world and shunning most human interaction. There are many such characters in the old stories, such as Suibne Geilt, Myrddin, and the Scottish Lailoken, who often carried apple branches as symbols of their passage through the otherworld. This is the silver branch featured in many myths, the branch often bearing apples, blossoms, and leaves at the same time, in addition to silver bells. The branch made sweet music that healed and soothed all who heard it. Sometimes it opened or heralded the way to the otherworld, such as in the story of Bran, who was summoned to the otherworld by a woman of the sidhe, who held such a branch as a symbol of her position.[115]

Associated with immortality and otherworldly paradise, apples are the ultimate symbol of vision and wholeness, reminding us of our divine natures and our perfection in the eyes of the gods. Magically it aids perception of all kinds, its links with madness revealing how our notions of reality are mutable projections. To have these notions changed can induce a crisis but they are sometimes able to leave us with a broader sense of the world than before. Potentially they leave us capable of communion with beings of all kinds, able to perceive the gods and the consciousness of the planet as a whole. Of course, the transition may be painful, even tragic, hence Oengus's words, *bríg anduini*—"substance of an insignificant person." To step outside ordinary consciousness may also mean stepping outside of society and losing the respect and protection it affords. The path of the lunatic and the path of the visionary may be equally lonely and hard. Yet in the magic of the apple, the challenge and the sustenance are one and the same; the traveller is able to draw from the well of spirit and receive nourishment from its otherworldly source.

In Greek myth, the garden of the Hesperides contained a golden apple tree which was given by Gaia to her daughter Hera when she married Zeus.[116] The apples from this tree brought the dead back to life and healed

---

115   Green, *Dictionary of Celtic Myth*, 49.

116   *Larousse Encyclopedia*, 164.

the sick. It was guarded by a serpent and nine goddesses, giving us clues to the apple's connection with life force and kundalini—the serpent and the spiral nature of our spiritual evolution—the nine goddesses. Apples are also sacred to Aphrodite, Greek goddess of love and sexuality, to whom the pentagram within the apple is also sacred, suggesting it is the apple's great life force manifesting sometimes in sexual energy that heals and transforms.

Apples were also important to the Norse gods, who remained eternally young and energetic thanks to the apples kept in a chest by Idun, the goddess of youth and renewal.[117] In the Celtic tradition, apples are associated with the magical Isle of Avalon, the Isle of Apples. It is an otherworldly place of healing and renewal where souls come back to wholeness by the grace of the goddess, who gives to all regardless of their status or worthiness.[118] This is another aspect of the apple, its connection with giving and as a heal-all, the promise that all, no matter how lost or wounded, can achieve healing. The apple is thus linked to Cuchulain's words, "dregs of clothing" or rags. The disenfranchised, the poor, the homeless, the weary, and the ill may all find comfort beneath its boughs. Our ultimate protection is inherent in the apple—the promise that our divine infinite nature can never truly be harmed or endangered, and we are all of equal value to the goddess.

Sadly, these positive aspects were turned on their head in the Old Testament, where apples became associated with sin, shame, and lust—the forbidden tree of knowledge. Its connections with vitality, pleasure, and otherworldly delight changed to a more fearful view. However, the apple's connection with knowledge remains in many cultures including the Celtic, where its ability to bestow knowledge of the otherworld (and thus the nature of the universe) is seen as a positive thing and a human's natural inheritance.

In the English west country there are two festivals honouring the apple. A relatively new celebration called Appleday, when the fruit is falling ripe

---

117   *Larousse Encyclopedia,* 270.

118   Green, *Dictionary of Celtic Myth,* 35.

from the tree, and the tradition of wassailing, held at numerous dates in December and January when the apple trees are fed with hot cider and drums are beaten to thank the apple spirits and cleanse the orchards of negative energies. Wassailing is an ancient custom still popular to this day; both celebrations are a focus of community spirit. Traditionally at the apple harvest, the last apple is always left on the tree for the apple-man, the tree spirit who blesses the apple harvest for the following year. The connections between apples and the Celtic peoples have always been strong; apples have been a reliable source of food and medicine since antiquity. The traditional custom of apple bobbing at Halloween/ Samhain comes from this, seeking the blessings of the apple spirits. The apple's connection with the Cailleach—the veiled one, the Crone— whose time is Samhain can also be seen here.

Apples are sacred to the Roman goddess Pomona, whose name means "fruit." Pomona oversees orchards and all fruit trees, rather than the harvest itself. She was said to be a wood nymph who was tricked into marrying Vertumnus, the god of the seasons, and a festival was held in both their honour on the thirteenth of August.

Practical and Magical Uses

Apple is a popular and kindly wood to use for a wand, and it is especially useful for healing and love spells. Both the fruit and the blossom are used to symbolise love, beauty, and immortality. They are commonly used in incenses, simple perfumes, and also sometimes rolled in beeswax to make candles for love and healing spells. One such spell is to carve your and your lover's initials into an apple and bury it. Should a tree grow in that spot, your love is said to be especially blessed.

Apples are also used in divination. The methods are varied, but burn-ing apple pips after assigning each one with a potential lover's name and throwing apple peel over the left shoulder to see if it forms a person's initials are both ancient ways reduced to parlour entertainment over the passage of time. Apples placed under one's pillow and asked with intent to aid the questioner are a powerful technique to induce prophetic dreams. There is an old Scottish tradition of eating an apple at Samhain whilst looking into a mirror—it is said you will see the person you are to marry over your shoulder.

There was a tradition in Germany until the nineteenth century to pour the water from a newborn baby's bath over the roots of an apple tree to grant the child good health, attractiveness, and fertility. Apple tree spirits are friendly and protective towards children, and it is excellent to take a troubled child to spend some time in an orchard and benefit from their gentle, soothing, unseen presence. Apple tree spirits will send the child good dreams and healing sleep.

Apples were used in Anglo-Saxon sympathetic magic, which depended on its associations. A holy name would be written on the apple which would be eaten on three consecutive days—three days often being a preferred span of time for such things. The apple would then cure all illness in the person—physical, mental, or emotional. Crab apple, known as *wergulu,* was also used in the famous nine-herb charm to treat poison and infection, from the tenth-century Lacugna manuscript.[119]

Apple wood is good for carving, particularly for magical wands, which can be carved with ogham or other sigils. The silver branch, adorned with bells or flowers, makes a particularly powerful magical tool for use with tree spirits and gaining entry to the otherworld. It is an especially good tool for otherworld journeying, where it can aid clear vision and effective navigation.

Healing

Apples are associated with cleansing and purification. Crab apple is a traditional herbal remedy for cleansing the body internally and externally; it is good for wounds as it is anti-inflammatory and antiseptic, and it is good for the internal system. It is particularly good for the bowels and stomach,

---

119   Eleanor Sinclair Rohde, *The Old English Herbals* (Newstead, AUS: Emereo Classics, 2010), 17.

and was once considered to be effective against poisons. Eating an unripe apple is good for curing diarrhoea, whilst eating whole ripe apples is helpful as a gentle laxative. Apple wine was a well respected cure-all in the ancient world, but it needs to be at least a year old. Apples are good sources of potassium, iron, and vitamins A and E. Apples also heal the skin; Gerard, writing in 1633, suggests an ointment made from boiled apples mixed with fat and rose water: fat serves as a binder and moisturises the skin, apple lends its antiseptic and anti-inflammatory qualities, and the rose gives healing and soothing qualities, combining to cleanse, heal, and rejuvenate rough or blemished skin.[120] The apple's anti-inflammatory qualities are also good for helping rheumatic conditions by rubbing the fruit on the affected area or making a warm poultice from the baked fruit.

Apple cider and cider vinegar both have excellent health benefits and can be drank warmed with cinnamon, ginger, and honey for colds and flu. Cider vinegar is very strong and should only be used in small doses highly diluted with water or apple juice. Apple cider left out in a warm room overnight can be taken to replace lost healthy stomach bacteria after a dose of antibiotics. Cider vinegar diluted one part vinegar to at least six parts water can be used as a facial toner, reducing blemishes and fading acne scars and age spots. Some studies report that taken regularly, it can help reduce cholesterol. It can also be used as a cleaning product around the home and to deter fleas.

As a vibrational essence, crab apple can be used externally or internally, working on the physical and subtle bodies, removing negative or unclean energies. It heals self-disgust, shame, fears of contamination, and poor body image. It is an excellent energetic cleanser particularly good for people who are very sensitive to toxic vibrations of all kinds. It is also good to use when fasting or to help cleanse wounds. It can also be used on animals for fleas and plants for mildew or greenfly infestations. Apple (crab, cultivated, or apple blossom) essence can also be used for soothing, and

---

120   John Gerard, "Of the apple tree" in *Gerard's Herbal* (1633). ([London?]: Velluminous Press, 2010).

gaining perspective and vision. It heals sexual issues, and connects to the Source and otherworldly energies, especially through dreams and healing sleep. It aids in transitions between the otherworld, which is good for those suffering from burnout resulting from strenuous psychic or magical work.

Ogham Divination Meaning

As an ogham, quert works with the connection between mind, body, and spirit, aiding the seeker in the quest for wholeness. It is a good magical symbol to aid in seeking inspiration from dreams and otherworldly connections, reminding us of the continual connection with the otherworldly paradise and our inner divinity. It suggests and helps in operating from "right action," coming from an inner sense of wholeness, and returning to wholeness. In divination it suggests that right action can be found when acting from a sense of vision and goodness. Kindness, to the self and others, as well as generosity and compassion are timeless heal-alls that lead the soul to wisdom.

Journal Entry: The Apples of Avalon Orchard, Somerset

Autumn here in Glastonbury is full of the scent of apples. The green and gold of the fallen leaves is studded with the rich red of ripe fruit lending extra loveliness to the air. Wandering through the orchards at dusk I can feel the presence of the sidhe around me, as if with every step I grow closer to the heart of Avalon and the deep healing of the otherworld. A stillness gathers in my heart, and I feel whole and at peace, at ease in my body yet as if all the world around is illuminated from within. The beauty of spirit in nature infuses everything. Asking for the blessing of the gods, Avaloch and Morgan, I gather apples for the Samhain ceremony, to honour our mortality, and slivers of apple wood for those who have come to me for soul retrievals—to encourage their wholeness to take root once more within them, to hold their soul in their body, re-remembering the delight of being here and now, a spirit delighting in the sensual world.

The Aicme of Muin

Blackberry/Muin *(Rubus villosus/Rubus fruticosus)*

....
Other names:
Bramble, cloudberry, American blackberry, goutberry
....

Word ogham of:
Morainn: *Ardi maisi* "Highest of beauty"
Tressam fedmae "Strongest of effort"

Cuchulain: *Conair gothar.i. tre muin*
"Path of the voice, three vines"

Oengus: *Áarusc n-airlig* "The proverb of slaughter"[121]

---

121 McManus, *Guide to Ogam*, 43, with additions by Calder, *Scholars' Primer*, 92–93.

Description

Blackberry in all its varieties is actually a member of the rose (*Rosaceae*) family, along with raspberry and apple. It is a trailing perennial plant that grows well in almost any soil. Blackberry grows biennial stems, known as canes, which only flower and bear fruit in the second year. Its slender branches have sharp curved barbs or prickles, often called thorns but are in fact much smaller and more flexible. It has hairy leaves with three to five leaflets. It has white five-petaled flowers which appear from June to September, and its fruit, the blackberry is edible and a favourite for children. At first the berry is green, then reddens before turning a deep red—black when it is ripe. Blackberry propagates by sending out strong suckering roots that lend a humped, hooping shape to the plant, as it anchors itself into the soil at numerous points. Bramble or blackberry grows prolifically in Britain and Ireland, as well as across Europe and America in various forms; however, it is often considered an invasive weed. There is evidence of human consumption of blackberries in the Iron Age, and probably far earlier, as it is no doubt a highly nutritious wild food.

Lore and Legend

Muin was sometimes thought to refer to the vine. However, there are no native vines in the Celtic world, and it is now commonly agreed that muin refers to the blackberry that grows up walls and over ground with equal ease. *Muin* is found to have three different meanings in Old Irish; firstly and most commonly as a cognate with the Welsh *mwn*, possibly referring to the throat or neck.[122] Other interpretations of *muin* are to be wily, a ruse, and love or esteem. We now enter complex visionary territory, where it is likely those originally using the ogham were aware of all three meanings and found within them poetic reference to the qualities and energies they wanted to refer to via the blackberry. This is perhaps what Cuchulain's word oghams refer to, muin calling to mind the throat, indeed the "path of the

---

122   McManus, *Guide to Ogam*, 37.

voice" that has three "vines," or strands of meaning. Using the voice was a primary tool of the fili (Irish poets), not only to entertain but to literally give voice to the spirits, expressing divine wisdom and prophecy. Both blackberry and the other plant most associated with muin, the vine, are both used to make wine, whose intoxicating properties were in ancient times often associated with inducing prophetic verse.

It is significant how quickly brambles can reclaim a patch of land for the wild, sending out tendrils which take root again, tethering the vine to the ground every few feet rather than growing from a single root stem. As a result, brambles grow in hoops. It was once traditional to pass babies through these brambles to secure good luck for their lives ahead. This practice is similar to the folk healing techniques associated with holey stones, because like the stones, the tethered bramble is strongly connected to the earth and its energies, drawing in the negative and emitting restorative energy. Eating blackberries is also good for the same reason. When gathered during the waxing moon, they are said to give good protection from ill will.

In folklore, blackberry or bramble patches are often linked with the faeries. In France, eating blackberries used to be considered taboo as it was kept as a food for the faeries alone. There is a still a tradition in parts of Britain that berries should not be picked after Samhain (October 31) as these belong to the fey and should not be touched. Blackberry patches are vast communities for beings of many kinds, faery and animal, as they provide excellent food, shelter, and protection due to its many thorns. It was a collective presence made up of many beings, fierce and armed, able to scratch, snag, and tear through even strong fabric; magically, the blackberry has many spears with which to protect itself and those it shelters. Oengus called muin "the proverb of slaughter" also referring to its fierceness; its berry juice is reminiscent of blood, and its extreme tenacity makes it comparable to a warrior's stamina.

The blackberry has a very strong life force and is certainly an important "power plant" in the Celtic tradition. Blackberry winters (when the dew on the blossoms is frozen in the spring) are said to be a sign of an abundant harvest to come, revealing the blackberry's intimate relationship to people of the land. In the Irish tale of the otherworld "The Voyage of Maelduin," Maelduin and his men arrive at an island covered with berries that save them from starvation and bring them renewal, easing the exhaustion of their long and arduous travels. The faery tale "Sleeping Beauty" shows the significance of brambles to protect, enclose, and contain in magical ways, providing the boundary for the spell of sleep, also serving as a test for the adventurous hero. In many ways, both the prince's quest for Sleeping Beauty and Maelduin's voyage can be seen as quests in search of the soul. The internal treasure gained by working with such strong earth energy and the inevitable tests of endurance it brings help the hero to discover his or her innate connection to Source and wholeness. This is the paradox of the blackberry—its fruit and thorns can illustrate the often contradictory human condition.

In Christian folklore, blackberry is sometimes said to be the thorns in Jesus's crucifixion crown, and Lucifer is said to have landed in a black-berry bush when cast out of heaven. This also illustrates the difficulties the human condition experiences in manifest reality.

Blackberry teaches the importance of harvest and gathering, as well as patience—getting through the brambles to gain the treasure, the vitamin-rich fruit. Thus the blackberry teaches humans the importance of living in harmony with nature and acting at the right time. Muin the blackberry is a food-producing plant, far more so than the other ogham plants, apart from the apple. It is concerned with attending to the body's needs, and the needs of the community to endure through harsh winter. It can do this only if the humans think ahead and gather when they can in preparation. It is not possible before or after the appropriate time. Many other things in life also have this quality, and it is an essential aspect of maturity for the individual to learn this. Thoughts, dreams, and talents also need to be harvested at the appropriate time and used appropriately. Conversely, all things also need to be released when their time has passed. Discernment is also required, as not all berries are safe or ready to eat; not all paths and choices in life are good to take. This discernment, timeliness and awareness of the present moment is also inherent in the seeker's quest for the soul; it is the only way connection with the soul, or the *all*, can be realised. This is the hard work that Morainn refers to, the "strongest of effort" that pays off in the reaping of a bountiful harvest—the completion of projects, within and without, as well as "the highest beauty."

The blackberry's extremely strong life force allows it to bear flowers and fruit at the same time, an almost miraculous feat of extreme fertility, and it can be almost impossible to eradicate from an area once it has taken hold. Its powerful, determined spirit teaches the importance of tenacity and effort, providing the stamina and life force to achieve things weaker spirits would not even attempt. It can grow in almost any terrain, going wherever it wants to go. This is a valuable skill for any seeker to acquire from a blackberry as ally, for its strength is from its self-determination and mobility, its ability to be both flexible and tough differing from, say, the oak.

Blackberry also connects areas of land and other plants and habitats, showing its ability to be an excellent networker by linking with different energies, binding and uniting. When working magically with the blackberry or the vine as an ogham stick or wand, the two species can be interchanged with each other, and they can also stand in for other woods when asked with respect, energy, and intent. This teaches how essentially all things are part of the whole, and the strong connection between all things can always be felt and accessed. In asking the blackberry or other wood to become your ogham stick or wand, this connection makes the magic possible. With an act of your will, the "strongest effort," blackberry will become your ally as surely as spring follows winter.

The blackberry or bramble is often considered to be sacred to the Great Goddess, especially to the goddess Brighid via its great protectiveness and generosity, being able to support and sustain a great variety and number of other life forms.

There is a Scottish riddle referring to the blackberry:

As white as snow but snow it's not
As red as blood but blood it's not
As black as ink but ink it's not.[123]

Practical and Magical uses

A useful technique to try with muin is to journey or visualise yourself as becoming the blackberry or the vine, and connecting a variety of other trees in turn. When this has been practiced a few times, it is possible to extend the exercise and try with a group of trees simultaneously. This powerful exercise can actually be quite grounding and develops skills in working multidimensionally and with a whole community of energies. Its binding abilities are also useful in cord magic and binding spells of many kinds, yet its friendly uniting capacity makes it ill-suited for spells of negative intention.

Blackberry leaves are often used in spells for protection, money, and abundance, as well as healing. One simple technique is to write your name upon a leaf in felt-tip pen, wrap it in deep blue cloth, and leave it in your purse or wallet.

Dried and powdered, the leaves are also used in incense blends for prosperity and protection. If you can, crawling through a blackberry hoop will banish negative energies, illness, and hexes. Alternatively, a prickly blackberry whip, swept over your aura or around your home will have a similar effect, but it must be buried as soon as its job is done.

The fruit, leaves, or stems of blackberry are used to invoke the goddess in all her aspects, and they can be incorporated into spells and ceremonies for this purpose in a variety of ways—flowers for the maiden goddess, fruit for the mother goddess, and prickly stems and dried fruit (gathered before Samhain, October 31, but used after) for the goddess as crone.

---

123   Carr-Gomm, *Druid Plant Oracle*, 23.

Blackberry is an excellent fruit to make wine and preserves, and it is traditional to eat blackberry pies or crumbles during the harvest festivals of Lughnasadh (if they are ripe in time) and the autumn equinox.

Healing

Herbally, blackberry has a strong curative tradition in the British Isles; it is extremely high in vitamin C, and blackberry leaf tea is very good for coughs (again associating it with the throat), colds, and upset stomachs. Its leaves can also be chewed to relieve bleeding gums. The fruit was an essential part of our ancestors' diet, and in medieval herbals, blackberry wine was taken to restore energy and hope—effects of its high life force and tenacity.

As stated above, crawling through a blackberry hoop is good to dispel illness, and it was once a cure for rheumatism.[124]

Blackberry leaves were once thought to help cure haemorrhoids, as they have astringent properties. Gerard writes:

> The leaves of the bramble, boiled in water with honey, allum, and a little white wine added thereto, make a most excellent lotion or washing water, to heal the sores in the mouth.[125]

As a vibrational essence blackberry is excellent for breaking inertia and stirring up energy to get on with difficult or tiresome tasks. It is an important essence to take to develop initiative and mobility in the world of work and emotional or spiritual quests. Anything being avoided can be faced and moved through, and things that seem impossible at the outset can be achieved with the stamina and effort the blackberry provides. It teaches the pleasure of harvesting your own work and achievements in due time, as well as revealing the folly of sowing negativity or nothing at all.

---

124   Grieve, A Modern Herbal, 109.

125   Gerard, "On the Bramble or blackberry bush" in Gerard's Herbal.

Ogham Divination Meaning

As an ogham, muin shows that the harvest you have sown is coming in due course; the fruition of plans are always in their timeliness and in the quality given to their achievement. Muin is a kindly ogham, revealing the bounty of the goddess and nature herself, which gives out to those in need and those who have plenty, the deserving and the undeserving in equal share. Muin concerns itself with the circular nature of life on earth and human existence. All things come around, good and bad, and the things that need learning or attending to will have another chance at a later time if the present opportunity is missed. Those goals achieved now also need maintaining into the future. These are the challenges of being alive in space and time.

Journal Entry: Blackberry Spirit of Dun Deardail, Highlands

Blackberry spirits are dear friends, luscious and full of the sensual joys of existence. I welcome the bramble patch in my garden as a place where both faeries and animals may gather and find shelter ... I work with my friends the bramble tribe when doing shamanic work out on the land, as a mediator spirit that helps me to connect with the deeper energies of the earth and those I may not have encountered before. Her rich spirit allows me to gather berries for preserves, and the dried leaves are good in incense to honour the powers of place. Once when walking in the Scottish Highlands by Dun Deardail ("the dun of Deirdre") I became tired and sat out on a promontory looking out at Loch Ness far below, when I had a clear vision of a beautiful woman with wild black hair and deep black shining eyes like berries ... she smiled and told me this land was hers. The air was filled with the scent of cooking blackberries although there were none to be seen. This warmed my spirit, gave me strength, and comforted me in this strange, wild place. The warm, delicious perfume of rich berries on a stove remained with me all the way, grounding and earthy yet full of delight, as if this wise woman of the hills had opened the door to her dun to wave at us as we passed by.

Ivy/Gort *(Hedera helix)*

....
Other names:
Creeping jenny, lizzie run up the hedge, alehoof
....

Word ogham of:
Morainn: *Glaisiu geltaibh* "Greener than
pastures"; *Millsiu féraib* "Sweetest of grass"

Cuchulain: *Sásad.ile.arbhar* "Sating of multitudes, corn"

Oengus: *Ined erc* "Suitable place for cows"[126]

Description

Ivy is a climbing evergreen plant that grows twenty to thirty metres high
on suitable surfaces, but is also capable of growing to a huge size along the
ground when it lacks support. It climbs by using aerial rootlets that are
capable of gripping strongly onto trees and shrubs, as well as stone, brick,
and the plaster of buildings and walls. It has alternate leaves 50 to 100 mm
long that are five-lobed and palmate (juvenile leaves), and unlobed heart-
shaped leaves on mature, fertile stems. Ivy flowers in small lime-green
clusters from late August well into autumn, providing precious nectar out
of season for the last of the insects before their hibernation. The berries,
each containing five seeds, begin yellow-orange and mature into a rich
red-black over the winter, when they provide excellent food for over-win-
tering birds and their young, right through into the spring. Ivy of several
varieties thrives in alkaline and chalky soils, but it grows well in most
types. It is widespread across Britain, Europe, and Scandinavia, as well as
North America. It is considered a pest in parts of the US.

---

126   McManus, *Guide to Ogam*, 43, with additions by Calder, *Scholars' Primer*, 93.

Ivy is the ultimate climbing plant; whilst dependent on a host tree or other support, it can grow almost anywhere and is strong enough to force itself into plaster and brickwork. It is a binding and uniting plant, its evergreen leaves growing all year round, and can trail through several trees or structures at a time. Whilst very strong and able to strangle a host plant by its persistent growth, it does not steal nutrients from its host. Instead, like its neighbours, ivy draws on food from the earth and provides extra protection for many life forms—spirit, insect, and animal—that shelter in its shadows. On buildings, it provides dryness.

Lore and Legend

Morainn refers to the ivy as "greenest of pastures" and "sweetest of grass" because the word *gort* can mean a green field or garden, as well as its associations with cornfields. This may be due to the collective and harmonious group effort required in order to sow and reap barley ("corn" in Ireland and the UK) and other agricultural tasks, which need the ivy's connecting and supporting energy if they are to be achieved. Cuchulain also refers to this (and to corn) as the ivy energy assists the group effort and makes the challenge of working with others go smoothly.

Ivy is often identified with immortality, resurrection, and rebirth due to the ivy's spiral growth. Often connected with wild or fey characters, ivy crowns were worn by the Greek and Roman gods Dionysus and Bacchus, who are associated with wine and revelry as well as the forces of nature. It was believed that steeping ivy leaves in the wine made it more potent whilst alleviating the aftereffects. In this aspect, ivy was associated with prophetic intoxication, something very important in the classical world, as well as to the Iron Age druids. The priestesses of Bacchus, known as Maenads, are thought to have drunk a poisonous entheogenic potion of ivy leaves, pine sap, and fly agaric mushrooms that led them to have ecstatic visions. They wore faun skins and carried a sacred staff called a thyrsus, which was wrapped in ivy leaves and topped with a phallic pine cone. In Euripides's play *The Bacchae,* the Maenads, here women driven mad by the god, are able to draw wine up from the earth by tapping their thyrsi upon the ground.[127] In later centuries, wine goblets were made of ivy wood, and by the Middle Ages in Britain, ivy wrapped around upright poles was used to advertise taverns.[128] It was thought that a handful of ivy leaves boiled in the wine or ale would remove its ability to intoxicate.[129]

Ivy wreaths were once worn in the classical world as a sign of intellectual accolade, as well as for newlywed couples, and this tradition was continued in the modern Welsh National Eisteddfod. In the nineteenth century, the Ivy Bush Inn at Carmarthen hosted the first druid ceremonies that honoured cultural achievements, and ivy wreaths were handed out to winners.[130] Ivy wreaths are also popular today with pagan couples during handfasting ceremonies.

Ruled by the moon, Ivy is also sacred to the Greek goddesses Pasiphae, Ariadne, and Artemis. In the Celtic tradition, ivy is sacred to the goddess Arianrhod, who is also associated with the moon and stars as well as the ever rotating wheel of the year. Her dwelling is the axis mundi, the spiral castle about which the stars turn, which can be seen in the ivy's spiralling growth, especially in its unfurling tendrils.

Ivy is particularly feminine in nature. In the British Isles during the Middle Ages was a winter solstice tradition with lingering pagan overtones: a boy wearing a holly crown and a girl wearing an ivy crown were paraded about the villages, poetically satirizing each other in a formalised battle of the sexes. The holly is ruled by the sun, and the ivy the moon, also repeating this motif of duality. Due to his crown, the boy symbolised the holly king, lord of the underworld and counterpart to summer's oak king. The ivy was given to the girl as a symbol of the goddess of the green world and also perhaps the faery queen, whose fecundity is never

---

127   Euripides, *The Bacchae,* trans. Gilbert Murray (bartleby.com), 828–835.

128   Carr-Gomm, *Druid Plant Oracle,* 59.

129   Grieve, *A Modern Herbal,* 441.

130   Ibid.

diminished. The ivy is an ideal representative of goddess energy at this time; unusually, the ivy flowers in autumn and seeds over winter into springtime, revealing its extra potent life force and its goddess-like ability to be fertile through the winter months. The youth of the holly and ivy at these festivals was also to signify the burgeoning sexuality that would ensure the fertility of the coming year, and this sexual energy can also be seen in the ivy's entwining and embracing patterns of growth.

Practical and Magical Uses

As already seen, the ivy represents the spiral path taken through life, the longer road through life and death to return again. The soul's journey is reflected in the route the ivy takes as it grows on and between trees in the woodland, and this may well be a major reason for its inclusion in the ogham. The leaves are heart-shaped and can also provide many clues to its nature and its usefulness to us. The ivy both supports and is supportive, binding together and uniting many other beings wrapped in its gentle embrace. Interestingly, when ivy grows on its own along the ground, it is far weaker than when it climbs and grows in union with other plants. Again, this is a good lesson for people who are similarly weakened by isolation and enriched by living as part of a community.

The ivy is an excellent ally for developing wisdom in social situations and to harmoniously bind communities. As related to magic, it assists with connectivity and group matters. It teaches that we need each other's support and shelter, and it stresses the importance of giving support and shelter to others. The hero Fionn mac Cumhail was kept safe and hidden in a patch of ivy when he was a child.[131] Yet the ivy also gives us a warning that this is a two-way process between people and energies that needs to be carefully regulated lest the power of the ivy burden its host or wilt and weaken all alone. Like the ivy, none of us is ever solely self-sufficient (and nor should we be), but neither should we be entirely dependent on

---

131   Carr-Gomm, *Druid Plant Oracle*, 59.

another for our needs. Carry an ivy leaf in your pocket or tell the plant your concerns if you feel socially awkward; learn from its example.

Ivy was often used as a winter fodder for cows, hence Oengus's reference to it being a suitable place for them. It was listed in the Irish Brehon laws with the *losa fedo*, "bushes of the woods." Ivy's association in the ogham texts with pastures and corn fields relate it directly to the idea of wealth and land ownership—as a feed for cattle, the greatest signifier for wealth, as well as the ownership of pastureland, both signs of status and power as well as abundance generally. Attaining this status relied (hypothetically) on good and honourable conduct, and it meant that one person was responsible for large numbers of other people who lived on the land and tended to cattle and other livestock. Again we see the idea of the ivy being attached to ideas of social connection and support, both given and received.

Ivy was thought to protect cattle from enchantment by the faeries, and it was worn by milkmaids for the same reason.

Ivy is under the rulership of the planet Saturn and is used for binding spells and underworld connection, as it was associated with the Egyptian god Osiris as well as the Greek Orpheus's journey into Hades. In binding spells, ivy wreaths are a good substitute for cords or threads, and the spirit of the plant may assist you in the magic if it senses your aim is just.

Ivy is often worn or carried to ensure fidelity between partners, as well as to grant fertility, particularly to older women. Ivy swept around an area is said to clear away negativity and bring good luck. Growing ivy upon the walls of a house is said to bring wealth and bind the family together.

It was once believed that dreaming of ivy meant that your lover was unfaithful, and that if ivy grew upon a young woman's grave, it meant that she died of a broken heart.

Ivy is an excellent plant to help connect with the goddess Arianrhod and her spiral castle of stellar wisdom. Use ivy to cast a circle in her name. Journey in vision to seek her wisdom on karmic issues, seasonal understanding, and astrological insights, as well as how to become a greater networker in order to achieve your aims.

Ivy's connections with intoxication continued through into the Saxon era, where it was used to flavour ale and clarify it as an alternative to hops. It was thought to be good for the health, and alleviate hangovers.

Healing

Herbally, ivy is now commonly considered poisonous, and it is certainly toxic to many and can cause allergies in some. Caution and common sense should be used. Historically, however, ivy leaves steeped in hot water were used for wounds and sores. Some old sources refer to ivy leaves being boiled and used as a salve for sunburn, vaginal infections, and skin irritations. Dried and powdered ivy leaves were a popular snuff to clear congestion.[132] According to the seventeenth-century Gerard, ivy-infused water was an excellent wash for eye infections.[133] Ivy berries are highly toxic to humans. Ivy should never be used medicinally other than by qualified herbalists. It is part of the mysteries of the ogham that as we progress through them in order, the practical uses for each diminish—and their spiritual aspects increase.

In medieval times, ivy was an ingredient in the *spongia somnifera*, where a sea sponge was soaked in opium, henbane, lettuce seed, and other opiates together with ivy as a form of anaesthesia. However, it is unlikely these were very effective and were certainly quite toxic and dangerous in their own right.

---

132   Culpeper, *Complete Herbal*, 201.
133   Gerard, "Of the Ivy" in *Gerard's Herbal*.

As a vibrational essence, ivy is good for learning to give and receive support and to learn to give and feel unconditional love. It is fitting that it follows on from muin (blackberry) as this also reminds us of unconditional love and the endless giving of the goddess. It helps with letting go in life and giving loved ones enough space and freedom, as well as giving this to yourself. It is excellent for connecting groups and communities and for understanding group consciousness.

Ogham Divination Meaning

As an ogham, gort indicates that good support is available, and it reminds us that none of us were ever meant to be isolated or removed from the loving ties that connect us to others. Its spiral form reminds us of our soul's journey through infinity and the balance between the self and the all/whole/collective/infinite. The ivy cautions us against holding on too tightly and smothering others; we are reminded that we are all safe to go with the flow. It teaches that love and connection are our greatest gifts. Sacred to the gods of revelry and the wild, it reminds us of our natural selves and inheritance—to find our place among our people and the universe as a whole. Sacred to the goddesses of the moon, it also reminds us of her gentle, all-embracing side that understands the subtleties of the human journey. We are reminded to view ourselves and others with compassion. None of us ever fully comprehends the true mystery of life, it is a journey without end, a question without an answer; all we can do is appreciate the effects of the unknown and unknowable upon us and value ourselves and each other as humans who are "being" and "becoming" rather than as finished, perfect creations. It is this compassion and acceptance of our human condition that can unite us all.

Journal Entry: Ivy of Glastonbury Tor, Somerset

Ivy is the wild lady of the greenwood; she gathers us all together, entwining and embracing. Invoking the spirits of the sidhe is made easier by her uniting touch. For mortals, connecting and working together is made easier by her presence. I use Ivy for binding spells of a positive nature, such as for healings, handfastings, and to ease discord in groups or families. It is also good around a ceremonial circle, at special occasions, and whenever we need to work together for a common goal. I love ivy as decorative magic, to invoke Faery and the spirits of the forest. I also use it to make ivy crowns, uniting all who wear them in delight and our wild and fertile natures. Whether we be of spirit or human blood, we are all children of the goddess of the earth. My favourite place to gather ivy is the base of Glastonbury Tor. The sacred hill has seen so many things over the years; the spirits there love to create unity between those of many different paths.

Broom/Ngetal (*Cytisus scoparius*)
Fern (*Dryopteris filix-mas*)

....
Other names:
Broom: Besom, scots broom, scotch broom
Fern: Shuttlecock fern, treasure fist, death flower, worm fern
....

Word ogham of:
Morainn: *Lúth lego* "Sustenance of a leech"; "a panacea"

Cuchulain: *Tosach n-échto.i.icce* "Beginning
of slaying/heroic deeds, healing"

Oengus: *Étiud Midach* "Raiment
or robe of physicians"[134]

Description

Broom, *Cytisus scoparius,* is a hardy, dense growing shrub with woody branches and small, hairy, trifoliate leaves. Its distinctive yellow flowers bloom from April to July, but can also flower at other times according to the weather. Broom can grow up to three metres tall, and has leguminous seedpods of up to three centimetres that blacken when ripe and crack open often audibly and violently, scattering the seed some distance from the parent plant. In contrast to the fern, broom prefers dry soils and sunny areas. It can be found commonly across Britain, Ireland, and Europe; in some parts of America it is now considered an invasive species. Broom is an excellent nitrogen fixer, ensuring soil fertility via a symbiotic relationship with bacteria that colonise its rhizomes.

---

134   McManus, *Guide to Ogam*, 43 with additions by Calder, *Scholars' Primer*, 283.

The male fern *Dryopteris filix-mas* is a perennial evergreen herb and is amongst the oldest of plants in the world. Ferns prefer wet areas, although shade and shelter are also important. They often provide dense cover in the understory of deciduous woodland. They can grow up to 1.2 metres and have distinctive feathered or ridged shuttlecock-shaped fronds, each crown coming from a single rootstock. Ferns propagate from spores that mature from August to November.

Lore and Legend

Ngetal is an ogham interpreted in many ways in modern times, and there is argument about whether it represents the broom, the fern, or (more rarely) the dwarf elder. The confusion is the result of the remaining source materials, which attribute different trees to ngetal. The twelfth-century *In Lebor Ogham* (Ogham Tract) attributes ngetal to fern. However, *The Scholars' Primer* (which may date back to the seventh century) attributes ngetal to the broom. To complicate matters even further, it is occasionally considered to be connected to the reed. That said, a connection between the reed and the broom does exist, as the Irish and Old Irish word *giolcach* means both "reed" and "broom"; it also can refer to raffia, bamboo, and rushes.

There is no *ng* in Irish. Instead, *ng* is a composite letter comprised of *n* from nion (the ash), and *g* from gort (ivy.) It is interesting that in the *Cad Goddeu*, the reed and the broom are also placed together, again suggesting a connection. Here we must remember that the ogham is represented by the trees but is not a "tree alphabet." In this instance, different plants are used to describe the sum of this ogham sigil's meaning and significance. The ogham is moving into a subtler level; ngetal is not dependent therefore on a single tree (or plant) but on a blending of these different meanings and the energies connected to these different trees and plants (the fern and broom would once have been considered trees), but its whole is greater than the sum of its parts.

The letter *ng* does not occur in Irish, so ogham scholar Damian McManus instead refers to it as *gg*, relating the word *getal* to an old word, *gonid* ("wounds, slays") and the Welsh *gwanu* ("pierce/stab"), both of which come from the root *ghen,* "to strike."[135] Together with the word oghams that relate ngetal to both wounding and healing (Morainn's "sustenance of a leech" meaning both blood and a healer, and Oengus's "robe of physicians"), this strongly suggests ngetal is related to surgery and the maintenance and development of potentially dangerous healing knowledge. By this stage in the ogham, the seeker is beginning to potentially hold and wield real power and must learn its correct use. From a magical point of view, it is significant that ngetal combines both a redundant *n* (it is silent) as well as the *g.* Placed after and yet containing *g* for "gort," ngetal is revealed as having uniting and binding qualities, gathering together disparate elements, while the sharp directness of intention revealed by *n* for "nion" (the ash, tree of spears) links it with ideas of incisions and stitches. Going further, the ability to wield power for wounding or for healing depending on the will and circumstances is also implied.

One tale in the Irish myths fits this paradoxical relationship between wounding and healing perfectly, the tale of Airmed's cloak. Airmed and her brother Miach were the children of Diancecht, the chief healer of the Irish gods, the Tuatha Dé Danann.[136] After the first battle of Moytura where the King Nuada lost his hand, Diancecht made him another out of silver. However, his son Miach went on to make him a hand of flesh and bone, restoring him completely. Diancecht was so jealous that he slew Miach. He attacked him three times and Miach healed himself, but when Diancecht attacked him a fourth time, he died. From Miach's grave grew 365 herbs with wonderful healing powers. His sister Airmed gathered them upon her cloak in the order of their properties. However, the jealous Diancecht scattered them to the four winds so that no human may know them all. It is said that Airmed decided to spend eternity searching for each of them and

135   McManus, *Guide to Ogam,* 38.

136   Ellis, *Dictionary of Irish Mythology,* 28.

relearning their properties. In this tale we see again the "robe of physicians" Oengus refers to as well as the "slaying" Cuchulain warns of.

The Celts had many healing techniques; herbal lore and surgery were both practiced together with healing incantations. There were plenty of female and male healers, and both were held in high esteem by their tribes. Later in Celtic Christian times, we know one of the Brehon law tracts, "The Judgements of Dian Cecht," is named after this mythical, divine healer. This sixth-century CE tract was on the practice of medicine and medical practitioners, and it suggests knowledge of the god in some form had survived to this time in legal as well as literary circles.[137]

Central to the work of the healer and magical practitioner is an understanding of hygiene, physical and energetic. Failure to keep our bodies, psyches, and energy fields clear from negative influences can result in feelings of being lost, disempowerment, and (likely) sinking into negative behaviours and depression. We may even fall ill on a physical or soul level. When this occurs, we must heed Cuchulain's advice, and accept that it is a time for "the beginning of slaying" or as it is sometimes translated, "the beginning of heroic deeds." We must challenge ourselves and any negativity around us, making the way clear once more with decisive, bold, and sometimes brave action. We must leave inertia, illness, wrong deeds, or bad environments behind and set ourselves on the right path once more. It may be hard, but this is the way of healing and of returning wholeness. Like the herbs on Airmed's cloak, what has been lost must be found.

The broom is commonly held as a plant of purification; it has a bright and fiery energy. Sometimes it is confused with gorse, which also features in the ogham, but the energy is quite different: broom is much gentler and has and none of gorse's spines and prickles. This shows how important discernment is with regard to our health and well-being. Like Airmed, we must learn to know one thing from another, to hold all this knowledge in our minds clearly, each in order. This lends an element of calm common

---

137   Ellis, *Dictionary of Irish Mythology*, 84.

sense to the process of purification, creating the physicians essential qualities of energetic and physical hygiene with practicality and wisdom.

At one time used as the brush part of actual brooms, the broom plant has been used for cleansing and protection from harm and illness as well as against negative spirits for centuries (it was once thought that all illnesses were due to spirit influence). For this reason it is traditional for a couple to jump the broom or besom at their handfasting or wedding, as it would leave all bad luck or negativity behind and draw in the blessings of the plant's bright, warming energy. Rather than gorse, which can induce rapid rises in energy and life force, broom is steadier and calmer. At weddings and handfastings, it encourages stability and an enduring steady rise in sexual energy or kundalini suited to longterm relationships. Broom creates an energetic fresh start, assisted by the gathering of forces and support of the ivy (g) made directly applicable by the ash (n).

Like the gorse, broom has strong visionary qualities and contains the chemical sparteine, which can induce hallucinations and euphoria. Also like gorse, it is intimately connected to witchcraft, and is of course used in witches' brooms, as well as traditional "flying ointments," where we see the shamanic aspects of the craft come to the fore. Broom can be used not only for cleansing and protection but also for seeking communication with the spirits via seership, vision, and divination. For this reason it is usually considered sacred to gods of communication, such as Mercury and Hermes. The sacred gathering of knowledge also has a part in the healer's art, where the promptings of spirit may inform and inspire.

As a cleanser and clearer of negative energies and a powerful teacher plant and ally, it can be seen that broom's qualities are essential on the path to healing. Without knowledge and the ability to clear the wounds or disease, no healing can take place. This ability is the "panacea" for all illness that Morainn refers to as well as the "sustenance of leeches" (healers), as it was a healer's art and knowledge that provided him or her food and clothing, giving them value amongst the people.

This resourcefulness—the ability to clear the way (broom) to achieve your objective (ash), supported by the ability to make diverse connections (ivy)—is a great and powerful ability, the preserve of heroes, physicians, and magicians—people beyond the ordinary. These qualities are a spiritual treasure, the attainment of which is a "mystery," the meaning of which is obscured by the fern, the plant attributed to ngetal in the *In Lebor Ogham*.

Ferns, one of the oldest families of plants on the earth, are excellent plants for camouflage, hiding even large animals in its foliage. It has long been considered able to lend invisibility to those lucky enough to have possession of its magical, elusive seed. This reputation survived well into recent centuries, quoted in Shakespeare's *Henry IV*: "We have the recipe of fern seed, we walk invisible."[138] It can also be seen in the fourteenth-century Welsh *Cad Goddeu* ("The Battle of the Trees") by Taliesin. In it, the fern is used to discover the god (and thus power) of the enemy: "I have plundered the fern, through all secrets I spy."[139] The fern's gift of invisibility helps it protect treasures of all kinds. It is traditionally thought to grow on burial mounds, lending it the names "treasure fist" and "death flower." It was said to be guarded by trolls who also frequented burial mounds and the fabled treasure within, the fern being a marker of the treasure's presence whilst obscuring it at the same time. This is similar to the Welsh mystery of the dog, the roebuck, and the lapwing, which guard, hide, and disguise the "secret" of bardic, divine knowledge. The fern flower is said to glow like an ember when discovered at night, its light being that of inner illumination, signalling the way through a complex mystery.

Like the broom, fern can raise the life force, and the male fern was considered to be an aphrodisiac. However, fern also has the magical reputation of being able to uncover secrets, and find secret or hidden knowledge, such as the herbs of Airmed's cloak. For this reason it is also useful in seeking

---

138   William Shakespeare, *Henry IV* act 2, scene 1, lines 81–81 in Norton
      Shakespeare, 1st ser., Stephen Greenblatt, ed. (London: Norton, 1997), 1173.

139   Graves, *White Goddess*, 46.

vision or divination. The moonwort fern was said to have magical influences over metals: inserted into a lock, it was said to be able to unlock it—another form of discovering secrets.[140]

Magically, fern seed is so elusive that there are many tales about how difficult it is to gather. British folklore attests that eleven pewter plates are needed to gather it, as it will slip through the first ten before landing on the eleventh. An Irish tale tells of a man who gathered fern seed in a box, while the faeries or sidhe whispered in his ears and beat him all over. When he finally got home, the seeds had vanished. Here we see the fern's close connection to faery magic as well as that of other "invisible" spirits.

Ngetal is the first composite letter of the ogham, the only one in the first and earliest twenty. It teaches the important qualities needed on a spiritual and magical quest. Psychic and psychological hygiene, flexibility, clarity, and resourceful initiative combine to make wisdom—not a passive thing divorced and remote from the world, but a grounded and applicable thing whose realm is that of the everyday world, the negotiation of life's varied obstacles. To achieve this is to truly attain a magician's treasure within, whilst in the outer world manifesting the effectiveness and healing abilities of the warrior physician. This is to be the true sovereign self, the hero—a panacea for the world.

Practical and Magical Uses

Broom is a highly magical plant also used in the creation of brooms or besoms. Broom is used to invoke the air spirits, linking it again with ideas about clear thinking and communication. It is used to sweep or blow away negative energies. Throw broom into the air to raise the winds, or burn it and bury the ashes to quieten them. Broom twigs bound with ivy or reed strips make a simple hand besom for magical purposes. Combined with birch twigs, they make a traditional witch's broom. Broom flowers can be used for blessings and protection of sacred spaces. They can be hung in

---

140   Carr-Gomm, *Druid Plant Oracle*, 44.

the corners of a room or any shadowy area that feels stagnant, such as fireplaces in summer. Make an infusion of broom flowers and leaves to sprinkle around for purification, blessing, and good luck. Broom also attracts faeries and can be worn by those seeking faery contact or earth healing. Sacred to Airmed, broom can be placed on the altar for any healing spells or when invoking her for assistance.

As discussed earlier, fern is considered to be a highly magical plant, protected by fierce spirits and the Irish sidhe and able to confer invisibility upon those who gathered its seeds. Ferns also make excellent protection for animals in the wild, sheltering small mammals from predators. These two aspects practically and magically intertwine in the lore of the fern and were no doubt used by hunters and later poachers who sought their prey without being discovered by animals or fellow humans. The magic of the fern is useful today in maintaining invisibility and protection when you want to go unnoticed. After leaving an offering for its resident spirits, make a vibrational essence or tincture of the fern at the summer solstice, when it is most powerful. Use it by scattering drops around anything you want to remain hidden, but beware: this will make the objects or area particularly attractive and visible to faeries and other spirits.

When making ogham divination in sets where each ogham is carved on its specific wood, broom is the more practical option to represent ngetal as it is easier to find a suitable piece. However, as with all trees and plants, permission should always be sought from the plant spirit first. Also remember to apply your inner guidance and common sense.

Healing

Herbally, male fern is known to be good for clearing the head via steam inhalation, and was once used as part of a remedy to expel tapeworms.[141] It is toxic, however, and should only be used by qualified herbalists. It is sometimes known in ancient literature as the "worm fern."

---

141   Grieve, A Modern Herbal, 310.

Broom is both cathartic and diuretic, being useful for the kidneys and clearing urinary infections and inflammations. However, it can cause vomiting if taken in larger doses.[142] As discussed earlier, broom flowers were used as a visionary herb for contacting the spirits because ingesting small quantities induce mild hallucinations and are said to grant access to the faery realm. A vibrational essence of broom is a far safer option that can assist in shamanic journeying, divination, and in the clearing of mind stagnation or stuck emotions.

Ogham Divination Meaning

As an ogham, ngetal increases resourcefulness and independence. Ngetal reminds us of the importance of combining skills and knowledge for the best end, being resourceful and flexible in our thinking and approach to life. Like the web of creation itself, ngetal draws from many aspects and areas, maximising the uses of all whilst depleting nothing. In this way knowledge is discovered, maintained, and preserved for future generations, in addition to serving as future steps along our own paths through life. This ogham encourages the seeker to think outside the box and maintain clarity of purpose and energetic hygiene. Ngetal also encourages the seeker to be discreet in sharing or broadcasting knowledge, choosing only suitable people and places. It reminds us to be conscious of the effects and consequences of disclosure. In this way nothing is lost, and new ground may still be discovered.

---

142   Grieve, *A Modern Herbal*, 127.

Journal Entry: Broom of Ham Hill, Somerset

Broom is special, and the plants gathered from a hillside where Iron Age Celts once made their home are especially precious. To me, these plant spirits are beings of light, dear to the goddess of spring and fertility. According to Welsh myth, broom was one of the ingredients when the goddess Bloddeuwedd was "made" by the wizard Gwydion. (I'm sure in effect that his spell merely bound her into a physical form, but that's another matter.) I use broom flowers to honour the goddess and decorate my besom each year around the summer solstice. To me, using them empowers and blesses the besom, and makes it especially beautiful. I am honouring it for its work.

Broom sprigs can be gathered into bunches to make hand brooms or brushes that are particularly effective, though it is unlucky to use them in May, as it is said it will sweep the head of the house out the door. I believe the reason is because it is so sacred to the goddesses; around Beltane, the broom should not be used for domestic work, in honour of this holiday.

Sitting with the broom as it begins to flower in April, it's clear that winter has now passed and the goddess of the green earth is burgeoning with life again. I have made potions with broom flowers, meadowsweet, and oak for invoking Bloddeuwedd, and I found them to be very powerful, inspiring me with visions of the wild goddess of the flowers. I have also used this potion as an offering to my plant spirit allies in my garden. However, Bloddeuwedd also takes the form of an owl, the wise huntress, so like her the broom should always be treated with respect and more than a little caution.

Blackthorn/Straif *(Prunus spinosa)*

....
Other names:
Sloe, the dark mother of the woods
....

Word ogham of:

Morainn: *Tressam rúamnai* "Strongest of red"

Cuchulain: *Saigid nél.i.adde suas* "Seeking of clouds"

Oengus: *Mórad rún* "Increasing of secrets"[143]

Description

Blackthorn (*Prunus spinosa*) is a deciduous shrub or small tree that grows up to five metres with blackish bark and stiff, spiny branches. Part of the family that includes peaches and cherries, it has oval leaves that are two to five centimetres long with a serrated margin. Its appearance in winter is similar to the hawthorn with its thorns and tangled branches, but unlike the hawthorn its small, white, five-petalled flowers open before its leaves, and its thorns are longer and far sharper. Blackthorn fruit, sloe, are small purple-black berries that are waxy in appearance and very bitter in taste. They are usually gathered in the UK in October after the first frosts and are used to make sloe gin. Blackthorns make excellent hedging plants and are commonly used for cattle enclosures. Native to Britain, Ireland, and Europe, it is widely cultivated in other areas including North America.

Lore and Legend

Straif means "sulphur," a substance with a long history of associations with the underworld, including the Christian hell.[144] It is also highly impor-

---

143   McManus, *Guide to Ogam*, 43, with additions by Calder, *Scholars' Primer*, 287.

144   McManus, *Guide to Ogam*, 38.

tant in the study of alchemy. Other translations hold that the name of the blackthorn fruit, sloe, and the word "slay" are connected. These all give excellent clues to the magical and spiritual significance of straif, the blackthorn. The blackthorn features in many Irish sagas, often as a metaphor for the destructive ability of warriors, or for death itself. Sometimes it appears as a symbol of a transformative vision of death as well and even of sacrifice. In the tale of Fionn, Sadbh eats sloes from the blackthorn and becomes pregnant from it, bearing a son who has a lump on his head. This lump is in fact a snake that can be killed in compensation for another man's life. This theme is repeated in *The Lays of Fionn*, where in the poem "The Sword of Oscar" sloes are again mentioned connected with someone dying on behalf of another.[145] Cuchulain's words that blackthorn is "seeking of clouds" is a kenning (a poetic reference) to death, the transmutation of the soul or spirit leaving physical matter behind. Like the snake on Sadbh's son's head, snakes are traditionally considered carriers of life force from this world to the underworld below. Morainn's words that blackthorn is "the strongest of red" refers to blood, another symbol of the mortal transformation into immortality.

Blackthorn's association with death, battle, and transformation can also be seen in the three colours that are found in it, red (blood), white (spirit), and black (death). These correspond to the red sap, the white of the flowers, and the black bark. These associate blackthorn with the triple goddess, and the tree is thus especially sacred to the Irish goddess the Morrighan, "the Great Queen" who oversees matters of war, death, and sexuality.

Blackthorn is usually thought of as a sister tree to the hawthorn, and it was sometimes used as a substitute for the hawthorn tree as a maypole during the May Day/Beltane celebrations. At new year, crowns of blackthorn were sometimes burnt as charms and their ashes scattered to fertilise fields. Blackthorn is one of the first trees to blossom at the end of winter, before its leaves have even unfurled; this associates it with the Crone or dark goddess (known in Scotland and Ireland as the Cailleach, or Cailleach Bheur, "the

---

145   MacNeill, *Duanaire Finn*, 154.

woman of winter") but also with fertility and endurance over tough circumstances. Cold springs, when other plants and trees blossom late, used to be called "blackthorn winters," as they were the only blossoms breaking through. In some parts of Britain, this was known as the "blackthorn hatch," and it usually preceded a much milder spring to come.

Often known as "the dark mother of the woods," again linking it with the Morrighan, blackthorn is always associated with magical binding and testing. This sort of relationship with the goddess as crone—the sometimes cruel, testing side of her—is balanced by her loving, beneficent side (symbolised by the apple), and her sexuality (the hawthorn, the blackthorn's sister). Connected to magicians and sorcerers, blackthorn cautions that access to the otherworld and its magical powers require clarity, caution, experience, and an awareness of the dangers as well as its blessings. This connotation is perhaps distantly reflected in the traditional tale that blackthorn comprised Jesus's crown at the crucifixion. It implies a shamanic and magical initiation was underway.

Blackthorn is also said to be sacred to the Irish god of death, Donn of the Milesians. At one time it was used to curse and discipline; blackthorn's testing qualities also control chaotic and chthonic forces, hence its association with death.

There is a strong connection in Celtic lore between the underworld, the dead, and the faery races. In Irish, the word *sidhe* means "ancestor," "faery," and "hollow hill," the latter referring to the burial mounds in which the faeries were said to dwell. Interestingly, these burial mounds also function as entry points into the otherworld. Because of this connection, blackthorn is a popular wood for calling up the faery Wild Hunt. The faery raid of the horned god and his hounds to gather lost souls and bring them to the realm of the dead. Blackthorn is sacred to and the dwelling place of the leanan sidhe, faery beings who are fierce lovers and highly protective of the tree. They will not allow any wood to be cut from it without permission, and never at the sacred faery times of Beltane and Samhain.

Blackthorn was also used to make Irish cudgels, the shillelagh, that in myth were often carried by giants and *gruagachs*: the wild men, nature spirits, and faery beings associated with earth and rock. Blackthorn would also come to the aid of heroes, and a single twig could magically turn into a hawthorn thicket to defend the good. Interestingly, the usher of the British House of Lords and the Order of the Garter is called "Black Rod" because he uses a blackthorn rod to ceremonially knock upon the door of the houses of parliament, a sign of its ancient authority and status as a weapon that continues to this day.

Blackthorn is always associated with traditional witchcraft, and was used in black magic and for "black" or "blasting rods," wands tipped with blackthorn thorns, which are very long and sharp. These rods were used for cursing, but the thorns also have applications for healing, rather like acupuncture needles. They can be used on poppets or dolls made of cloth or wax used to represent a particular person in distance healing. Sadly, the association of blackthorn with black magic also led to superstitions where the Christian devil was said to prick his initiates on the finger or shoulder with a blackthorn needle, leaving a "witch mark." These marks added to the hysteria of witch hunts; they served as "evidence" to accuse anyone with scratches or birthmarks of any kind. Such was the connection between the blackthorn and witchcraft that as an insult, blackthorn was reputedly used in pyres for burning witches at the stake. There is another connection between the blackthorn and the fingers in the little-known subject of hand ogham, where each joint of the finger represents a different tree or meaning. In this way, witches and druids are able to use their hands for spell casting as well as perhaps for secret communication.

Blackthorn had the same connection with the devil and bad luck in the Scottish Highlands, recorded in a proverb in the *Carmina Gadelica:* "Better the bramble than the blackthorn, better the blackthorn than the devil. He who would go in the bramble for me, I would go in the thorn for him."[146]

---

146   Alexander Carmichael, *Carmina Gadelica, Volume 2* (http://www.sacred-texts.com/neu/celt/cg2/cg2108.htm), 275.

In Ireland it was considered taboo to burn blackthorn wood; however it was classed in the Brehon laws with the *fodla fedo*, "lower classes of wood" useful for field boundaries and hedges. It is mentioned in "The Song of the Forest Trees," part of the Middle Irish tale "The Tragic Death of Fergus mac Leide": "The surly blackthorn...a wanderer, and a wood that the artificer burns not; throughout his body, though it be scanty, birds in their flocks warble."[147]

Practical and Magical Uses

Considered to be under the astrological rulership of Scorpio, Pluto, and Mars, blackthorn wands are extremely powerful but only safe when used by those with extreme clarity and experience, as the energies they invoke are really not controlled but rather allied with, and only when justly in need. They should only be cut or gathered by the person intending to use them, and great care and respect should be involved in its preparation. Be sure you work with the highest intent, lest the blackthorn turn against you. It is also advisable to have learnt from the lessons of ngetal the broom beforehand so you have good energetic and magical hygiene, clarity of purpose, and experience with responsibly wielding the power the blackthorn may grant you, if you are worthy.

Blackthorn is frequently used in hedgerows to create impenetrable barriers. One of the first hedgerow trees to flower, its distinctive white blossoms lace the dark wood while the leaves are still only just budding, lending an eerie glow to the hedgerows at night. Blackthorn makes such strong barriers that it is said it helped keep the Romans out of Anglesey, the druid stronghold. This physical quality reflects its psychic qualities of creating excellent psychic barriers and boundaries that grow stronger still by gathering, transmuting, and returning the negative energy of trespassers. The blackthorn is totally impenetrable against all attack and can only be crossed with love and trust, as seen in the tale of Sleeping Beauty. The thicket surrounding

---

147   (no author), "Fergus mac Leide."

the enchanted castle is made of blackthorn and together with hawthorn and wild rose, they weave a spell of protection for the young princess and her emergent sexuality. The prince, in turn, is initiated into manhood and becomes worthy of the princess by his love, the test of which is facilitated by the fierce blackthorn and its fence of spears.

This testing and initiating leads the seeker closer and closer to karmic issues, thus its relation to the transformation of the spirit after death. Magically, it helps us initiate changes in ourselves and our circumstances, making it the archetypal magician's wand capable of making great shifts of reality. It does this with great ruthlessness and severity if necessary, concerned more with the soul's growth than our comfort. In this way the Crone's face can be seen, bringing on the transformations of death and rebirth, full of contradictions as the impersonal force of nature. Yet its beautiful white blossoms remind that even in the darkest places, the light can still be found; in the most trying of times, dawn grows ever nearer. This is referred to in Oengus's words for the blackthorn, "the increasing of secrets." Beyond the veil of mortality and the wielding of magic are other wonders, other "secrets" that lead us beyond our horizons. Befriend the blackthorn tree when you are encountering difficulties or initiations, and if you have permission from the tree spirit, carry a little of its wood or leaves, or burn some leaves as a protective charm or incense.

Magically, blackthorn boughs can be burnt as an offering to the sun at the winter solstice, as a sign of the end of the reign of the winter king, Arawn, or Gwyn ap Nudd, who is the lord of the Celtic underworld, Annwn. It can also be used to honour the Wild Hunt at Samhain, particularly to help guide on those who have passed from life to death but may have difficulty doing so. In cases such as these, extreme care, caution, and respect should be used.

Practically, it is not surprising that blackthorn was traditionally used to make fighting sticks, given its fierce nature. Its strong, tough wood was also used for the teeth of rakes and for walking sticks. The juice of its fruit was once used as ink.

Healing

Warning: the leaves and seeds of the *Prunus* family contain cyanide, which can be fatal if ingested in excess. Sensible caution should always be used. Always seek the advice of a qualified herbalist before taking regularly or in any quantity.

The culinary uses of blackthorn include making sloe gin as well as jams and jellies from its round, bitter black fruit. Herbally, blackthorn flowers and fruit are both tonic, and an infusion of either the flowers or fruit is useful for stomach problems and urinary infections. It is also good for helping defend against colds and flu, as well as sore throats, mouth infections, and rheumatism. It is sometimes said that an infusion of the bark is good for nervous disorders. An infusion of blackthorn flowers was sometimes used to treat diarrhoea in children, as it is quite mild. Blackthorn flower infusion is also used to clear the skin of toxins by cleansing the blood and liver.

As a flower essence, blackthorn can be used to bring about change from hardened, ossified circumstances. It gives the strength to deal with karmic issues and to heal the shadow side of our natures. It brings light to those stuck in severe darkness. For this reason, it also helps heal trauma and soul damage. It helps in contacting the wild spirit of nature; reconnection with this energy restores our natural state and vital well-being.

Ogham Divination Meaning

As an ogham, straif the blackthorn reminds us that magic is the nature of the universe and that wonders are the normal reality of the world. Accepting the darkness is the first step to enlightenment, giving balance and clarity to see and acknowledge our pains and difficulties, paradoxically leading us back into the light. Through challenges we are born anew. After the maturing lessons of the broom, blackthorn gives true power and the ability to wield it well. Straif, the composite of *s* for saille, the willow, and *t* for tinne, the holly, show that this is a combination of movement to and from the otherworld as seen in the willow together with the energy and vital life force of the holly. The movement of this energy from Source to the outer world is magic, *s* to *t*, the blackthorn. This can only be held by the gaining of wisdom, the initiation into love which is its great test for us. If we are worthy, the power is ours.

Journal Entry: Blackthorn of Compton Dundon, Somerset

Blackthorn is a tree of the wild edges, full of thorns and hidden mysteries, a tree of the wisewoman and the magician, *pellars* and cunning men. As the year turns to spring, it lights up the shadowed lanes with millions of blossoms like tiny stars defying its black, leafless branches, and showing us that warmer days are ahead. My dearest blackthorns are those nestling around a certain Iron Age hill fort near here; they are guardians to the deep faery and sacred spirit enclosures hidden at its feet. While walking there one day, following a small stream to its source, I was greeted by someone unseen calling my name, and suddenly a spear of sunlight broke through the trees and touched a blackthorn covered in rich black sloes. The air buzzed with magic and spirit presence, and I was given a very special gift—my blackthorn *keppen*, a wand of especial power to be used only in the greatest need. I come to these trees when I am in need of blackthorn spines for the greatest defence and healing in the direst of circumstances, examples of which it would not be suitable to write of here.

Elder/Ruis *(Sambucus nigra)*

....

Other names:
Ellhorn, lady ellhorn, hylder, alhuren,
eldrum, pipe tree, sweet elder

....

Word ogham of:
Morainn: *Tindem rucci* "Most intense of blushes"
"reds a man's face through the juice
of the herb being rubbed upon it"

Cuchulain: *Bruth fergae.i.imdergadh*
"Glow of anger, punishment"

Oengus: *Rúamnae drech* "Reddening of faces"[148]

Description

A member of the honeysuckle family, elder is a deciduous, broad-leaved
shrub or small tree which can reach up to ten metres. Its twisted, rugged
shape, arching branches, and grey-brown furrowed bark are distinctive as
it forms many hedges and small copses across the British Isles, particularly
near water sources or in rich, moist soil. It is also found across Europe and
as far as Siberia and Turkey, as well as in North America. It has slender,
oval-pointed leaflets of approximately thirty centimetres long that grow
from a central stalk in March and early April. Its pale creamy blossoms
also spring from a central stem into an almost umbrella formation of hundreds of tiny flowerets known as panicles, which have a distinctive, heady
smell. Its tiny dark purple berries form in masses on the same stems, and
are edible in September.

---

148   McManus, *Guide to Ogam*, 43, with additions by Calder, *Scholars' Primer*, 93.

Lore and Legend

Elder has held a special place in the human mind for millennia; its powers have been respected across Europe by the Norse as well as the Celts and Saxons. Elder is one of several trees that has particular regenerative abilities, recovering easily from damaged branches and brutal pruning. By extension, this suggests its life-giving qualities and thus its association with magic, the goddess, and female energies, all of which have long been feared and respected.

Elder is known as being the home of the Elder Mother (also known as Lady Ellhorn) in folklore, especially in Britain and Scandinavia. As guardian and protectress of the tree and its surrounding area, the Elder Mother is a form of genius loci. In Denmark, the Elder mother is known as the Hyldemoer, the mother of the elves, and is said to live in the elder's roots. For this reason, it was considered dangerous in early Christian times to make cradles out of elder in case the Hyldemoer should try to take or torment the child, as the gods of the old ways became the demons of the new religion.[149]

Often growing near a sacred spring or well, elder was also traditionally planted near houses, particularly in Britain, to grant the inhabitants the Elder Mother's protection and assistance, although later Christianity transformed her into a wicked witch—her transformative, testing qualities became subverted and misunderstood. However, since Pagan times it has been held taboo to ever cut the wood of an elder unless granted the Elder Mother's express permission, lest you suffer her terrible wrath. Such things are achieved by magical deals, offerings, careful and respectful communication, or by cunning such as the traditional folkloric prayer: "Lady Ellhorn, give me some of your wood, and I shall give you some of mine when it grows in the forest."[150] The Romani would go to great lengths to go through each bundle of firewood to make sure none of it was elder before casting it upon the fire, so fearful were they of the elder tree's wrath.

---

149   Thomas Keightley, *The Fairy Mythology: Illustrative of the Romance and Superstition of Various Countries* (London: G. Bell, 1892), 93.

150   Grieve, *A Modern Herbal*, 266.

Elder is sacred to the Germanic goddess Holda, or Frau Holda, a protectress of women's crafts who brings unborn babies to their mothers and rocks the cradle when everyone is asleep. Here we see the same association of the Elder Mother rocking the cradle but with benevolent intent. She is said to have a pool where the souls of unborn children reside, and she watches over all children and women, helping those who keep their homes in good order. Holda is also known to be the old woman of winter, a crone goddess who leads the Wild Hunt, guiding souls to the underworld. In this aspect she is also known as Frau Woden, or Frau Odin, showing the connection with elder as an old wisewoman. Holda is also considered to be a faery woman called a *huldra*, a forest spirit known for being a beautiful, powerful seductress, with a hollow back like an old tree trunk and a cow's tail. Huldras are usually benevolent, the friends of charcoal burners and woodsmen, as well as dairymaids, another form they sometimes take.

The elder tree is also sacred to the crone goddess Hecate, and the tree has its name due to its associations with crone goddesses, the Cailleach in particular, the wise woman of winter. Here we see the goddess as wise old woman, keeper of the mysteries, midwife, and preparer of the dead. The Elder Mother's chastising and testing qualities are revealed here; she is an initiator of souls from one realm to the next. In many ways, the Elder Mother is the archetypal witch, feared for her magical power and sacred knowledge, but also desperately needed. As shall be discussed later, the elder is a treasure chest of healing medicine as well as a master teacher for magical practice. As such, hers is a unique position in our ancestors' consciousness, holding both the supportive and constrictive power of human elders over generations. Despite the Christianised negative view of witches, in the Western world various forms of magical wise women and men have held core knowledge from the distant past into the present day, and this gift of continuity in the relationships between mortals and the earth and its spirits is signified by the elder tree. In the fearful past, witches were said to be able to transform themselves into elder trees, a superstition that made the elder more feared than honoured, but its reputation of bestowing magical abilities and making magical spirit connections has remained to the present day. This magical side is accompaniment to the earthly lessons it presents, namely the duties of elders in the community, showing you where your obligations and commitments lie and helping and teaching how to meet them responsibly.

It is said that the scent of the elder is mildly hallucinogenic, though there is little proof of this. However, tradition states that sleeping beneath the branches of the elder grants access to the otherworld, sometimes physically and sometimes through magically empowered dreams. It is also said that standing beneath an elder tree at midsummer grants the vision of the sidhe as they ride by on their quarterly migrations.[151] In times past, the Elder Mother spirit and her connection with the faeries was considered so powerful that sleeping beneath the tree could actually lead to being carried off by the faeries permanently, never to return.

Association with the tree was seen perhaps as signifying the intention to build spirit contact and embark on or develop magical training to such a degree, and it has been used in this way in modern times. Central to this is the elder's ability to assist in changes of consciousness and the development of visionary skills. The elder's visionary qualities also reveal the tree's position as a gateway to the otherworld, be it faeries or indeed the ancestors and the realm of the dead, known as Annwn in the Celtic tradition. In the ancient Irish collection of stories known as *The Lays of Fionn mac Cumhail* is a tale known as "The Headless Phantoms." In this tale, Fionn stays in a strange, otherworldly house where elder logs are burnt upon the hearth, and Fionn spends the night being forced to face a series of horrible, taunting monsters.[152] Due to its connection with the crone and the underworld, the elder has associations with the dead, contact with spirits, and the ancestral realm. This goes back as far as the Neolithic period; funerary flint

---

151   Grieve, *A Modern Herbal*, 267.

152   MacNeill, *Duanaire Finn*, 129.

arrowheads that appear to be shaped like elder leaves have been found in megalithic barrows.

The elder's presence in invoking spirits of the underworld also reveals its assisting role in facing the internal shadow dwelling in the underworld within, the subconscious. Facing the shadow is a perennial task for heroes of all cultures as well as an essential in spiritual training. In addition, confronting our shadow has a beneficial effect on healing on all levels. Once the shadow is faced, energy and potential are unleashed, bringing change upon the seeker psychologically, energetically, and by extension, physically and magically as well. This is the metaphysical side of the elder's healing qualities, and a gift from the ancestors. *Ruis* means "red"; facing our shadow (and thus our failures and hurts) as well as our achievements induces the "blushing" the elder invokes according to the word oghams of Morainn and Oengus.[153] Working to correct the problems and faults discovered also leads to the anger and punishment (or rectification) referred to by Cuchulain. Dealing with these difficulties is an essential part of the elder's lessons and gifts. However, doing so results not only in the increase in our well-being, but also in our reputation and legacies to future generations, when we join the ranks of the elders in turn.

To become worthy of the term "elder" is not only about age; it is also about responsibility and the fulfilment of duties and responsibilities to our communities and loved ones. It is about acquiring the wisdom and insight to support and guide future generations. Becoming an elder includes sacrifice and restoration, working hard for the betterment of others and leaving a positive effect or contribution to the world, family, or community. Nearly all the parts of the elder have some beneficial or medicinal use, and the tree encourages us to be similarly useful to those around us, giving in balance or even more than we take from the world. It is a rare thing in modern Western culture.

---

153   McManus, *Guide to Ogam*, 38.

Thus it can be seen that the elder's gifts revolve around ideas of trans-formation and regeneration resulting from death, rebirth, and the changes that accompany this journey. In our lives are many deaths and rebirths, lessons learnt and repeated in new forms as life experiences lead to devel-opment and renewal. By sacrificing the past, new energy is released, ben-efitting from the nourishment produced from the healthy decay of things that have passed their time. This links it not only with the crone but with the other phases of the women's and goddesses' cycle from maiden to mother to crone in turn, as well as a man's journey from youth to wise man. Each develops as a result of the karma and patterns of growth the past has provided.

Practical and Magical Uses

Elder is very useful for spells of closure and banishing. Its dried and crushed leaves are a good addition to incense used at Samhain, for clearing negativ-ity, as well as at other threshold times such as births and marriages, where its protective energies come to the fore. Elder is also one of the best trees to use for working with the faeries and attracting other nature spirits.

Elderflower water, especially when made with spring water or dew, can be charged up in the light of the full moon and used for beauty spells and connecting to the goddess and the faery queens. Use the water to wash your face, anoint your eyelids, or drink with a blessing.

There are many techniques and spells involving the elder to increase clairvoyance or seership; one such involves anointing the eyes with elder sap or juice. This is of course only successful if suitable offerings have been given and the tree has granted permission.

Elder pith can be soaked in oil and burned in a bowl, serving as a lamp for magical purposes, but great care should be taken and again, the tree should have granted permission beforehand. The wood burns very poorly; it and the inner pith should only be used in special circumstances for magi-cal uses, and even then with extreme care and respect.

Both the flowers and fruit make excellent jams, wines, and teas, and they have cosmetic applications as well: the berries were once used to add blush to lips and cheeks, and as a shampoo to darken the hair. Elder is also useful for making natural dyes: black from the bark, green from the leaves, and blue from the flowers. The wood (with permission!) can be used to make small objects like combs and wooden spoons, as well as whistles and peashooters for children, as the stems can be hollowed out easily. Whistles fashioned from elder wood can also be used to attract faeries and air spirits.

Healing

Medicinally and in healing, the elder's berries are mildly laxative and a rich source of vitamin C. A distillation of the flowers is a good facial cleanser that can also be drunk as a very pleasant tea that is helpful for bringing down fevers. The distillation can help soothe colds and flu, and it is a good blood purifier. Fresh leaves make good compresses for surface wounds, and elderflower water makes an excellent eye lotion.

As a vibrational essence, elder assists in dreams and the balance between the realms within and without. It can help those who are excessively earthy or excessively dreamy. It also helps faery and ancestral contact in magical and shamanic work.

Ogham Divination Meaning

As an ogham, ruis the elder shows sacrifice must be made in order to gain in the long term. It reveals the need to balance energies to restore equilibrium, health, and well-being. Mistakes must be corrected and wrong deeds put right lest the blushing of embarrassment and shame follow as well as the red of wounds. It reveals the possibility of forgiveness and redemption in these circumstances if right action is taken to restore and repair the situation. Often this rebalancing means cooling one's temper and releasing resentments, calm wisdom reflected in the soothing effects the flowers have on the body's feverishness. As within, so without. Cool, calm thinking often guides the way out of the troubles hot-headedness can unwittingly create.

Elder encourages us to face our shadow selves and come to a state of peace with our less graceful or positive aspects. It reminds of the need to be responsible, upright, honest, and honourable. It also shows the time has come to move from one phase of life to the next—moving through transitions with grace, ease, and honour. On its deepest level, the elder shows the presence of the ancestors and their guidance. It counsels the proper conduct necessary to be worthy to join the ancestors in due time.

Journal Entry: Elders of Avalon, Somerset

Elder trees are the most magical beings. Wise mothers watching over the land, they are nature's medicine chest, and also powerful otherworldly spirits. The heady scent of their blossoms on the air on a summer's evening sweeps aside the veil between the realms, attracting the faeries and other magical beings, expanding my seer sight. Sitting beneath the branches as dusk gathers, I enter into a deep communion with the sidhe and the guardian spirit of the land herself. Snatches of song and rhyme pass through my mind like clouds illuminated by the setting sun, streamers of golden light. My cousins and co-walkers, my faery spirit kin show me deeper ways of working, healing spells for tree and river, becoming one with the soul of the world...

I lay a bowl of spring water in the branches as the glimmering full moon makes its way above the horizon to energize the potion. This vibrational essence shall help those in need of renewal and those who seek to work with our faery kin. With the tree's permission I gather some of the blooms to make a healing and refreshing cordial, empowered by its magic.

The Aicme of Ailm

Scots Pine/Ailm *(Pinus sylvestris)*
Silver Fir (*Abies alba*)

....
Other names: Scotch pine
....

Word ogham of:

Morainn: *Ardam íachta dha* "The loudest groan,
that is, wondering. For 'aaaaah' is what a man
says when groaning in disease or wondering,
marvelling at whatever circumstance"

Cuchulain: *Tosach garmae* "A beginning of calling"

Oengus: *Tosach frecrai* "The beginning of answers,
that is, the first expression of every
human being after birth is 'ahhh.'"[154]

---

154   McManus, *Guide to Ogam*, 43, with additions by Calder, *Scholars' Primer*, 281.

Description

The scots pine is an evergreen conifer reaching up to forty metres tall. It has blue-green needles that last for three to six years and short-stalked, oval cones. It can be found across northern Europe, and is the only native pine tree of Britain. Despite its recent widespread use in artificial-seeming plantations in Scotland, it once covered most of the country before the great fellings of the Neolithic and the increase of agriculture that have affected the landscape for millennia. It grows mainly in the lowlands but can grow in the mountains up to 2,000 metres. In lowland environments it can have rounder, irregular crowns; trees growing in mountainous areas are narrower and more pointed. It is very hardy, and its deep roots allow it to colonise some of the more extreme climates, from very dry to boggy to even sandy environments. To the casual observer, it is distinguished from the silver fir by its bark, which is fissured and brown at the base and rising to reddish as it reaches the upper half of the trunk. Scots pine grows well in northern Europe and Scandinavia, and was one of the first trees introduced into the US, around 1600.

The silver fir, also associated with ailm, grows up to fifty metres and has grey, smooth bark. It does not generally reach as far north or as high up mountainsides as scots pine, populating the Alps up to 1,600 metres. Its needles last eight to twelve years—twice as long as the pine. Its crown is conical at first but flattens with age; it is then described as having a "stork's nest" crown. Silver fir is not as hardy as the scots pine, although it does well on most terrain; it prefers moist soils and areas with high humidity. The silver fir is a threatened species in its natural habitats, largely due to poor forestry practice and pollution. Yet it is grown commercially in quite large numbers as it is commonly used as a Christmas tree in Europe. Its relative, the Pacific silver fir, *Amies amabilis,* is native to the Pacific Northwest and has similar attributes.

Lore and Legend

In the early Irish Brehon laws, the pine was one of the seven noble trees and was called *ochtach*, not *ailm*. Felling it unlawfully incurred the harshest penalty—death, which was reserved for felling the pine, the apple, the hazel, and entire groves.

Ailm is thought to mean "pine tree" although in *The Ogham Tract* it is referred to as the fir tree.[155] In European and British popular usage, these two trees are often interchangeable due to their similar appearance and qualities. Ailm is the first vowel sound in the ogham, and as said in the word oghams, "aaah" can be said in a variety of contexts, giving it different meanings. It can be said in pain, wonder, revelation, and sympathy, and its interpretation is affected by its context and association with other ogham trees. It can be said to be an ogham about impetus, breaking new ground, and motivation. Promoting perspective and clear-headedness, its energy helps to overcome knotty problems and stuck circumstances, resulting in either the relief or inspiration that signifies such a release—hence Morainn and Oengus's interpretations of ailm … "aaah!" as well as the energy to achieve the necessary breakthrough and to move forward. As Oengus points out, such breakthroughs begin at birth, with the new life emerging into the world.

The pine's common use today as a Christmas tree is a modern incarnation of its long-standing association with the winter solstice. With its red trunk and evergreen needles, pine stood out across the bleak and grey landscapes of the northern winters. Its prominent vitality and hardiness promise that life continues through the harshest of seasons, and that in the darkest times the sun's journey has already begun to swing towards the earth once again. Its reputation as a tree of regeneration also has a practical manifestation: when cut down, the tree may appear dead, but new stems will appear from the still-growing roots.

The tradition of decorating the tree at winter solstice/Christmas goes back millennia, to when the spirit of the tree was honoured and asked to

---

155   McManus, *Guide to Ogam*, 38.

bless and support the people through the cold season, conveying its vitality upon them. In Scandinavia's Viking eras, boughs of pine or fir were brought indoors and decorated to entice or honour the spirits of growth to return in the spring as precursors to the modern Christmas tree.[156] Pine or fir was also used to decorate the Yule log, which was usually oak or ash itself. The Yule log was burnt for protection and blessing, and a small piece was kept as kindling for the following year's Yule log. Although the Yule log is now associated with Norse Yule celebrations, it is thought that this was part of a continuous practice from much earlier times and cultures. Pine's association with vitality and continuity was held across Europe; the fir was associated with the Phrygian lover of the goddess Cybele, Attis, who was sacrificed at the winter solstice by being gored by a boar only to rise again the following year. During his time in the underworld, Attis's body was transformed into a fir tree.[157] This naturally translated itself later into an association with Christ's resurrection, thus becoming the Christmas tree we know today. The baubles and tinsel of today are a remnant of the tree's Pagan past, the offerings to its spirit made across heathen Europe.

The fragrant pine was often burnt at the winter solstice, its fumes purifying the air, stimulating the circulation, refreshing the mind, and clearing the house energetically. Together with the practice of bringing the evergreen boughs indoors, pine's presence in the household during the coldest months formed a continual relationship between the tree's spirits and the home, maximising the blessings and assistance it offered. People could feel confident once they had pine's promise; the previous winter was survived and the continuity of the seasons and the family was maintained. Culpeper attributes the pine under the rulership of Mars, with its fiery, robust,

---

156   Esaias Tegnér, *Frithiof's Saga: A Legend of the North*
       (Stockholm: A Bonnier, 1839), xlvi.

157   Graves, *White Goddess*, 191.

masculine energy.[158] The silver fir, so popular as a Christmas tree today, is under the rulership of Jupiter, who oversees matters of abundance and jollity.[159]

The scots pine and the silver fir rise above the heads of other trees in the landscape and are used by shamans to assist in their envisioning of the upper realms. The trees also served as lookouts, giving a view of the distant horizon even across wooded areas. In Yakut mythology, the souls of shamans are born in fir trees, the greatest position in the highest branches.[160]

The pine's and fir's associations with regeneration and resurrection, to-gether with their magnificent height, naturally suggest a connection with the upper shamanic realms, the seat of the gods known as Gwynfyd ("the white life") in the Welsh Celtic tradition. Gwynfyd is accessed by many means, often with the assistance of bird spirits, but by visualising the pine or fir tree and asking its spirit for permission, the upper realms can be accessed by means of imagining yourself to be climbing its branches, guided and held by its steady yet clear-headed presence. Here the perfect vision of all things is held; it is the realm of ideas and ideals, heroes and divinities, existing out of time in a state of perpetual grace and light, the balancing counterpart to the underworld, Annwn. In Gwynfyd everything is unsullied and uncomplicated by contact with the mortal realm of experience. The visionary blueprints, the potential, and the divine spark within all things are held in the upper world, influencing the world below by its very existence and the possibilities that it represents. From this comes pine's old poetic name, "the sweetest of woods."

The trees associated with ailm lend themselves to attaining clear-headedness and vision on many levels. By reaching above the clutter of the forest canopy (the mundane day-to-day distractions of the mortal world), it is a great teacher of perspective. The viewpoint above the world allows patterns and threads of meaning to become apparent, enabling the seeker or

---

158 Culpeper, *Complete Herbal*, 278.

159 Ibid., 144.

160 Nevill Drury, *The Dictionary of the Esoteric* (London: Watkins, 2004), 105.

shaman to find solutions and predict likely future events. A higher perspective can also be useful to understanding the past. We can see how events unfurl in streams of cause and effect and witness seeds of destiny and fate grow and take root along ancestral bloodlines. Once we understand the past using the gifts of foresight and insight, we are granted wisdom and the ability to implement divine, upper-world vision; we are capable of restoring health, wholeness, and healing, correcting mistakes and negative patterns.

Energetically, pine clears confusion and stuck energy, an action that reveals hidden things and truths we would rather avoid acknowledging. It helps to take not only a long-term view of events, but it also clears the way for implementing the changes necessary to usher in a new phase. It is these qualities Cuchulain refers to in his word oghams as "the weaver's beam," a poetic kenning for the spear. The pine helps the seeker perceive the web, the warp and weft of life patterns and events, thus the symbol. Yet the spear also has the ability to strike directly at the heart of the matter, pinpointing issues and crucial junctures from afar. It is therefore a spear of vision and activation rather than base aggression. As Taliesin's *Cad Goddeu* reveals, the fir is "uncouth and savage" in contrast to the "courtly pine."[161] It can therefore be seen that the ogham ailm represents the key to transforming ignorance and inexperience, the passive victimhood of a lack of perspective into clarity, wisdom, and thus ability and effectiveness.

Practical and Magical Uses

Practically, pine and fir have long been used for ships' masts, house joists, rafters, floors, telegraph poles, "wood wool" (a cushion filler and packing material), and much more. Pine is also used to make chipboard, as it is not a strong wood despite its long fibres. It is made into turpentine, and vegetable tar from the roots has been used to stimulate hair growth. The resinous wood burns well, producing a strong flame.

---

161   Graves, *White Goddess*, 37.

Magically, pine is excellent for cleansing and prosperity spells, as well as calling upon upper-world spirits for assistance in bringing changes in fortune. Pine also helps build magical endurance and restores hope and positivity to those who have been suffering for a long time. It can be burnt as wood upon a hearth or as an incense for these purposes, and blessed pine needles thrown into boiling spring water form a sort of magical aromatherapy.

Pine cones can be used as fertility charms, especially for men, as the Martian, phallic energy helps to build up vigour and robust good health. Pine cones were placed along with acorns on the mythical Maenads' wand tips and were used to draw water or wine from the earth. Likewise, a pine cone-tipped wand can draw the earth's fertility and abundance into your life. They are powerful magical tools of manifestation and sacred sexual union.

Pine cones and branches hung over the bed ward off illness and are especially useful placed near the ill or weak. Likewise, they can be hung about the home to draw their evergreen strength and vitality.

Pine and fir can both be used in herbal sachets and charm bags to ease depression, fatigue, and overturn bad luck.

Healing

Herbally and in aromatherapy, pine is very useful for clearing cold and chest infections as well as killing germs. Its scent is warming and cheering, instilling hope and positivity. The needles and branches were used medicinally by the Greeks and Romans and are still used in saunas in Scandinavia to this day. The vapours and resin pine releases are excellent for the respiratory system and boosting circulation, easing aches and pains, and clearing toxins from the body. The aromatherapy oil extracted from the needles, cones, and twigs should only be used diluted in a carrier oil to clear germs from the air. As an additive to cleaners it can disinfect floors and surfaces, hence its common use in detergents.

As a vibrational essence, pine decongests mind, body, and spirit, clearing blockages and bringing clear vision. It assists in developing awareness and a sense of purpose, showing the way ahead out of stale or congested circumstances. It is also used to help clear the conscience and alleviate feelings of guilt, whether deserved or imagined, a quality attributed to its ability to clear the head and see ways forward to correcting the situation and rectifying any hurts caused. This also brings on a renewed state of creativity, as the stagnant energy is released, transforming it into something positive.

Ogham Divination Meaning

Ailm the pine suggests that clear-headedness and a calm viewpoint should be sought—quiet, contemplative times between periods of action. Listen, both to the prompting of spirit and the words and implications of those around you. You have a great opportunity to affect change by becoming present in each moment and aware of your surroundings physically, psychologically, and energetically. This is your route to empowerment and your protection. If you have lost clear perspective in the situations around you and are instead propelled by people or events that are no longer under your control, you are urged to seek clarity and vision through stillness, cleansing, rectification, and the detoxification of your being. Sitting at the crown of the tallest of trees, you will receive new vision, wider horizons, and in time, perceive the way ahead to a better future.

Journal Entry: Scots Pine of the Great Glen

These tall trees see high above the forest, reaching the high slopes of the mountains, their first branches only greening at their neighbour's canopy. I sit amongst the roots of a tree I call the lord of these woods. He must be of great age, for he has the widest trunk of all his kin in the area, reaching high above them. As I came to sit by him, I felt a great sense of softness and welcome; warmth surrounded me even though the first leaves were turning golden as autumn took hold. But he shall stay green all winter, his fresh needles clearing the senses of all who pass.

I let my breathing settle and slow, stretching out to him in kinship. I place my back against his strong but soft trunk. I feel the stillness he holds and his calm confidence, and it seems to me that his spirit is like warm silver light. He teaches me to rise higher and feel the tips of my hair drinking in the sunlight far above. He shows me the sight of the eagle, the valley impossibly far below, wrapped in a mantle of green and gold with the secret silver dark waters of the loch and the golden and grey mountain ridges thrusting into the sky like naked shoulders slipping free of an emerald shawl.

The air is cool, setting my whole body tingling far below, fresh bright light enlivening my being. I feel my heart and mind expand in a thousand ways I cannot describe, drinking in new vision. I feel the upper world, Gwynfyd, all around me; the very air is luminescent and swirls around me, *is* me. Here in this place, I am one with the vastness of creation, my body a tiny moment and place in time, far, far below. A spiritual gift more than a magical one, the pine lends vision, perspective, and blows fresh air through my mind, alighting me with inspiration and *glefiosa*, the bright knowledge of spirit.

Gorse/Onn (*Ulex europaeus*)

....
Other names:
Furze, frey, prickly broom, whin
....

Word ogham of:
Morainn: *Cognaid ech* "Wounder of
horses" *onnaid* "Wheels of a chariot"
Aliter comquinidech "Equally wounding"

Cuchulain: *Lúth fiann.i.fraech* "Sustaining equipment
of warriors, or hunters"; "fierceness"

Oengus: *Féthem soíre* "Smoothest of
craftsmanship"; "gentlest of work"[162]

Description

A member of the pea family, gorse is a dense and very prickly evergreen
shrub that can grow up to two metres. Its bright yellow flowers blossom
in spring and summer, but it may flower year-round depending on where
it is situated. The flowers have a very sweet scent and produce copious
amounts of pollen and nectar, making it a favourite of bees. It prefers to
grow on acid soils, sandy heaths, moorland, and common land in windy,
exposed positions. Growing on the poorest soils, it prefers sunny positions away from trees. Gorse is distinguished from the broom by its long
thorns, which grow up to two centimetres. They almost entirely replace
the leaves as the main photosynthetic organ on the plant. Young gorse
leaves are trifoliate, but as they age they become scales and thin spines.
Gorse has adapted to become what is called a "fire climax" plant—that

---

162   McManus, *Guide to Ogam*, 43, with additions by Calder, *Scholars' Primer*, 281.

is, whilst highly flammable, can withstand fires. Its seed pods are largely opened by fire, ensuring the plant's regeneration. The root stumps also regenerate rapidly after fire where the ground is cleared. The branches would have been shaded earlier, as other plants would grow and provide cover. Gorse is an excellent nitrogen fixer and is used to reclaim ground for cultivation. It grows so well in poor soil that it is now considered an invasive species in some parts of North America.

Lore and Legend

Gorse or furze was mentioned in the Brehon laws as one of the eight bramble trees. It was known as *aiteand*.

The word *onn* is Old Irish for "ash tree," pointing to the meaning and energy of this ogham sigil.[163] However, *The Scholars' Primer* (*Auraicept na n-Éces*) refers to onn being the furze or gorse bush.[164] Gorse is often considered to be almost the same plant as the broom, yet while it is in the same family it differs significantly in its sharp thorns, which the broom lacks. The similarity between them exists in the yellow flowers and the freshening, clearing energy. Gorse is also a great provider of fertility; it increases life force, creativity, and vitality. Sacred to the Irish sun god Lugh, it is associated with the summer festival of Lughnasadh, August 1. In Brittany, which still has a strong Celtic tradition, especially at Pont Aven, Lughnasadh was known as "the Festival of the Golden Gorse." The tradition continues to this day.[165] Lugh is associated with light, inspiration, and skill. His spear of light, one of the "hallows" (sacred treasures of Ireland), is said to induce ecstasy. This ecstatic energy is invoked by the gorse in many different aspects, drawing inspiration as well as passion and lustiness, a rise in life force spreading across the body. The connection to Lugh also reveals gorse to be a powerful "warrior" plant, a fierce ally helping with mental agility and the ability

---

163   McManus, *Guide to Ogam*, 38.

164   Calder, *Scholars' Primer*, 287.

165   Moe Jorgen, Peter Christen Asbjornsen, eds., Fodor's *Normandy, Brittany and the Best of the North* (http://books.google.co.uk/books?id=JbyMN6oZK8MC&, 2011).

to sweep away and destroy redundant or negative thoughts. Similar to the broom, it has these energies in a more powerful and intense configuration, hence Cuchulain's words on the gorse being "sustaining equipment of warriors" and "fierceness." It is not only muscle that comprises the warrior's strength but also skill, mental and physical agility, and the courage and energy for sustained periods of action. Interestingly, gorse was also used as a favoured fuel in bread ovens, another "sustenance" of a warrior that was also particularly significant at Lughnasadh, which later became Christianised as Lammas ("loaf mass") honouring the wheat harvest.

Gorse has another side—eroticism and desire. The old saying "when gorse is in bloom, kissing is in season" is a reference to the fact that love is a perennial and permanent aspect of life, just as the gorse can blossom year-round.[166] The sweet smell of gorse—as with the hawthorn—has been associated with the scent of female genitalia and arousal. Its great life force also links it with the fires of passion and sexuality.

The queens of Faery are said to hold gorse as especially sacred, and the flowers have been eaten in times past to induce visions of Faery, which are often accompanied with a sense of the great and primal eroticism present in the natural world. As mentioned earlier, gorse blossoms are a favourite of the bees, another signifier of the erotic and sensual aspects of the wild to which the gorse is inextricably linked. With its five petals reminiscent of the pentagram and the sign of the goddess, it draws seekers back to a simpler, more primal, and animalistic side of themselves, where the tangles of the intellect are unravelled by the instinctual knowing of the body. It is this sexual aspect of onn that Oengus refers to when he calls the gorse *Féthem soíre*— "the smoothest of craftsmanship" or "gentlest of work," for gorse is an ogham of lovemaking, partnership, and desire. As such, it is useful in love magic—especially in acquiring skill as a lover—although the results may be more passionate than anticipated!

---

166   Grieve, *A Modern Herbal*, 367.

Gorse is traditionally burnt at the spring equinox across the Celtic diaspora as an offering to the returning sun and to destroy the plant's hard thorns to encourage fresh and softer new shoots. The new growth is used particularly in Scotland as valuable food for livestock. Spring equinox is a time when the sun is entering into its most powerful phase: the winter has passed and summer is ahead. Sap is rising in trees and animals alike. Gorse's tendency is also to raise the life force and the passions, and the resurgence of the life force across both the body and the earth itself.

Burnt as fuel, gorse creates great heat and is good kindling, and its fiery solar attributes make it a favourite to place in the fireplace in summer as the hearth fire. Gorse lends its protective and clearing energies to the house, encouraging blessings upon the home. These properties are again due to its connection with the faeries and the sun. Whilst gorse is said to attract and be sacred to them, it is also used to repel faeries and even witches, whose fondness for the gorse is also well known. Thus we see how the power of the gorse has remained acknowledged and respected over the centuries despite the contradictions of cultural and religious opinion.

Whilst in some parts of Britain gorse is said to be a marker of faery dwellings and to be a favourite place for their revels at the festival of Beltane (May 1), bestowing the blessings of the sidhe, in others it is associated with many tales of "wicked" faeries. In nineteenth-century Anglesey were several recorded cases of faery abduction; one woman used bundles of gorse all around and over her bed to protect herself from being stolen.[167] The woman stated on many occasions that she could have no peace unless the gorse was upon her somewhere.

Like the hawthorn and the blackthorn, gorse's thorns create an energetic "sacred enclosure" of sorts, protecting those within from those without. Just as with the other two trees, this particular protective aspect seems to be especially potent when women and/or children are seeking sanctuary, giving more clues to its magical and spiritual nature.

---

167   Wirt Sikes, *British Goblins* (London: EP Publishing, 1973), 116.

The gorse's life force-boosting ability and its association with fire and solar energies are not only physical matters. Using it can also lead to a surge in intuition and imagination, increasing the flow of awen, divine inspiration, poetically referred to by W. B. Yeats as the "fire in the head" in his poem "The Song of Wandering Aengus." Such a state is one of heightened visionary knowledge as well as spiritual and intellectual expansion. It is the radiant brow of initiated and illuminated mystics like Merlin, Gwydion, and of course the bard Taliesin, whose name itself means "radiant brow," a description of his visionary prowess. With its yellow flowers, gorse has also been associated with the element of air, the direction of the east, and thus magically with intellect, the "fire in the head" here meaning great bursts of mental agility and intellectual fertility. Such bursts of genius can lead to clever solutions and achievements as well as the ability to empower thoughtforms and visualisations. It is this deep place where the source of visionary and bardic inspiration can be accessed; the gifts of prophecy and ancient knowledge can be absorbed and understood. The other side of this is an overactive mind that leads to inflation, overstimulation, and even divine insanity. Contact with the more earthy aspects of life may become difficult, and thoughtforms may take on undesirable lives of their own. If this happens, gorse's thorns and the cleansing, warrior qualities should be sought to clear the ground and deflate the energy to a more earthed and balanced state. In this way, gorse can act in a similar way to broom but in a more powerful mode when more serious clearings are necessary.

One of gorse's important aspects is its ability to house and host many life forms. Its thorns and tangled branches provide protection from the elements and make a suitable habitat for many insects, small creatures, as well as nesting birds. Gorse's new shoots and copious amounts of nectar also provide an abundance of food. This providence in turn provides a good example to humans, and teaches that abundance is ever-present in the natural world. We are counselled to wisely gather resources and give generously, reminded of the need to regularly seek nourishment for our minds, spirits, and bodies. The result of all that vitality is thus to serve and embrace life in all its forms.

Practical and Magical Uses

Gorse is usually considered to be under the rulership of the planet Mars, or sometimes the sun, as both refer to its bright, fiery energy and magical uses.[168] As already described, gorse is an excellent kindling fuel that makes hot, brief fires good for baking. Gorse is also used to make hedges and boundaries, as its sharp thorns prevent animals and people passing easily, hence Morainn's practical comments on the gorse: *cognaid ech,* "wounder of horses." Morainn also links the gorse with horses when he says it equals the "wheels of a chariot," and to its thorns when he calls the gorse "equally wounding," the flowers and the thorns being of equal help and harm. Gorse can also clear and maintain your energetic boundaries around the home or metaphorically in your life and personal relationships.

Gorse flowers make a beautiful yellow dye, and young gorse shoots make excellent nutritious fodder loved by horses and cows, the latter of which were said to make richer milk as a result.[169] At one point, the seeds were considered nutritious, but this may be due to the gorse's life force-enhancing qualities rather than due to a specific nutritional value. The ash from burning gorse is particularly alkaline and makes excellent food for the soil.[170] The ash was also once used as a substitute for soap—another aspect of its clearing properties.

Gorse is an excellent flower and wood for love spells and amulets to attract good luck, igniting passions and enthusiasm for life with its solar and martial energy. Gorse also has an excellent effect on the solar plexus; wearing it is good to draw in and develop your personal power or for after shamanic power retrieval ceremonies. Scattered around the home, it attracts

---

168   Culpeper, *Complete Herbal,* 160.
169   Grieve, *A Modern Herbal,* 367.
170   Ibid.

good luck and prosperity. The golden flowers are also great substitutes for golden coins in prosperity spells; they can be carried in gold cloth in your wallet or purse to attract more gold, to see that your coffers are never empty.

Gorse is also helpful burnt as an incense or thrown upon the fire when feeling stuck or stagnant in any way. Blessed spring water can also be "asperged" or sprinkled around the home using a sprig of gorse to bring fresh energy, prosperity, and good luck.

Healing

Medicinally, gorse was thought to be useful for dissolving kidney stones and clearing jaundice; young shoots were made into a tea. Gorse is also taken sometimes to ease depression and feelings of being lost or stagnant. However, Culpeper warns that while it may take away melancholy, gorse may "send up strong fancies, and as many strange visions to the head … therefore [it is] to be taken with great moderation."[171] This warning most likely comes from gorse's subtle visionary qualities, working as unintended side effects. While its fiery, enthusiastic energy may indeed help with depression or melancholia and set you back upon your true path in life, Culpeper's warning should always be heeded—this is a powerful plant and should not be taken if you are undergoing any significant mental or emotional instability or repression. Guidance is a must.

As a vibrational flower essence, gorse is excellent for increasing mental and emotional energy as well as restoring hope, one of its most notable qualities. It achieves this by refreshing the person's point of view, empowering positive thinking and resourcefulness, and clearing negativity. However, gorse's vibrational essence doesn't contain any of the herbal matter and the accompanying visionary side effects. It is a much safer alternative for those with delicate psyches, which will be built up and made stronger gradually and steadily by its support.

---

171   Culpeper, *Complete Herbal*, 160.

Ogham Divination Meaning

As an ogham, onn signifies a time of resurging life force and inspiration, and guidance from the visionary within. It ushers in a time of new ideas and great fertility. It is a fiery catalyst for change. However, it also warns of the potential for life force to burn out of control, or even burn out entirely, when primal or inspirational energies simply cannot be found or they have become so imbalanced that they no longer have a basis in the health and right action of a properly functioning life. Gorse brings cleansing, as well as renewal and restoration, so that properly balanced energy and inner equilibrium will return. Onn reminds us that a time of high power, pride, and the inner light of an empowered soul are our birthrights. The light of summer is ahead.

Journal Entry: Gorse of Priddy, Somerset

I am walking on the high Mendip hills where the gorse grows thick by the field of round barrows. Golden on the green-grey hillside, they mark a place of the sidhe, an excellent spot for seeking visions of the otherworld. Here the spirits of the ancestors gather at dusk as the wild wind blows over the moor. I eat a few flower tips to ease my weariness, and the world around is illuminated from within before my mortal eyes settle again into the everyday. I am granted the gift of gathering a few blooms and spiky sprigs for a house-clearing spell and to ease a friend troubled by nightmares.

Tying them into a bunch, I bless the house by sprinkling spring water from the well around the walls and hang them in dark corners and around the bed, before sending the spirits that trouble her on their way. She will sleep soundly from now on.

Heather/Ur *(Calluna vulgaris)*

....

Other names:
Scots heather, ling
....

Word ogham of:
Morainn: *Gruidem dal* "Terrible tribe"
Úaraib adbaib "In cold dwellings"
Ur "The mound of the earth, heath"

Cuchulain: *Forbbaid ambí.i.uir*
"Shroud of a lifeless one"; "the grave"

Oengus: *Sílad cland* "Growing/propagation of plants"[172]

Description

Heather is an evergreen shrub of the *Ericaceae* family that usually grows up to half a metre but can grow a full metre on occasion. Its small pink-purple or white bell-shaped flowers grow along one side of the stalk, blossoming from August to October. It is extremely hardy and woody, growing on heaths, moorlands, as well as woods and bogs in acidic soils. It is a favourite of bees, and the two have long been linked together in meaning and tradition. Heather is one of the first plants to propagate an area after a forest fire, and its ability to grow in rough terrains is exceptional. Heather has short, tough leaves and purple stems, which are a favourite food of the red grouse and other heathland birds. Heather grows across western Europe and Asia, North America, and Greenland.

---

172   McManus, *Guide to Ogam*, 43, with additions by Calder, *Scholars' Primer*, 283.

Lore and Legend

Ur once meant "earth" but in modern Scottish and Irish Gaelic it means "new" or "fresh," whereas the word "heather" is *fraoch,* which means "fury" and "wrathful."[173] Fraoch is the name of a warrior of the Tuatha Dé Danann, the husband of Findabair, the daughter of Maeve and Ailill.[174] Fraoch had a particularly powerful and fiery lineage, as he was the son of the hero Cuchulain and the lady of the sidhe, the otherworldly Aoife. Other sources say his mother was the sexually insatiable queen Maeve.

Fraoch was killed by his father and is associated with a cave at Cruachan, part of Maeve's territory, where an ogham inscription was found that reads "the cave of Fraoch, the son of Maeve." Maeve is notorious for her sexual appetites and erotic nature, and Fraoch is connected with warriorhood and sexual energy, the rhythms of life and death. The next stage in the journey after the fierce, warlike energy of life and its natural conclusion, death, is ur—the new, a return to the earth.

The common thread of meaning between these two words, fraoch and ur, has to do with transformation, the cyclical gateway of life and death, the fierce energy that wipes away the past and ushers in the new. This is sexual energy not merely of individuals, but on a planetary scale. In the eternal cycle of life, death, and decay, new life is nourished and sustained. It is true on the forest floor as much as it is in human lives, when the lessons—those many lives and deaths of our ancestors—provide context, meaning, and support to our own. It exists in microcosm as much as in macrocosm, for there are many deaths in a single human life, the endings that inevitably mark stages upon the road of life, and each gives way to beginnings, new life sustained and altered by the experiences of the past. The energy that moves the leaves from trees and feeds the ravens upon the carcass is the same which brings new life to the world, upends that life to the underworld, and returns it to the soil, transformed into a source of new life once

173   McManus, *Guide to Ogam,* 38.

174   Ellis, *Dictionary of Irish Mythology,* 129.

more. This is sexual energy in one of its myriad forms, the very impulse of life itself.

Heather's association with life and death is potent. The purple flowers are said to be stained from the blood of fallen warriors, like Fraoch himself. The "cold dwellings" and "the mound of the earth" Morainn refers to are the houses of the spirits of our ancient dead as well as the sum of our past experiences. These ancient dead are said to dwell in the barrow mounds and tumuli scattered across the British and Irish landscapes, their bones lying within whilst their spirits feast in otherworldly halls. This underworld is only accessible via the earth mounds themselves and the visions of the shamans who held their rituals and trance journeys within their cold sheltering cysts.

Indeed, heather often grows upon burial mounds. Cuchulain refers to this when he calls ur "the grave" and "the shroud of a lifeless one." The completion of lifelessness is not death but that which lies beyond. New life is fed from the death of the old. It is the "growing of plants" as Oengus calls it, from the soil nourished by corpses of the past.

Heather is always associated with the bees that swarm around it and produce excellent honey from its nectar. The spiritual importance of bees is a worldwide and ancient phenomenon, often connecting the plant with numerous goddesses, teaching many lessons on our erotic, primal state, community, and of course, fertility. The importance of bees to the fertilisation of crops and the survival of the environment as a whole was always known, but the modern world is only beginning to regain the understanding and respect the earth deserves. Bees in many ways are linchpins in the earth's fertility and the continuation of life itself. Thus ur is connected to the newness of life, and the fertile earth, "the growing of plants" to which Oengus refers.

Heather is sacred to goddesses of fertility and sexual love such as Venus and Isis, whose sexual impulses also reveal the darker side, the link between life and death. Both are two sides of the same essential sexual energy, the thread upon which all life is strung, moving from birth to death and beyond.

The thread upon which our lives travel is similar to notions of the great web, the strands of destiny woven by the triple goddess in the underworld, called the Norns in Viking mythology. It was said that the thread of our lives was spun before we were even born and is cut by the crone goddess when it is time for us to die and our energy take on a new form. The thread passes from the spiritual realm into manifest reality and back again, only to continue weaving between the worlds, one life form and the next. Heather, particularly white, is said to be lucky for this reason, as the Romani people well remember.[175] Its connection with the threads and the flow of our life along it is so strong that it encourages us to make right decisions and follow the right direction through our lives. Bad luck can be considered the opposite of this, those moments when our inner balance and innate connection to the universe is off-kilter. Nothing seems to go right, and wrong actions create momentum that leads from one mistake to another. Right action and the restoration of our lives requires awareness to see the problem (scots pine), the rectification and clearing (gorse), and the restoration of flow along the paths of our destiny, facilitated by the heather. Right action and "luck" are restored by our ability to move naturally along the current of life without blocks or resistance. This is the gift of the heather. Life in all its forms blossoms and moves along in natural rhythms when balanced between life and death; beginnings and endings flow smoothly and continuously, one into the other.

There is another facet of this current of energy, this thread of life along which we travel. It is the link between our inner and outer selves, the healing that takes place when the flow between them is restored, the wisdom and wholeness of our inner selves drawn up from the depths of our souls to nourish our surface lives, giving it meaning and harmony. The same is true for our relationships with each other. When the flow between giving and receiving and the individual and collective is in balance, healing and wholeness ensues. Between collectives and communities, peace is

---

175   Carr-Gomm, *Druid Plant Oracle*, 56.

encouraged and created. When this flow develops harmoniously between individuals, love is the inevitable result. Between couples, it becomes sexual and soulful love; the journey between one life to the next continues as one generation conceives and gives birth to the next.

Thus in many ways heather's energy functions as a gateway, a channel between worlds, the river of energy that flows along it between inner and outer to access the wisdom of the ancestors, the gifts of spirit, the fertility of the goddess, and the knowledge of our own souls. It is the flow between our conscious and unconscious selves.

Practical and Magical Uses

Astrologically, heather is considered to be ruled by Venus. The plant and its accompanying bees have an excellent effect on whatever grows around it. Apple trees bear much more fruit when growing near heather. The same can be said for us—our lives and bodies bear fruit from our connection with the flow of life, the cycle of fertility and decay that is the goddess herself.

Practically, heather has many uses. It used to be considered a good fuel for fire, especially in conjunction with the peat upon which it often grows. It was also used for fences and to make ropes, as well as in the manufacture of several dyes. Heather is still used to make brushes and brooms, and it was used to stuff mattresses—it was said then to have healing qualities as well as induce restful sleep and insightful dreams. Honey made from heather is particularly delicious and healing, as is tea made from its blossoms.

Another aspect of heather is the legendary heather ale. The earliest traces of it go back to 2000 BCE, where a Neolithic pottery shard found on the Isle of Rhum was discovered to have traces of a fermented drink made from heather flowers.[176] The ale was loved by the Celts and all tribes of northern Europe including the later Vikings, but sadly the recipe was lost centuries ago. It was said to be an excellent cure-all, fortifying warriors before and after battle. It increased agility, endurance, healed wounds, and restored

---

176   "Did You Know? Fraoch Leann (Heather Ale)" (http://www
.rampantscotland.com/know/blknow_heatherale.htm).

spirits after the horrors and trials of battle. In restoring flow and harmony, the sense of self is restored and the path to healing is begun. Various new recipes for heather ale have since been reconstructed.

Heather is great for spells calling upon the Great Earth Goddess as well as Isis, Venus/Aphrodite, and the Melissae—sacred semi-divine priestesses who served the Great Goddess (most famously in her aspect as Artemis) Gaea, the original goddess served by the Oracle at Delphi who was known as the Delphic Bee. The Celtic goddess Brighid also has many bee and heather associations; she can be called upon using heather flowers scattered around sacred space, or burnt as incense. Carrying heather is known to bring good luck, and it is also an excellent talisman for connecting with the Great Goddess and tuning into and harnessing empowered feminine energy. Heather can be used in charm bags to protect women, owing to the shamanic assistance of its fierce spirit. However, there is no substitute for common sense and practical caution; it is better to use heather to see how you can protect yourself more effectively than to rely on it to do the work for you.

Heather has been used magically to open portals between this world and the realm of the sidhe, and purple heather especially was used to help contact the dead. Together with fern, it can be used in spells to call upon the rain, but only in real need.

Healing

Heather flowers are antiseptic and expectorant, making it good for coughs and wound or facial washes.[177] It is said to be good for insomnia as well as stomach pains and skin complaints. It is diuretic, so heather tea is a good general tonic that flushes toxins from the body, again increasing the flow. As a vasoconstrictor it is also good for the heart and is said to slightly raise blood pressure. Traditionally it is also said to be excellent for rheumatism

---

177   John Lust, *The Herb Book* (New York: Bantam, 1986), 215.

and gout, especially when the fresh flowers are poured under hot water in a bath.

As a vibrational essence, heather is said to be good for talkativeness and for healing obsessions with troubles and illnesses. It can be said that such a person is "stuck," lacking connection to the flow of life. Excessive talkativeness can be seen as a form of purging, an attempt to restore the flow, by using words to push the energy along. Unfortunately it can create yet another pattern of stuck energy, as we focus only on what has hurt or disturbed us. Our energy and thoughts merely rotate around yet another cul-de-sac without progress. Heather's essence corrects this, repairing the threads and the flow, restoring harmony and our relationship with the world and each other. It does this by being a great comforter, nurturing and encouraging. Sometimes it encourages a great outpouring of tension so that finally ease can follow. It gives reassurance that we are cared for just as we are. It is excellent for the wounded inner child and restores bonds between people, helping them feel the love that others feel for them, as well as the love they feel for others.

Heather's vibrational essence is also good for healing the sense of the feminine, restoring a sense of respect and empowerment for feminine energy.

Ogham Divination Meaning

As an ogham, ur reminds us of the love of the goddess and the love the universe has for us. It encourages us to reconnect with ourselves and each other. We are encouraged to follow our passion and desire. It is that which propels us forward in a never-ending cycle through seasons, lifetimes, birth and death, in an eternal dance with life itself. Even death is a part of life, and as our consciousness flows between one life form and another we enact and embody the relationship between the individual and the infinite, of which we are always a part. We are connected by the web of life and are also the web itself, the conduit through which other forms also travel through time and space, as we do. Ur encourages us to be children of the universe, beginning, ending, and beginning again, opening up to the kindness and comfort of the divine. We are reminded that if we simply follow what feels comfortable and wholesome, only goodness follows. By trusting our luck, we open ourselves in innocence to the bounty of the universe, and that makes us lucky; we receive the goodness that is always available. New doors of opportunity are opened, and Spirit is allowed to lend a hand. We become more confident and positive, and our lives are filled with ease and playfulness. Growth and abundance is our natural state; healing and wholeness are restored by listening to the body, rediscovering our ability to love, restoring the flow and our connection to the life around us.

Journal Entry: Heather of the Great Glen, the Highlands

Purple heather covers the hillsides here in great swaths like a vast company of warriors. Centuries ago this land knew so many battles, and the purple heather signifies their blood spilt upon the earth. The pain of their loss can still be felt, as if the very soil still grieves. But there is another presence here, too. This is a goddess place; the fierce spirit of the warriors guards and honours a deep feminine energy. The land itself gathers these souls to her breast, and they rest in her ancient embrace. Beneath the earth, in the air, and in the icy waters running down the rugged hillsides into the great lochs below, the sovereignty of the land remains—a fierce goddess full of mercy and endless love. I am granted her permission to gather a little of her blooms, that I may use to restore some of that sovereignty in myself and others in charm bags to grant sleep and deep healing. I also make a flower essence, resting a crystal bowl of spring water amongst the flowers and the bees to ease those who are stuck reliving their miseries and grief. A few drops of the potion every day, and the goddess will set them free.

Aspen/Eadha *(Populus tremula)*

....

Other names:
Test tree, trembling tree, quaking ash,
quaking aspen, pipple tree

....

Word ogham of:

Morainn: *Érgnaid fid* "Discerning tree/man"

Cuchulain: *Bráthair bethi.i.e* "Kinsman of the birch/aspen"

Oengus: *Commaín carat* "Exchange of friends";
textual reference: "horrible grief"; "test tree"[178]

Description

Aspen and its very close relatives the white, black, and grey poplars are members of the willow family. They are quick-growing deciduous trees that can reach up to thirty metres tall (black and white poplars grow up to thirty-five). Aspen grows by sending out suckers that can develop into new trees; a single aspen can generate hundreds of others that are all joined at the roots, creating their own grove. The grey-green trunks darken with age, developing diamond-shaped lenticels or ridges over time. The oval-shaped leaves are shiny on top and paler beneath; hairs develop with new shedding as the leaves mature. The dense profusion of dangling male catkins develop in March and April and can measure up to eleven centimetres long. Though sensitive to drought, aspen tolerates a wide range of soils and terrains, and it will colonise poor or rocky soils although it prefers moist, fertile areas. Aspen interbreeds with other poplars with ease, and there is a wide variety of hybrids. It was introduced to the British Isles quite a long time ago and is considered one of the oldest native species. Aspen is particularly prolific in Scotland and can be found

---

178   McManus, *Guide to Ogam*, 43, with additions by Calder, *Scholars' Primer*, 93.

in the ancient Caledonian forest and as far north and west as the Shetland Isles. European aspen also grows as far north as the Arctic Circle in Scandinavia and as far south as equatorial Africa; it is also found in Asia. Other forms of poplar are found across North America.

Lore and Legend

Known as the "trembling tree," aspen features in *The Ogham Tract* under several spellings: eadha, edad, ebhadh, and ebad, to name a few. It also features in the later five double letters known as the forfeda, which were added to the ogham several centuries later to accommodate vowel sounds absent in Gaelic but present in Greek and Latin, the *lingua franca* of the early Middle Ages. This modification was similar to the addition of further letters in the Latin alphabet, a seventh-century accommodation of the "barbarian" tongues.

Aspen is strongly associated in Celtic traditions with the festival of Samhain, and it has a history of use in spellwork for helping the alleviation of fears, controlled contact with beings of the underworld, and peaceful contact with the spirits of the dead. In Ireland, rods of aspen called *fe* were used for the measuring of dead bodies for coffins.[179] Thus aspen was deemed a respectful tree to use for this delicate and sacred task. Conversely, in ancient Wales, the tree was considered cursed because of its connection with the dead; it was thought to be the wood from which Jesus's crucifixion cross was made. Aspen's connection with the dead goes back as far as 3000 BCE, where golden headdresses and crowns of aspen leaves were placed upon the dead in burial mounds in Mesopotamia (modern Iraq and Syria), a practice thought to ease entry into the underworld.[180] The association with death also connect aspens with the autumn equinox, the "old age" of the year, a threshold between death and renewed fertility. Perhaps this is why Cuchulain called the aspen "kinsman

---

179   Graves, *White Goddess*, 193.
180   Ibid.

of the birch," referring to its position as liminal, the closing of one phase inevitably ushering in another's new beginning (birch). As Oengus puts it, it is an "exchange of friends"—a time of transition and "passing on" which suggests a safe, assisting energy, an ally and support. As "friend" to the birch, duality and relationship is suggested; it is a fluid and easy ("friendly") transition from one realm or state to the next.

Aspen is associated with fear and fearfulness because of its role as a threshold tree. It is thus referred to in *The Scholars' Primer* as "horrible grief … test tree." Thresholds mean change, and it can be a terrifying thing on many levels. As fear develops, it sucks life energy and causes us to resist change, making the transition harder—a self-perpetuating cycle that strips us of strength and makes us more vulnerable. Fearlessness and courage, on the other hand, naturally make us more robust and present; we are more able to deal with whatever comes our way. Of course courage and reckless-ness are not the same; the former is an aware willingness to endure and overcome challenges with the trust that we are capable of enduring.

Aspen is also a powerful goddess tree, with its different species being attributed to the various aspects of the triple goddess. Thus the aspen is the tree of the Maiden. The white poplar is associated with the Mother goddess and the black poplar the Crone. The goddess embodies the threshold and portal into life, serving as caretaker and later she who lays out the dead, and aspen can be seen as accompanying that experience—youth through death to life again. It has great sympathy and understanding of the human condition and an awareness of our frailties and vulnerabilities. Aspen is par-ticularly sacred to the Greek maiden goddess Persephone, who wed Hades and lived there with him for six months of the year, causing autumn and win-ter in the world above. In Greek mythology, it is said that aspen trees stand at the threshold to the underworld, marking the boundary between the spirit world and the world of mortality. White poplars were said to line the banks of the river Styx; they needed to be crossed to enter the underworld.[181] Poplars

---

181   Graves, *White Goddess*, 375.

also featured in the Elysian Fields, and Hades's lover Leuce (a daughter of Oceanus) was turned into a poplar by him after her mortal death.[182]

The aspen's trembling leaves link it with the presence of spirits, particularly wind spirits but also otherworldly and ancestral beings. As such, it was also associated with oracles and augury. It was used in making divinatory incense, and listening to its leaves rustling can invoke trance states. The rustling is sometimes believed to be the tree itself communicating, and in the Gaelic-speaking lands aspen leaves were sometimes placed upon the tongue to encourage eloquence. The aspen's "voice" was also attributed to faeries and otherworldly beings who gathered around its shade. For this reason, aspens and other poplars are considered to be gathering places for all sorts of spirits and energies; important events occurring near them took on added significance, as if portended, blessed, or cursed by spiritual forces.

It was thought that the voices of the dead could be heard in aspen's rustling leaves, understood only by seers or shamans. These trees are especially significant, serving as threshold and visionary trees where messages from the otherworld can be accessed. Aspen grants assistance in the ability to receive these messages, helping us develop the courage to do so. In the alteration of the shaman's or seer's vibrational rate, contact between the worlds is made easier. In this way, aspen also teaches right use of magical power, as connection with the otherworlds and multitudes of Spirit grants access to greater abilities and knowledge. Here is the hidden side of cause and effect that can so often create difficulties for the unwary or irresponsible. Seekers realise they are not engaged in parlour games when magically working with spirits; they realise instead that they are participating in a magical universe far larger than their perceptions. Working with the aspen increases awareness of this universe and helps the seeker adjust and cope with the increase in perception.

The name "aspen" comes from the Greek *aspis,* which means "shield." Aspen was used by the Greeks as well as the Celts to make shields, and it

---

182   *Larousse Encyclopedia,* 189.

was almost as popular as the alder for this purpose. Like the alder, aspen also makes good shamanic shields, giving courage when embarking on new terrain, assisting the spirit of the fallen warrior to move on and find a way to the next world should the worst happen. Shields made of aspen were perhaps especially precious and used for only the distinguished warriors. It is said that the hero Cuchulain's shield was made of aspen and that he received his final training on the Isle of Skye from a woman called Scáthach, which means both "shadow" and "shield." To pass the tests and learn the lessons of shadow is to come to terms with the underworld and otherworld inside and outside ourselves; gaining courage and going beyond our limitations and perceptions is crossing the threshold between what we are and what we could and will be. This is aspen's lesson, and once we have passed we are marked as experienced, proficient, and seasoned— hence Morainn's word ogham for aspen as "discerning man."

The Greek hero Hercules was given a crown of aspen after killing the giant Cacus to mark his achievement, as was the Irish hero Oscar who is said to have fallen on the battlefield heroically after killing the high king in defence of the Fianna, of which he was a member. After slaying the king, Oscar is said to have fallen like an aspen tree—bravely and with awareness, his spirit leaving "like leaves on a strong wind."[183] This wind is the north wind that carries the spirits of the dead and their voices to and from the mortal world.

Practical and Magical Uses

The magical uses of aspen are all related to thresholds, shielding, building confidence, attuning us to be able to cope with the vast increases in energy coming from the spirit world, and the qualities of air—communication, augury, and messages to and from the spirit and mortal worlds. For this reason, aspen is used in sympathetic magic to heal nervous complaints, illnesses, and conditions that induce shaking and trembling, and the overcoming of

---

183   Gregory, *Irish Myths and Legends*, 395.

anxieties and fears. An old Lincolnshire charm refers to this as well: "Aspen tree, aspen tree, I prithee shake and shiver instead of me." Sometimes a lock of a person's hair was buried beneath an aspen tree or hung in its branches so that the tree would take the illness from the afflicted.

Aspen is also used in various traditional recipes for flying ointments, as its magical properties (and of course its indwelling spirit) are excellent for helping to cross into the spirit realm and seek spirit vision. In reality, flying ointments of all kinds—even those with toxic hallucinogenic ingredients— are entheogenic potions that assist the seeker with finding spirits and "spirit flight," accessing the divine via shamanic experience. Aspen's spirit is an excellent ally, giving protection as well as extra "lift" thanks to its connections to the air element. Aspen is also a good addition to Samhain incense or to scatter about the circle, for the same reason.

Aspen is traditionally placed under the astrological rulership of Saturn and is used in spells relating to legal worries and protection against theft.[184] Gathered with the tree's permission, a small bundle of aspen wood or bark tied with red thread and buried at the threshold is good against thieves and malicious intent.

Aspen is also sometimes considered under the rulership of Jupiter due to its connections to the god Zeus, and it is used in money spells. Due to its connections with eloquence, aspen is also associated with Mercury and can be used for communication spells as well as to help with writing legal letters or application forms. Poplar trees are associated with moon magic due to the connection with Persephone. Similarly in the Celtic tradition, aspen and poplars are associated with the Faery Queen who grants the seeker a "tongue that cannot lie"—an ancient reference to the gifts of prophecy and magical eloquence.

---

184   Culpeper, *Complete Herbal*, 278.

Practically, poplar is not used for many things as it is quite a weak wood, but it is very buoyant so was sometimes used to make paddles and oars. Aspen is excellent for carving, and as it does not burn well, white or grey poplar (a cross breed between poplar and aspen) was sometimes used to make floorboards in houses. As discussed earlier, aspen was used to make shields due to its strength.

Healing

Herbally and practically, aspen has much fewer uses than the trees featured earlier in the ogham. As mentioned, aspen was used for measuring rods and shields, but it also makes rulers and plywood. Medicinally, it has been used for fever and nervous complaints, and tea made from its buds is said to be good for cuts as well as sore throats.[185]

The buds from black poplar can be used to make a healing salve good for bruises, aches, and pains. Balm of Gilead, made from the balsam poplar (a relative of the aspen), is used as an expectorant and relieves congestion. Both poplars and aspen contain salicin, a compound found in pain relief medicines, good for mild external aches, pains, and minor injuries.[186]

As a vibrational essence, aspen is used to heal and alleviate fears of the unknown and unseen, such as a fear of the dark. It helps alleviate shaking and trembling, and relaxes the light body, helping an agitated vibrational rate (the result of communicating with spirits, or simply being close to them). It makes the spirit communication experience easier, replacing fear with trust of self as well as others. Using aspen, peace and calm are achieved, and the vibrational rates become more in tune or resonant so that communication and interactions become easier. Aspen also restores flow and motion to those who are literally paralysed by shock or fear or stuck in a fearful state. Less well known is aspen's value in peaceful banishings and space clearings, especially relating to rites

---

185   Lust, *The Herb Book*, 318.
186   Ibid.

of the dying and dead, when it can be used to anoint, spray (as part of a dilution), or burned as fragrant oil. Using aspen can help the spirit's transition and attract beneficent guides and ushers to lead the way to any lost or fearful spirits. As such, is it valuable for shamanic "soul leading" work and others who assist such transitions. Aspen can of course also be burnt or made into a tea or tincture for this psychopomp purpose as well as in its vibrational form. However, its essence spirit must be actively asked for assistance, and when using the tree's physical matter, permission should always be sought and the material magically charged with specific intent.

Ogham Divination Meaning

As an ogham, eadha relates to communication and connection between worlds, peoples, and individuals. It encourages animation and urges you to get things moving, drawing in life force and enthusiasm. It also urges you to remember that life is always in a state of flux; to stand still for too long is to stagnate and resist the very flow of life itself. There is always more life, just as there is always more death. In balance, this knowledge can be a great source of comfort and support. Listen to your inner promptings and the messages of spirit. Consider advice from your elders. Attend to and value your inner rhythm.

Aspen may suggest becoming imbalanced with the ebb and flow of life, either in overload—shaking and trembling with fear or unused energy—or in a state of inner drought and stuckness where life needs stirring up and quickening once more. Breathe in the connection you have with the infinite, trust, and take steps to restore your balance. Consider this a threshold, and cross over. You have nothing to fear.

Journal Entry: Aspens of Ebbor Gorge, Somerset

Aspen is such a vital tree for seers! So many of us feel afraid when we begin to experience the presence of spirits; it's as if the very air shakes around us. In fact, it is the difference between our energetic and vibrational rates … it's hard for beings of two worlds to stand close to one another. But aspen stands at the veil between the worlds with ease and can smooth the discord. I gather aspen leaves to help those new to the path who feel fear, and I make essences and potions with the tree spirits by placing a bowl of spring water in the branches for a night and a day. I have a favourite aspen near here. The wind in the leaves carries the voices of those long passed, and as Samhain approaches I sit in vigil at its base at the dark of the moon. The ancestors pass on their messages, sometimes clearly, sometimes as a deafening chatter, sometimes as a fleeting vision as if in a dream, but they are heard and heeded and may rest knowing they are remembered and honoured by those who no longer fear the dark.

Yew/Idho (*Taxus baccata*)

....

Other names:
The ancient tree, English yew,
lubhar (Gaelic), ywen (Welsh).

....

Word ogham of:
Morainn: *Sinem fedo* "oldest
tree" *Ibur* "Service tree"

Cuchulain: *Lúth* (no lith) *lobair.i.aes* "Strength/energy
(or colour) of an infirm person"; "people or an age"

Oengus: *Caínem sen no aileam ais*
"Fairest of ancients"; "pleasing consent"[187]

Description

Yew trees are evergreen shrubs or smaller trees that grow up to fifteen metres that can be far wider than they are tall. The broadly conical needles grow radially on upright stems and last for up to ten years. They often have many trunks which can form into a single deeply ridged central trunk that can even have gaps allowing access within its central space. The trunks often become hollow over time. Yew bark is soft, flaky, thin, and red or grey-brown in colour. The hard, green, oval seeds ripen into red or yellow berries by October. Growing all across Europe and north Africa, yew prefers damp, milder climates, but can grow in mountainous regions up to 1,400 metres in the Alps. It also grows in the understory of deciduous woodlands, particularly in more open areas and on slopes and gulleys. All parts of the yew are poisonous except the fleshy part of the berry, but even

---

187   McManus, *Guide to Ogam*, 43, with additions by Calder, *Scholars' Primer*, 93.

the seed within is toxic, containing the poisonous alkaloid taxine. Yew sadly has become much rarer in its wild habitat and is now protected in the UK, but there are many cultivated yews in gardens, parks, and of course church-yards, which often contain yews of exceptional antiquity.

Taxus brevolia, the Pacific yew, grows in the Pacific Northwest, as does *Taxus canadensis*, the Canadian yew. Both have similar properties.

Lore and Legend

Yews may well be the longest living trees on earth. Often found to be sur-viving in some of the oldest British churchyards, some yews vastly pre-date their accompanying churches and are thought to be as much as four or five thousand years old. They survive the modern era by their connection to these churches, themselves often built in places of local preexisting spiritual significance. It is now thought that the importance of these sites has been marked over the millennia by the presence of the yews, giving rise to the church's long association with them. The oldest living thing in Britain (and probably Europe), is the Fortingall yew, which stands at the geographical centre of Scotland in Fortingall churchyard. The tree's age is estimated to be at five thousand years old.[188] It is thought that the yew trees achieve such long life spans via their constant regeneration, causing their ages to be mis-calculated in the past. This is why Morainn refers to the yew as "oldest tree," revealing a depth of practical knowledge we have clearly lost.

Yew is also listed as one of the oldest things in the fourteenth-century Irish *Book of Lismore* which states "three lifetimes of the yew for the world from its beginning to its end."[189] Two of the five "great magical trees" of Ire-land used as gathering places for armies and druid convocations were yew trees, providing testimony to their great importance in the Celtic world. (Early Christians cut these trees down, unfortunately.) Yews were once

---

188   "The Forestry Commission Scotland: Fortingall Yew" (http://www.forestry.gov.uk/forestry/INFD-6UFC5F.)

189   Whitley Stokes, trans., *Lives of the Saints, from the Book of Lismore* (London: Clarendon Press, 1890), xii.

considered to be the species of the great World Tree particularly in the Heathen traditions and across the Northern Hemisphere due to its incredible life span. In Norse tradition, the World Tree Yggdrasil is thought to have originally been a yew, although later Yggdrasil was considered to be an ash, perhaps signifying a cultural change to a more ordered and goal-orientated society suggested by the ash's magical qualities, as opposed to the yew's contemplative and meditative qualities, concerned with the balance between mortality and infinity. For this reason yew trees are sacred to Odin, who used Yggrdasil as his "horse"—the means to traverse the nine realms.

The yew has several names in the Celtic tradition—idho, ido, io, and eo. Eo is also the name of the mythical salmon of knowledge. Said to be one of the oldest animals in existence, this salmon knows the mysteries and magic of the universe and is able to pass on enlightenment—"the bright knowledge"—of bardic inspiration, also known as awen, which makes the shaman/druid/bard able to prophecy and wield great magical power.[190] This provides a clue to yew's mysteries and the gifts it holds—a still point in the universe present in time and space, yet able to witness the unfolding of the world from a perspective of such large spans of time to have a unique and incredible gift for us. It provides access from our mortal viewpoint into something much larger— from the Celtic viewpoint it may be considered as the infinite, a place where millennia blur into one another, enabling patterns and threads of meaning to be detected and understood. We are allowed a glimpse of the wider universal perspective, the view of the gods.

Yew provides a link between this world and the next but not in the guiding and transitional way of the aspen. Instead, it represents that which lies beyond: the void that must be crossed between this life and the next and the solid presence of the unknowable and inevitable that accompanies all our lives. Should we look in its direction, we see the greater universe all around us; our lives are as mayflies in comparison to the infinite enfolding us, a fact both terrifying and reassuring. We may end, yet something—indeed,

---

190   Matthews, *Aquarian Guide*, 144.

everything—continues. Idho signifies this awesome truth and as such is associated with endings and beginnings, rebirth and mortality, the fact that death and life and the ever-turning wheel between the two are our only known certainties.

Yews often grow upon barrow mounds and places associated with our ancient ancestors as markers of the world beyond and our eternal spirits.[191] For this reason, yew trees were often planted on the graves of fallen lovers, and tales abound of the trees linking the two graves, joining the souls in death. Legendary lovers Tristan and Isolde were reunited in death by the yew as were the Irish Deirdre and Noisiu, whose separate yew trees were said to have grown over Armagh Cathedral to embrace. The yew tree's root system is vast and can be seen disturbing the surface soil in many grave-yards, even breaking up the capstones of graves as the centuries pass. For this reason, the yew is traditionally sacred to crone goddesses and deities associated with death such as the Greek Hecate and the Irish Banba, they who hold the mysteries of death and infinity in their strong, ancient hands. In Rome, black bulls wreathed in yew were sacrificed to Hecate as food for the dead.[192]

The yew also holds special importance at the festival of Samhain, the day of the dead and the ancestors' presence and wisdom. It was burnt at Samhain to lend protection and balance these energies, negotiating rela-tions between the living and the dead.

There is a mention of yew trees in *The Lays of Fionn* known as "The Lament of the Fianna," which heralds the end of the legendary band of heroes. Fionn makes a prophecy: "On Samhain's eve, in the yew glen, that the faultless Fianna should depart, and that it should be an end of us tonight. Tonight it is an utter end."[193]

---

191 Westwood and Simpson, *Lore of the Land*, 807.

192 Graves, *White Goddess*, 193.

193 Mac Neill, *Duanaire Finn*, 153.

In the *Rennes Dindshenchas* (a collection of lore connected to Irish place names) the Yew of Ross is associated with the goddess Banba, and was known as "a firm, straight deity...the renown of Banba."[194] One of Ireland's five great magical trees as mentioned earlier, this tree and the knowledge associated with it reveal this link between death, knowledge, and infinity. Other names for the yew were "spell of knowledge" and "the king's wheel."[195] The king's wheel referred to here is a special brooch worn by the high kings of Ireland, passed from one king to the next as a reminder that each king was part of a whole. The king's role required this knowledge, and was a caretaker with responsibilities to future generations. It was a reminder that the wheel would always turn, and that duty to the past and future should be paramount in the king's mind. The same could be said for all magical workers and wisdom seekers in the Celtic tradition, where the honouring of ancestors and the consideration of future generations is of utmost importance. This explains Oengus's word oghams associated with the yew—"fairest of ancients" or "pleasing consent," as well as Morainn's addendum to his kennings for the yew as "service tree." The duty of honouring ancestors and looking to the future is required of us whether we undertake it or not. To ignore the call of our responsibilities to the past and future is to abuse our ancestors. The duty need not be unpleasant; it is an aspect that lends new context and depth to our actions and motivations with great enriching and enlivening results. With steady and patient progress we may acquire the "pleasing consent" of our ancestors and feel their support and gentle guidance steering us into better and more fulfilled lives. As a symbol of the ancestral support available to us, the yew is indeed the "fairest of ancients."

A sense of eternity reveals the patterns only visible in the longest-term view, illustrating how themes recur and evolve over massive spans of time,

---

194   Whitley Stokes, ed., "The Prose Tales in the Rennes Dindsenchas" in *Revue Celtique XV* (Paris: Librarie Emille Bouillon, 1894), 278.

195   Ibid.

undergoing subtle shifts and adjustments on a theme until time itself is no longer linear but spiral, evolving, expanding into existence rather than cutting through space in a straight, logical progression. The yew tree's physical growth reflects this, as the branches take root into new trunks that all feed from the same roots. The yew maintains its impressive lifespan by spiralling in and out of the earth, enacting the spiritual knowledge it symbolises.

Yew can be seen to represent the total of all the other ogham in the sense that all the lessons of the other nineteen take place beneath its aegis. As it allows access to the infinite, it naturally reveals the connection between all things, time, space, and points of consciousness—the sum of all knowledge. And yet yew's position reveals an innate paradox, that whilst containing the ever-changing All, it itself holds a position of utter stillness and reflective silence. The only response to such staggering enlightenment is to learn the difference between doing and being. This is what Cuchulain is referring to when he says yew is "the strength (quality or colour) of a sick man, people or an age." He is referring to the gift received in coming to terms with death and the endless movement of time, when it is realised that one's actions or errors mean little in the face of eternity. It is in being, not doing, that we learn to be truly alive. That quality of existence relies on an accumulation of wonderful precious moments, not great long arcs of achievement and activity. In this way, yew teaches stillness and meditative presence, contacting the All via an awareness of each individual moment in time as it is experienced—a powerful magical tool as well as spiritual truth. Following this path yields far greater self-empowerment and inner transformation. It is only by being utterly present in the moment that the crack in time may be discerned, like the crevice in the yew's ragged trunk. We may reach within and touch the face of the gods.

Magical and Practical Uses

Yew leaves were once burnt as divinatory incense in addition to their ritual use at Samhain, but only when outside. Their toxicity is so powerful that it was once thought that to sleep beneath a yew was certain to lead to death.

It is now thought that the sap produces a vapour that can invoke altered states of consciousness, but real and extreme caution should be exercised, of course. Yew wood was never needlessly cut for this same reason, in addition to the great respect given to the tree.

With its connections to the underworld and infinity beyond, yew is used in all sorts of ancestral magic, as well as to protect against negative forces or unwelcome ghosts. A few yew leaves placed upon the altar or worn when journeying or invoking ancestral assistance can be very effective, but as stated, caution should be used when handling all parts of the tree; it should not be in contact with bare skin for any length of time. The wood is less toxic, but it is best oiled or varnished to provide a barrier.

Yew is an extremely dense close-grained wood excellent for carvings. Votive offerings made of yew wood have been found in British holy wells and springs. However, it was also used to make wheels, cogs, and handles. Archaeologists have found various objects made of yew in the UK dating back as far as the Neolithic era. Yew is most famously used in making excellent longbows and knife handles, where the wood's great strength and durability were valuable characteristics. The earliest longbow ever found was discovered at Ashcott Heath in Somerset, England, dating to 2665 BCE.[196] Modern archers report no ill effects from using yew bows.

Yew wands are particularly powerful, preferably when made of wood fallen from a tree with its permission and with whom you have already established a relationship. (When working with a yew wand, always oil, wax, or varnish it before use.) The yew wand not only proffers the great knowledge of infinity and ancestors, it also may assist in contacting deep land-based ancestral lines—following in the very path of the druids who walked the land before us.

---

196   E. Bacon, *Archaeology: Discoveries in the 1960s* (Lincoln, UK: Praeger, 1971), 16.

Healing

Yew has a unique quality amongst the ogham: it is the only poisonous tree. In many ways, the poison serves to protect its powerful energies and guard access to its knowledge. The tree requires careful handling, as does our magical and spiritual work. Yew needs to be physically respected, just as we also need to respect our own physical bodies, maintaining the balance between the present and eternity. Too much of one is bad for the other, and balance must be prioritised if we are to progress. Perhaps notably, yew has no herbal qualities as it is so toxic that care should be taken when near or handling it; hands should be washed before touching the mouth or eyes after contact. The chemical taxol in the yew has been found to have some use in cancer treatments, particularly in high amounts in the Pacific yew. That said, herbally yew has no place whatsoever in common use—it's just too dangerous.

Energetically, yew can help us come to terms with our own death and find healing and solace in the realms beyond. To our eternal souls, this is the greatest healing of all. It also helps balance psychic burnout or times when our awareness has expanded excessively fast, leading to inflation, fear, or mental illness.

The best ways to work with the yew for healing are to make a vibrational essence (where the water used only comes into the energy field of the tree and no physical matter is used), or to commune directly with the tree spirit. Both of these approaches are recommended so long as the tree is regarded with the utmost respect and care. This is not a tree to impose your will or wishes upon; the benefit lies in its example, in *being* rather than *doing*, allowing its influence and energy to affect us as it sees fit.

As a vibrational essence, yew is very grounding and heals psychic burnout from excessive spiritual or magical work. It lends perspective and a calm, steadying presence, understanding a mortal's challenges in an infinite universe. In this way it balances the micro- and macrocosm, soothing any anxiety this shift in perspective may provoke. It also helps with issues relating to grieving and aging, as well as helping to prepare the soul for the inevitability of death—and the promise of rebirth.

Ogham Divination Meaning

As an ogham, idho counsels patience and perseverance if either has been absent. Yet it also may suggest the need to rebalance the other way, seizing the day or the moment wholeheartedly, as if it were the last. The ending of one thing inevitably leads to the beginning of another, and this process may become a wonderful, joyous dance just as easily as it may invoke mortal dread. Yet the truth remains the same; trying not to hold on too tight and carry the infinite lightly is the best way. After all, in the Celtic tradition the afterlife is a splendid, beautiful place full of wonder, joy, and love. Finding this in the mortal world and the easing of difficulties is achieved through small, simple acts of progress and tenderness towards ourselves and others. It is our subjective experience that we have the most power to change, and peace is something that is therefore best sought within rather than without. In the face of eternity we are all divine children, and it is our task to remember this. In doing so we honour the past, present, and future with equal compassion. Idho asks us to enter into silence and surrender to creation with joy.

Journal Entry: The Yews of Chalice Well, Glastonbury, Somerset

I am blessed to live near a great many ancient yew trees. So many yews grow in sacred, ancient places: in churchyards, on barrows, upon ancient alignments, and many near holy wells. The yews at the Chalice Well stand in a place held sacred for millennia. With ancient, steady grace, they breathe out deep silence and peace. Sitting in their shade, one once blessed me with a vision of the infinite, spiralling out from a single point of consciousness into a vast multitude of beings, each as shining and precious as a star; unique and yet bound to each other in kinship, endlessly embodying and expressing their diversity and their communion with the whole, by turns... a breath in, a breath out... The yew is not a tree for practical magic, standing as a reminder of this sacred principle, the source of our magic, its cause and also its effect. Without spirit or our connection to the infinite, magic, like mortality, has no context, becoming empty of meaning. To be blessed with the awesome wonder that is manifestation, there must also be the wonder which the yew trees hold. There must be silence and dissolution into the infinite. Idho is often pronounced "9o," and when spoken slowly, becomes an intonation of great power, the Celtic om— "IIIIIIIIIIIIIIIIIOOOOOOOOOOOO"—the all-encompassing whole.

The Forfeda

The forfeda are five additional trees and plants considered to be a far later addition to the ogham, less directly magical in use. They are included in *The Ogham Tract*, and are commonly thought to be the addition of letters and sounds absent in Old Irish but present in Greek and Latin, which were in common use at the time.

Magically speaking, they are far more obscure, although contact with their plant spirits reveals them to be as much plants of power as the first twenty ogham trees. They are included here for thoroughness and as first clues for the seeker's magical investigation. The forfeda lack a complete set of word oghams to accompany and elucidate their meanings; there is some debate about which trees are referenced, as the source materials have many discrepancies.

The forfeda are EA for ebadh, the poplar; OI for oir, the spindle; UI for uilleann, the honeysuckle; IO for iphin, the gooseberry; and either AE for eamhancholl, the witch hazel, or PH for phagos, the beech.

EA/Ebadh (white poplar)

The white poplar, *Populus alba,* was discussed earlier in this book in relation to the ogham eadha, aspen. Its function is a gateway tree to the otherworld, helping to assist with acclimatising to increases or dramatic changes in energy or atmosphere, especially when encountering the dead or the otherworld, as both eadha and ebadh stand on either side of idho, the yew, the entrance point to infinity. Here the seeker can access another chance to come to terms with the transition as well as the energies and beings encountered. The aspen and the poplar stand on either side of the great womb and tomb of the goddess, guiding us smoothly and compassionately through death into what lies beyond.

OI/Oir (spindle)

Spindle, *Euonymus europaeus,* is primarily used to make spindles in weaving, hence its name. Weaving has a special place in magical lore, especially in Celtic and northern European folk tales, where it is always associated with fate, destiny, and weaver goddesses, such as the Norse Norns, who wove the fate of every living person, cutting the threads when their time was up.

Named after Euonyme—the mother of the Furies, or goddesses of vengeance—the spindle is intimately associated with women's magic and skills. Weaving cloth is connotated with fate and destiny in addition to domesticity, and thus security and peace. Where the weaver goddess goes, women and children are safe, resources are abundant, and creativity (not basic survival) comes to the fore. These gifts are as much due to the goddess's ferocity as her kindness.

In pre-dynastic Egypt, the weaver goddess Nit (or Neith) was considered to be the most ancient one to whom the other gods went for wisdom.

In Greece, the Moirai or three Fates were three ancient crones who controlled human destiny. The Norse and Germanic goddess Frigg is always associated with weaving, as are the Valkyries, who feature in "The Song of the Spear" as weaving with human heads to weight the thread, and human guts as the thread for the warp.[197] The German Frau Holda is also associated with weaving, as is the Greek Athena, and the Roman Minerva. In the Celtic world, Brigantia—often associated with Minerva—may also have been considered a weaver goddess, overseeing the sovereignty of Britain and its people.

Spindle is common in Britain, Ireland, and northern Europe. A variety of spindle, *Euonymus atropurpureus,* is common in the eastern United States.

UI/Uilleann (honeysuckle)

ഐ

Lonicera periclymenum, the honeysuckle, is associated with the sign of Cancer and is usually considered to be a very feminine plant.[198] Culpeper suggests it is useful for sore throats, while modern writers sometimes associate the honeysuckle with Jupiter and thus consider it useful for money spells and matters of love and friendship. The great beauty, delicious scent, and climbing and twining properties of the honeysuckle suggest that, like ivy, its place in magic is related to community, relationships, and binding disparate groups together harmoniously (time spent connecting with its spirit confirm this), together with the assistance it can grant in matters related to romance and of the heart. Honeysuckle is associated with courtship in lowland Scotland, where young men would carry a stick of honeysuckle

197 "Darradarljod: The Battle Song of the Valkyries" (http://www.orkneyjar.com /tradition/darra.htm).

198 Culpeper, *Complete Herbal,* 190.

for good luck in love. It was also said to be good to draw good luck into the home and protect from malicious faeries.[199]

The vibrational essence of honeysuckle is usually used for dealing with feelings of regret and sadness, releasing the energetic and emotional tendrils that hold us in the past. Honeysuckle is wonderful for opening the heart centre and making us available to the unconditional love of divinity. It encourages us to become fully present in the here and now.

IO/Iphin (gooseberry)

Gooseberry traditionally has been used in childbirth and for menstrual problems; the early herbal writer Gerard suggests that it can be used to staunch bleeding and stop "the menses or monthly bleeding."[200] Later herbals suggest it is useful taken monthly as a tonic for pubescent girls.[201] For this reason, gooseberry was considered sacred to the goddess Brighid and goddesses like her who oversee matters of childbirth and women's cycles, such as Diana and Arianrhod. In modern times, gooseberry is primarily taken as a food, in sauces, tarts, and pies.

The gooseberry has uses in all sorts of magical healing charms and spells; its thorns direct away illness in a similar fashion to that of the blackthorn but with a gentler energy. It also helps with issues related to eyesight and vision, the berries themselves resembling eyeballs. Gooseberry thorns were used in Ireland as a form of sympathetic magic to heal styes. Point the gooseberry thorn at the eyelid, and say, "Away! Away! Away!" Doing so is said to make the stye vanish.[202]

---

199   John Matthews and Will Worthington, *The Green Man Tree Oracle* (New York: Barnes and Noble, 2003), 100.

200   Gerard, "Of goose-berry," *Gerard's Herbal*.

201   Grieve, *A Modern Herbal*, 365.

202   Lady Wilde, *Ancient Legends, Mystic Charms, and Superstitions of Ireland* (London: Chatto and Windus, 1902), 198.

AE/Eamhancholl (witch hazel or wych elm)

The witch hazel referred to here is the British name for the witch elm, not the common witch hazel cultivated in North America. Also seen as "wych elm," *Ulmus glabra* is the only native elm in the British Isles. The "witch" or "wych" in its name is in fact drawn from the Middle English word *wice* or *wiche,* meaning "supple" and "bendable."

The wych elm or witch hazel was commonly used to make cart wheels, as its strength and suppleness make it good for bending. It was also used to make bows. Culpeper places elm under the rulership of Saturn.[203] In Celtic and later Saxon lore, the elm was associated with the underworld, the sidhe, and the elves, who were said to live in burial mounds and Neolithic barrow tombs. In Gaelic the elm is known as *leven* and is found in many place names such as Loch Leven in Kinross, Scotland. There, the wych elm was used for dyeing, where strips of elm were used to tie strands of cloth in a form of early tie-dye. The boiled bark of the elm was also used to treat burns and other wounds.

Witch hazel's ogham is usually the same as the one for beech.

PH/Phagos (beech)

The beech tree, *Fagus sylvatica,* is traditionally called the "queen of the woods" because of its great beauty. In Britain it is often associated with snakes and earth energies due to its serpentine root system. Beautiful examples of this can be found at the ancient stone circles of Avebury in Wiltshire, where the serpentine roots of beech trees encircle much of the henge or ceremonial ditch. The circle complex itself has a reputation as a

---

203   Culpeper, *Complete Herbal,* 131.

dragon temple (another serpentine association), sacred to earth energies and the earth herself. The Gallo-Roman god of beech trees, Fagus, is known because of altars dedicated to him in the French Pyrenees, suggesting their importance to the Celts who lived there.[204] The Roman writer Pliny describes how an orator worshipped a beech tree in the Alban Hills as a personification of the goddess Diana.[205]

Beech is intimately associated with learning and knowledge. The Anglo-Saxon word for "beech" was *boc,* the source of the word "book." The first runes and the first oghams were said to be carved on slips of beech, and for this reason the beech is said to be sacred to Ogma as well as the goddess Danu, a goddess of knowledge and learning, mother of the Irish gods the Tuatha Dé Danann.

The medieval Welsh poem "The Battle of the Trees" (*Cad Goddeu*) by the bard Taliesin refers to the beech as a tree which "prospers through spells and litanies," showing its close associations with magic and magical lore.[206] Any spells or prayers spoken at beech's roots were said to come true, and curses said under its boughs were said to be more effective—so long as the goddess approved. Spells of any kind can be written upon beech wood or a beech leaf and buried to draw the attention and support of the earth goddess.

Water from the hollow of a beech tree is excellent for spellwork, blessing, healing skin complaints, as well as gaining the goddess's beauty. As a vibrational essence, beech is used to increase tolerance, compassion, and gentleness. Again, beech allows us to draw in the qualities of unconditional love the Great Goddess offers.

---

204   Green, *Dictionary of Celtic Myth*, 95.

205   James George Frazer, "The King of the Wood," chapter 1 in *The Golden Bough* (http://www.sacred-texts.com/pag/frazer/gb00103.htm).

206   Graves, *White Goddess*, 45.

Climbing the World Tree:
The Ogham as a Spiritual Quest

Now that we have considered each of the ogham trees in detail, we can see that each tree leads to the next in an evolving stream of consciousness that takes us from a single point of awareness and perspective to a point of universal awareness and communion. The ogham as a whole therefore represents a map to lead us through an evolutionary spiral up and around the World Tree, from birth to death and beyond, or on a smaller scale, through the process of manifestation for all creative projects and processes.

The following shamanic journeying exercise can be performed as a whole, or in four sessions, each time working through a complete aicme (tribe) in order. Please note that this is intense, and you will need to allow enough time to see it through. You may wish to record the following description, or hold the details in your memory before proceeding.

First prepare your sacred space as you wish, and raise some energy from the earth, or in a way that suits you best. Then take several deep breaths, and when you are ready, visualise an oak doorway or gateway to the great forest ahead of you. Take a few moments to acknowledge this place and moment as the beginning of your journey. Pass through into the forest, seeing clearly a distinct shimmering path of pale stone before you, winding its way through the trees ahead. As you pass through the oak doorway, you are met by your tree spirit ally, and together you progress to your sacred inner grove. Call upon all your allies and the great forest itself to assist you and guide your way. Follow the path.

When you come to your grove, you see a bright light at its centre. As you focus upon it, you see that it shifts and changes form into many different types of trees—sometimes it is an oak, sometimes an ash, and sometimes a yew tree. The very air about it shimmers with sacredness and power. Take a moment to consider this.

At the great tree's base, you see the guardian of the grove, and as you draw closer, you see the light is in fact a tall being that appears to be part of the tree and then separate from it by turns. The air is full of whispers, and all the trees of the grove are shaken in a gentle breeze. This is a being of particular power. When you are ready, approach and meet the guardian and the being of light.

"Hail to Ogma!" calls the guardian. Immediately all the trees grow silent, and you see that at this being's feet, silver serpents coil and rise out of the earth.

Allow time here for your communion with Ogma in this hallowed, sacred place of power. He may have words or visions to show you, or you may simply have a feeling or sensation. Do not analyse it; allow it to be as it is, a mystery teaching from the god himself.

When the time is right, either Ogma or the guardian will hand you a wooden staff. It is plain and unadorned but as you move to take it, they suddenly thrust it into the earth between you. Immediately it begins to grow into a giant tree, carrying you with it in its branches. The tree grows so quickly and into such a vast, incalculable size that the branch before you and under your feet becomes a path, and each twig and leaf coming from it becomes a huge forest all around.

Before you on the path is a slender young birch tree. Its trunk is straight and white and its delicate leaves shimmer. Out from the tree steps a being, the spirit of the birch. This being stares into your eyes and says:

All beginnings necessitate a period of cleansing and careful preparation with rectification from the past where necessary, and a guarding of boundaries to keep the new life safe from intrusions and pollution.

Reaching out with a bunch of birch twigs, it scatters water around you, waving and shaking the twigs around you briskly, as if sweeping away any old and stagnant energy. Pause to reflect on this, and gain your own insights from the birch spirit.

When it is time, the birch spirit returns to the tree and you continue along the path. Ahead you see a rowan tree, its leaves a deep, vibrant green against its rich red berries. As you approach, the rowan spirit steps out from the tree, and stares into your eyes. It says:

As the new spirit grows, so does the need for greater awareness and protection.

With this, the rowan spirit anoints your eyelids, granting you greater vision. Again, pause to reflect on this and allow the rowan spirit to share any other insights with you that it chooses.

When it is time, the rowan spirit also returns to its tree, and you continue along the path until you reach an alder tree. Its whole form is shielded from view by its rounded leaves. The alder spirit steps from the tree and stares not at your eyes, but your heart. It says:

When awareness is achieved, it is possible to move forward, shield raised to defend and protect whilst in motion.

With this the alder spirit reaches out and places a leaf against your chest, like a tiny shield, but you sense its power. Pause to reflect on this, and any other message the alder spirit gives to you, before it returns to its tree, and you continue along the path to the willow tree which stands near.

The willow tree waves its branches gently as you approach, and its spirit steps forth.

> We travel the World Tree, in a quest to seek the soul's vision, drawing it from the otherworld, across the deep waters of the heart.

The willow spirit touches your heart, and a feeling of ease and harmony comes to you. Allow time to pause here, and reflect on this, and the presence of the willow tree, in your own way.

When it is time, the willow recedes into the tree, and you continue to the ash tree you see ahead. It stands tall and straight before you.

> When we have vision, we learn how to reach an objective and grow strong, how to negotiate the interaction between spirit and the manifest world. No one can do this for you; you must learn this lesson yourself, by experience.

The ash spirit lays a hand upon your shoulder, and you stand straighter and feel greater strength up your spine. Allow time here to commune with the ash spirit as it directs. In time, it returns to the tree, and you remain alone upon the path.

> *This completes the first circle of learning, the first branches of the tree. From here you may continue on the path or return the way you came. Go past the trees, stepping lightly into the grove, through the forest, and back to your body to return another day.*

Should you wish to continue, follow the path until you see a hawthorn tree. Its shape is a mass of flowers and thorns. The hawthorn spirit speaks to you:

*If you would grow to maturity, you must learn the challenge of
the heart. Will you rise to the test?*

Here you must answer truthfully. Allow space for the hawthorn spirit
to speak to you as it chooses. If you pass the test, it places a leaf upon your
breast.

When it is time to go, the tree spirit recedes and you continue along
the path until you reach a mighty oak tree.

The oak spirit stands before you and reaches out, directly touching
your heart. In a deep voice it says:

*To those who pass the challenge of the heart comes inner sover-
eignty.*

With this, the oak spirit touches you between the eyes, and you feel a
crown of light encircle your brow.

Pause and reflect upon this, allowing space for the oak spirit to guide
you as it chooses. When it is time to continue, the oak spirit returns to the
tree. Ahead you find a holly tree, deep green and full of shadows.

The holly spirit speaks:

*It is one thing to gain inner sovereignty, and another to maintain
it, through all adversities.*

And with this, the holly spirit also touches your brow. Allow time here
to reflect on how it feels and any other wisdom it shares with you at this
time. When this is done, the holly spirit returns to its tree. You continue
onwards to the hazel.

The hazel tree and its spirit are light and fast moving, shimmering before
you. The hazel spirit bows before you and says:

*When sovereignty and endurance are achieved, we may gain ac-
cess to divine inspiration.*

And with this, the hazel spirit breathes gently upon you. Allow a pause here again to be open to any wisdom the hazel chooses to share. When ready, it turns away, back into the tree. Ahead you see an apple tree, full of fruit.

The apple tree spirit smiles as you approach, and says:

Access to divine knowledge leads to healing and communion with the soul and the gods within you.

And with this, the apple spirit touches your brow and then your heart. You feel your whole being soften and grow whole. Pause here to reflect upon this, and spend time with the apple spirit as it directs.

This completes the second circle of learning, the second set of branches. From here you may continue on the path or return the way you came. Go past the trees, stepping lightly into the grove, through the forest, and back to your body to return another day.

Should you wish to continue, go ahead along the path until you come across a blackberry thicket. The blackberry spirit speaks with many voices:

To take your gifts into the outer world, you must apply strength appropriately so that it may become tenacity and manifestation.

Pause here, and allow the blackberry to guide you as it will. When you are ready, continue along the path. Eventually you see a tree covered in ivy. The ivy also speaks with the voice of many:

We must give as we receive to flourish in the world, joining with others in blessing and embracing what we find.

Once more, allow space so the ivy spirit can advise you as it chooses. When it is time, you continue until you see a patch of broom. The broom spirit speaks:

On every quest, we must learn to make course corrections and re-
solve difficulties; we must learn what to keep and what to surrender.

Again, allow time so that the broom spirit may share what it will. You
then continue on to the next ogham tree, the blackthorn.

The blackthorn spirit is crowned with white flowers. It speaks:

In surrendering we discover hidden knowledge.

Bow to the blackthorn in silence and heed its wisdom. When it is time,
the blackthorn spirit recedes. Ahead on the path you meet the elder tree,
richly perfumed. The elder tree speaks with a voice as old as the world:

Maintaining a balance with all things leads to the wisdom of
elderhood. The heart's willingness to sacrifice the self for the well-
being of others and the future is its greatest gift.

Pause to reflect upon this and any other wisdom you may receive.

This completes the third circle of learning, the third set of branches
upon the tree. From here you may continue on the path, or return the way
you came. Go past the trees, stepping lightly into the grove, through the for-
est, and back to your body to return another day.

Should you feel it is right for you to continue on to this final stretch of
the path, you carry on along the path until you reach the scots pine tower-
ing above you with its red trunk and deep green needles. The scots pine
speaks with the voice of the wind:

Elderhood leads to a widening and far-reaching perspective,
where all things may find a place in your heart and in your vi-
sion, that you find your way according to the roads of spirit, the
great web that connects us all.

Pause to reflect on this, allowing time for the scots pine spirit to share what it will.

When you are ready, you see a gorse bush ahead. The gorse is covered with yellow flowers and shines with its own light. The gorse spirit steps forth with a golden mane that flows and blows about it like flame.

Encompassing the All, we find the vivifying currents of life itself … so that we are ever renewed.

With this, it places a yellow gorse flower to your lips, and you taste its nectar, rich and warm. Delight fills you. Allow time to feel this, and benefit from the gorse spirit's presence.

Next you are drawn to a patch of purple and white heather ahead. The heather spirit steps forth, a beautiful woman with kind eyes.

The cycles of life and death all turn within the heart of the earth goddess, and all receive her love and care unconditionally.

With this, she touches your heart, and a single tear falls down your cheek, as something long held in your heart is released at last.

Stay with this as long as you need, sharing with the heather spirit as she directs.

When it is time to leave, ahead you see the shivering branches of the aspen tree, blowing in a wind you cannot feel. The aspen spirit steps forth.

I show the way, and mediate between the worlds. On one hand, the living. On the other, what lies beyond.

Listen to the aspen spirit, as it speaks for those beyond in all their forms.

When it is time at last, far ahead you see a yew tree. Its trunk is huge and wide; its branches bow to the earth and others spring up from where it touches. As you approach, you see that beneath it and in gaps within its trunk, stars and darkness can be seen. You feel its spirit but it cannot be seen, although the air seems to vibrate to an endless intonation.

Iiiiiooooooooooo

Take time here and look deep into the branches and the space in its trunk. The darkness enfolds you and the stars reel overhead, spiralling into infinity…

We may dwell here in communion, or when we choose, re-embark into creation and rebirth via the birch. Thus the tree is climbed and descended into the mortal world, at will.

In time, the vision fades and you are back in your sacred inner grove. Ogma has gone, but the guardian remains and you still hold the staff in your hands, only now it is marked with each ogham sigil inscribed in light, rising along its length.

Rest here as long as you need before thanking the guardian and your allies. Return along the path through the trees, through the oak door, and back to your body.

When you are ready, flex your fingers and toes. Feel yourself fully back in the here and now. Eat and drink to ground yourself, and record your experiences in your journal.

Ogham Staves and Wands

Working effectively with the ogham relies on a closely built relationship with the trees and their spirits. In this way, every ogham stave— whether inscribed upon wood or written upon paper—becomes an embodiment of the tree's particular energy and spirit. The ogham thus becomes an ally in divination, contemplation, and magic. Therefore in this section we will turn our attention to making and preparing ogham staves that still contain and are empowered by the tree spirits themselves for a variety of magical and spiritual uses.

Ogham staves can be prepared using the wood of each tree or a single type of wood; beech and birch are good for this purpose, as is simple box wood or pine. Ideally the wood should be gathered from the wild trees themselves with the permission and assistance of the tree spirit (and any landowners). Gathering may not always be possible, however. Ogham staves inscribed upon wood purchased in DIY stores may be charged and blessed for use quite effectively. Care must be taken, however—the wood should be from a sustainable, ethical, and ecologically conscious source. This is for our own magical and spiritual integrity as well as to encourage the tree spirits' support.

When gathering wood from a specific tree, time should be spent in a meditative state in the tree's presence for a time, and decisions need to be made as to whether the wood should be cut from the living tree or gathered from the fallen twigs and branches beneath it. There are two schools of thought on this: the wood gathered at the tree's base is better as it does no harm, but the wood cut from the tree contains its living essence and is thus superior. In practice, there is no substitute for feeling the guidance of the tree itself. Some trees will want you to gather from fallen branches and twigs, and others will guide you where and how to cut a small piece from a slender branch. If the wood is gathered with the tree's permission, the spirit of the tree will accompany the stave and empower it. If permission is not granted, the stave will not hold this energy and will be a mere symbol and unusable for magical purposes.

Ideally, you would spend time with each tree and plant spirit represented in the ogham. If you can, you will be able to slowly enter into a relationship with each tree in its physical form. When ready, you will be able to ask each specific tree in turn for a piece of its wood. Seeking each ogham tree in sequence is an excellent magical quest and meditative process in its own right and is by far the best teacher for tree magic and the ogham in all its uses. The very process of seeking out each tree in turn becomes as much a spiritual journey as a magical one, and your soul will gradually align to the ogham patterns of growth with tangible results in your day-to-day life. This "walking with the ogham" aligns you with nature and the great spirits of the green world in a very distinctive way.

Gathering Wood

When you feel you have a sense of the tree spirit of your chosen wood, you need to seek its permission to gather a piece of its wood for your use. Bear in mind that the ideal size for an ogham stave for use in divination will be relatively small, perhaps three to five inches long and the thickness of a pencil. Any larger quickly becomes impractical for ogham casting, although it may be appropriate for wands or staffs.

Sitting at the tree's base (or if this is not possible, as near to its presence as you can be), ask the tree out loud if you may have a piece of its wood in order to make an ogham stave. Allow yourself to fall into silence, and focus your attention on your breathing and your chest area. Then gently expand your awareness again towards the tree. How do you feel? What sort of response are you receiving? Do you feel any unease or discomfort in your chest or stomach? Do you feel any resistance? Look to your subtle emotions, as these may in fact be the tree's feelings. What is your initial immediate feeling? If you feel nothing negative, take this as a sign that you may proceed. Next, feel out whether you may take a living or a fallen piece, remembering that fallen pieces may still have the tree's energy and spirit present in them if the tree wishes it.

Let your eyes and focus soften. If a piece of wood catches your eye that seems suitable in size (especially width rather than length), consider if this is the piece you may have. If there is any difficulty acquiring it, take it as the tree refusing permission for that particular piece, if not your request in general. At each stage, you must be alert, respectful, and sensitive to the tree spirit before you.

If you feel you have permission to cut a piece, then you must use good equipment. Sharp secateurs are good for this—do not cut a piece any thicker than these can handle. Tell the tree what you are doing, and be sure to make the cut clean and tidy, at an angle so that any rain water falling on the cut falls away from the tree's trunk rather than further into it. When you have made the cut, lay your hands upon it. Raising some energy from the earth, send it into the wood with your heartfelt thanks, and "seal" the area with energy.

Whether you have gathered a fallen piece or cut from fresh wood, you must leave an offering. Sometimes a tree will very clearly tell you what it wants. If this is the case, heed its request to the best of your ability. Spring water is an excellent offering, as is a small lock of your hair to show your equality with the tree spirit and to encourage a lasting bond of good relations between you. Offerings of song and sacred dance are also acceptable, but physical offerings should always be biodegradable and do no harm to the tree or its surrounding area. Gathering any rubbish if you see any is also a valued offering, and should be a continuous part of your work with tree and nature spirits of all kinds whenever it becomes necessary.

This same initial practice is perfect for gathering wood for wand use, with the only change being that a wand will usually be a larger and longer piece of wood.

Charging and Blessing

When wood has been gathered, it needs to be charged and blessed for magical use. If it has been bought rather than gathered, it may also need ritual cleansing by passing it through sage or mugwort smoke and leaving it upon the earth overnight, perhaps longer. Alternatively, it may be cleansed by leaving it in cold running water, but care should be taken to ensure it is dried again thoroughly and without damage.

To charge and bless an ogham stave or wand, you need first to create a simple sacred space, be it a magical circle, a working space in a woodland grove, or some other calm area. Whatever your location, you will need to be uninterrupted and able to work in a sacred and conscious manner.

Take the piece of wood in your hands and breathe deeply, feeling your feet on the ground and your connection with the heart of the earth. Next, turn your attention to the tree from which the piece was gathered, whether you encountered it in the physical world or not. If you are working with each ogham tree and its wood in turn, ask the spirit of the tree to be present and charge and bless the piece with its energy, that you may use it for magic and the seeking of wisdom. Use our own words, but be honest, simple, and respectful. Hold the tree in your vision, and see it sending some of its energy into the wood.

If you are using a different type of wood for your ogham stave, first ask the spirit of the tree that gave the wood for its blessing and assistance, and then ask that the spirit of the specific ogham also be present to bless and charge the piece. Take your time, and wait until each stave feels full of energy and spirit presence.

Next you need to carve, draw, or paint the specific ogham sigil upon the blessed wood. There are various ways to do this: permanent ink, pyrography (burning), or with a sharp knife (bronze or flint knives are the best for this, as they are compatible with the trees' energy in a way that iron or steel are not). Practicality must come first at this stage; inscribe the sigil in a way that is clear and at your comfort or skill level so that it easily carries your sacred intention. You may need to cut a small sliver of the wood away in order to create a smooth enough surface to mark clearly.

Mark the sigil onto the wood, again asking that the tree spirit charge and bless the sigil. Verbally call the ogham sigil itself (beith, luis, etc.) as well. When you have finished, again hold the piece in your hands. Raising energy up from the earth, and holding the feeling of conscious connection with the tree, see the sigil charged with energy in your inner vision.

You will need to repeat this process with every ogham sigil and stave to make a complete set.

If you are making your own set of ogham cards, thank the wood that made the paper, and then ask for the energy and blessing of the ogham tree you are inscribing upon it. From there, the process is the same.

Wand Charging and Blessing

If you are making a wand rather than an ogham stave, ideally you have gathered the wood yourself and know which tree the piece has come from. Wands gathered and prepared in this way are always better than purchased ones, even though they may be far simpler and more rustic in appearance.

Again, call or invoke the tree's presence and ask that it charge and bless your wand. Use your own words, but approach the tree spirit in friendship and respect, asking that it be your ally from this point. Feeling your feet upon the ground and your connection to the heart of the earth, hold the wand in your hands. In your inner vision, see the wand being charged, blessed, and filled with light from the earth and the tree spirit's presence.

You may decide to inscribe the wand's type of tree in ogham upon it or other symbols and sigils that come to you during this process, but remember that a powerful and effective wand is not necessarily one with a lot of decoration. The source of the wand's power is the connection with the tree spirit more than any other detail.

An effective wand doesn't necessarily need to have a point or tip to be cut or shaped into it. Take your time; feel the wand's indwelling spirit and let it guide you as to its use. Each piece of wood will have its own energy current (usually from the trunk to the tips of the branches), and the direction of the energy in the wand will follow this pattern. Get into a calm, meditative state and use your instincts and powers of observation to support your inner vision. In this way, you will find which end to hold, and which end to use in order to direct your will and magic into the world.

Using a Wand

To effectively use a wand, you need to repeat the energetic pattern of the tree itself. Draw energy up from the earth—your roots—and raise it up your body, trunk, and along your arm. Call upon the spirit of your wand aloud or in your inner vision, and together direct the energy through the wand into a single point in the manifest world.

Wands are particularly effective when casting a circle in this way or for inscribing energetic ogham spirit sigils either on surfaces such as objects, doors and walls, parts of the body for healing, or "in air," marking energetic boundaries or to invoke a specific energy into a space.

Drawing Ogham Spirit Sigils

Ogham spirit sigils can be drawn using a wand or your hand. Raising energy from the earth, call upon the spirit of the tree and ogham you have chosen to cast, and energetically "draw" it either in the air or upon your chosen surface.

Oghams can be cast in this way for a whole host of reasons, calling upon their various qualities. Try birch for cleansing and new projects, rowan and/or oak for protection, apple for healing, elder to attract faeries, and blackberry for money spells.

Combination Oghams

Oghams can be combined to fine-tune your intentions and spellwork. Each ogham may be used to represent a letter to write out spells in Gaelic or English, or their energies can be combined. For example, birch, broom, holly, and apple can be combined on a single stave for a healing spell. Birch and broom combine to cleanse away illness, holly increases life force, and apple restores wellness and wholeness.

Combination oghams should be drawn vertically up the stem, with a "mouth" at the top and roots at the bottom (see figure 2).

Figure 2:
Combination
Ogham

Ogham Divination

Ogham can be used for divination in various ways. Ogham staves can be drawn at random from a bag and cast upon a cloth for "open" divination methods, or they can be chosen at random and placed in a sequence or pattern for interpretation in relation to their position.

Preparing for Divination

Divination is the act of accessing spirit or divine wisdom for application and guidance in the everyday world. Divination can be used to seek support and extra insight into a whole host of issues from magical and spiritual matters to the mundane. However, the power to change and act in relation to fate and circumstances is always in the hands of the seeker. No divination technique ever presents the future as if it is carved in stone. As such, it is a tool for advice that suggests layers of meaning. It comments on the spirit threads that connect all things, aiding in our navigation through life, but it does not prophesise.

That being said, all forms of divination involve some level of contact with spirit, often in very subtle ways. We must remember that when we perform a divination, we are not alone—we are interacting with spirit in a very real way. With regards to the ogham, we are interacting with the spirits of the trees and the presiding spirits of each ogham sigil. We also access the ancestral wisdom of the druids and their forebears. For this reason, divination should not be a casual act but one that is performed in a sacred and conscious manner, respectful of the energies and spirits we contact.

Effective divination requires us to consider our tools as sacred, keeping them safe and away from casual observers. Keeping our ogham staves in a purpose-made bag or box is good for this. We also need a surface upon which readings are performed, such as a special silk cloth, or a piece of wood or leather used for this purpose only.

We need to be in a sacred and calm space physically and psychically before performing an ogham reading. Switch off the TV and eliminate any distractions. Clear a space on a table to do the reading. Take some deep breaths, and call in your spirit allies before beginning. Alternatively, only perform divination within a magical circle or other sacred magical space such as a grove.

The last and most important detail is to call upon the spirits of the ogham themselves for assistance. Doing so is very simple: take a deep breath, feel your connection with the earth, and verbally ask the ogham spirits for their help in your own words. Without this conscious connection, we are drawing only on our own innate wisdom, missing out on the hosts of support the ogham trees themselves can offer us. Using the ogham without this conscious connection becomes an empty gesture that exercises our self-reflection rather than our interaction with the web of creation.

Framing the Question

Sometimes framing the appropriate question can be quite straightforward. However, when matters surrounding your enquiry are complex, it can be a good idea to make the question as open as possible to receive a message from spirit that may help you to think outside the box or draw something to your attention you were not aware of. Questions such as "How shall I proceed for my highest good?" are very useful. Another to consider is "What guidance does the ogham offer me at this point in my life?"

Single Ogham Stave Reading: A Message from the Gods

In some ways, this is the simplest way to use the ogham for divination. A single stave is drawn at random from a bag, or from the complete set held bunched in the hand. The single stave thus holds all the meaning and advice given. The message is direct and simple but may hold many levels of meaning—no further elucidation is offered. Drawing a single ogham is good for quick and direct advice, but it may sometimes be the hardest to interpret and follow, as no further oghams are present to assist understanding.

Three-Ogham Stave Reading: The World Tree

This layout uses three ogham staves chosen randomly and placed in a vertical line.

Starting from the bottom and ascending, each of the three positions represents wisdom in relation to the lower, middle, and upper worlds.

1. The lower world
   This position relates to the roots of the World Tree, and the roots of your query and situation. The underworld is the place of rest and regeneration, the realm of ancestral wisdom, that which has passed, and the earth's deep energies. It is the realm of the sidhe, the faeries, the weaver goddess, and the three Fates. The underworld, called Annwn in the Celtic tradition, is said in Taliesin's poem "The Spoils of Annwn" to hold a great cauldron, the sacred womb of the goddess which is attended to by nine otherworldly priestesses. An ogham

Figure 3: Blank Ogham

placed in this position advises you on what has brought you here and what is at the core of the situation. It suggests avenues for transformation and what constrains you due to past actions.

2. The middle world
The middle world is called Abred in the Celtic tradition. This is not only physical matter, but the indwelling spirit present in all manifest reality as well. This position highlights your present circumstances and the issues and support that surround you in the everyday mortal world. The middle world is often overlooked and disrespected, and an ogham placed here serves as a reminder of how to relate to the sacred earth and the human world around you in a more effective and conscious manner; that is where real change, healing, and empowerment can occur. The middle world is also the place of our animal and elemental allies, the spirits of nature and seasonal connection. The middle world is subject to constant cyclical change, as are our mortal selves. Even mundane and practical issues are subject to this pattern, and are manifestations of spirit as much as anything else. The ogham placed here reminds and advises you how to act for the best outcome as well as how to embrace the present effectively.

3. The upper world
The upper world is called Gwynfyd in the Celtic tradition and is the place of divinity and of our highest selves. Here the blueprints of all creation are held in their most perfect form before they interact with manifest reality. In the upper world, we may find our first and best intentions, reconnecting with our original potential. As a place at one with Source, our divine aspects, as well as the gods, it is somewhere from which we can draw energy and ideas. Contact with the upper world allows fresh starts and the endless compassion of the Creator in whatever form resonates with us.

Here is the place our destiny is held and remembered, as well as the place from which we may draw support and effect change. The ogham placed here reminds us of our highest aims and potential, suggesting a possible future should we navigate true to our soul's purpose. It may also point out how to reclaim a positive perspective or come to terms with the effects and consequences of our actions, should rectification need to occur.

Sample Reading

Roy wanted a reading concerning how to progress his career and insight into how he should best focus his energies most effectively with career in mind. As a creative person, he was often commissioned, and this provided a focus, but other times he was inundated with ideas but unsure which ones to choose. This led to times of intense activity followed by periods of inactivity and lean finances. The three staves that appeared in his reading were as follows.

3) Eadha /
Aspen

2) Saille /
Willow

1) Idho /
Yew

Figure 4:
Three-Ogham
Stave Reading

1. Underworld: Idho/Yew

   The yew counsells perseverance, patience, and small steps towards progression. Roy was either working or had little income, leading to an imbalance. Yew in the underworld suggested a need for in-between commissions, other more long-term creative projects, or tasks that could shore up and develop his reputation to create a sound foundation. Yew also encouraged a more compassionate and positive attitude towards his accomplishments, seeing times of focused activity and repose as part of the rhythm of his life. With greater perspective, yew suggested he would see that he had in fact been making steady and fruitful progress all along; a positive future lay ahead.

2. Middle world: Saille/Willow
   Willow in the middle world suggests a need for balance and harmony, in all different aspects of life. It suggested here that Roy needed a flexible attitude about his creativity and career. He was encouraged to go with the flow, seizing upon inspirations and opportunities as they arise. Having a harmonious, grounded environment in which to nurture his creativity would also be conducive to seizing opportunities and ideas, and being able to make the best of them.

3. Upper world: Eadha/Aspen
   Aspen in the upper world suggests that creative ideas and inspiration would be especially forthcoming for Roy, but that an imbalance with the earthy and practical aspects of his job would lead to difficulties in turning these ideas into grounded manifestation. Time needed to be taken to correct this imbalance, and to create an environment and attitude that held this creative flow in balance. Trusting that there would always be more ideas and more commissions was a basis for greater confidence and the instigation of more long-term plans. Communication and communal effort were also highlighted here, suggesting collaborations would also be worthwhile.

Five-Ogham Stave Reading: The Celtic Cross (Also Known as Brighid's Cross)

In addition to the three-stave spread, we may choose to use an additional two oghams on the left and right of the tree. These refer to our feminine side or ancestral line and our masculine side or ancestral line respectively. The spread can also be interpreted as a breath in on the left and a breath out on the right. Thus the ogham placed on the left side suggests that which supports us and from where we may draw energy. The ogham on the right suggests what needs our attention and where we should place our energy and best efforts. Taken as the four points of the compass with a central point in the middle world, directional and elemental correspondences may also be gleaned. This spread is best read going first around the compass points and then to the central, middle world position.

Figure 5: Blank Five-Ogham Stave Reading

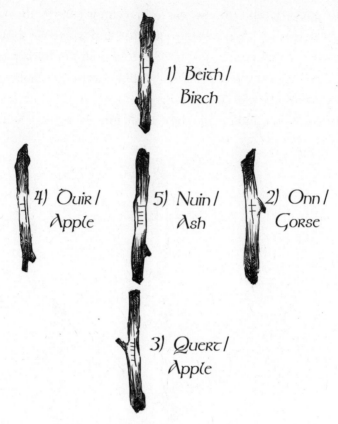

Figure 6: Five-Ogham Stave Reading

Sample Reading

Morgan had long-standing chronic health issues that conventional medicine helped only a little. She requested a reading to gain a deeper insight into her condition and what could be done generally to improve her health and well-being.

1. Upper world, North, Earth: Beith/Birch
   Birch counselled a fresh start, especially so in the position of the upper world and the north, the place of earth. Here, the birch suggested that this was an auspicious time for renewal, and that

cleansing needs to take place in order to make way for this new fresh energy and vision. Birch advised that it was time to let old patterns of behaviour or stuck, stagnant energies be cleared away and released—an emotional, energetic, and physical detox. It was time for a new phase of life and renewed energies. As the north also represents the element of earth, a new fitness or diet regime was advised as a way for Morgan to reconnect with her highest potential and greatest health.

2. Male line, East, Air: Onn/Gorse

   Gorse's wild, fiery energy in the east is like the sun—bright and full of illumination. Placed here, it suggested that Morgan had a highly active mind, readily inspired and creative. Periods of excessive highs and lows of energy were also indicated where creative or intellectual fires would burn fiercely (and potentially out of control), leaving her drained in the aftermath. The pattern could have been inherited from her male line, as it certainly pointed to her more active side, suggesting she could physically burn off energy in action and achievement. Held in balance, Morgan could be extremely productive and inspired, but out of balance the effects on her health would be profound. Gorse counselled her to learn to mediate these energies more calmly, and that cleansing and rectification may be required to restore this balance.

3. Underworld, South, Fire: Quert/Apple

   Morgan received apple here, suggesting that her health problems stemmed from a mind/body/spirit issue, where emotional or spiritual pain or wounds were taking their toll on her physical body. Apple encouraged her to consider how things felt, rather than rationalise her condition, and take an instinctual feelings-and-intuitive approach to her well-being. The need for greater compassion and kindness towards herself and others was also highlighted.

The presence of apple suggested that Morgan needed to be "in her body" more often, rather than distancing herself from her physicality due to her discomfort. Positioned in the south and relating to the element of fire, apple also suggested this attitude towards her own body affected her energy levels, vitality, and sense of enthusiasm. An approach more in tune with her subtle senses and their effects on her body would have corresponding effects upon her physical stamina and general well-being.

4. Female line, West, Water: Duir/Oak

   Oak in the west suggested great emotional security and strength. Stability and experience led to a grounded understanding of the watery realms of emotion and the intuitive realms of spirit, implying that Morgan was able to practically apply this with maturity. Oak, the tree of sovereignty, in the west also showed that this was where Morgan was at her strongest and healthiest. That strength could have been inherited from her female line, or it could have suggested that she was very comfortable with her own womanhood, finding it a source of power. Oak's presence here meant that she was very present in her emotions and intuitions, and in turn they were a place of internal growth and well-being that could then lead her into better health in other aspects of her life. If emotional pain was the cause of her illness, as suggested by the apple, she had undertaken considerable emotional healing by this point; the effects of it upon her physical state would be felt at some point in the future.

5. Middle world, the Self: Nuin/Ash

   The World Tree positioned in the middle world and place of the self suggested that Morgan was determined. She had reserves of inner strength, and better health and well-being would come from maintaining balance in all the various aspects of herself and her life. Here we see the axis mundi, or divine centre, in the central position—highly auspicious. An upright, focused, and centred approach bears the best fruit. A balance between *being* and *doing* is highlighted here, as is harmony between the three worlds and the inner masculine and feminine. Here ash advised the famous spiritual adage found above the entrance to the Delphic Temple of Apollo—*medén ágan*, "nothing in excess"—breathing in and out, times of action and rest in equal measure lead to the great improvement in health she longs for. Ash also represents the lightning flash; it may be that, should she seek that balance, she may find that a surprise improvement in her condition takes place sooner than previously thought.

Open Ogham Reading

An open ogham reading is when the ogham staves are gently thrown upon a surface to all fall where they may. This relies on the visionary abilities of the person casting the ogham to interpret their various positions in relation to each other. The divination may be further assisted by the reader's spirit allies and the ogham spirits themselves via inner journey or seership.

Open Ogham Reading: Fionn's Window

Named after the Irish hero and magician Fionn mac Cumhail, Fionn's Window is an arrangement of ogham sigils including the forfeda in concentric circles. Another name for it is the Fege Find. A *fege* is the central ridgepole used to hold up an Iron Age round house. Ridgepoles have been used for divination and shamanic purposes in numerous cultures where the central pole represents the great World Tree, granting access to the other worlds.[207] Fionn mac Cumhail was a powerful magician due to his consumption of the mythical salmon of knowledge that contained access to all magical lore, history, and spiritual experience. He is a deeply shamanic character, and it may be that Fionn's Window demonstrates a shamanic divinatory technique particularly Celtic in detail but universal in nature.

---

207   Ananda Coomaraswamy, *The Door in the Sky* (Princeton, NJ: Princeton University Press, 1997), 18.

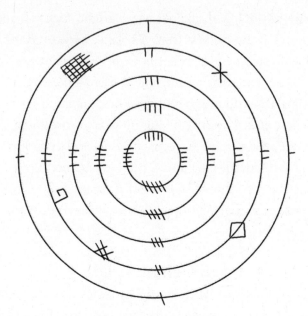

Figure 7: Fionn's Window

In the diagram, we see each of the four aicmes or tribes placed in the four directions, one ogham of each aicme occupying the same circle as those of the same position in the other three. Thus the aicme of birch lies vertically along each circle, descending from the north. The aicme of the hawthorn descends along each circle from the east, the aicme of the blackberry ascends through each circle, coming up from the south, and the aicme of the pine does the same from the west.

Each circle may be seen to represent a different layer of existence spiralling back and forth from Source into the material world. In this way, the relationships between each ogham and thus the journey of the seeker begins with birch. It then develops through that aicme and continues to the outer realms of the next, weaving in and out until it reaches the yew in the position of the furthest inner point of the west. Here is the direct interface point with the spirit realm and our eternal selves. Here we meet the gods, and may choose either communion with them or return to be reborn via the birch.

We have a map of our spiritual journey that may also be used metaphorically to answer some of our lives' most complex matters, granting us direct insight from spirit.

Each ogham and the aicme to which it belongs can be ascribed to have a direction and elemental aspect (north, earth; east, air; south, fire; west, water) to aid in their interpretation. When casting oghams upon Fionn's Window, we may also have the added insight of how each ogham relates to the position in which it lies.

Obviously this technique is quite advanced and relies on the experience and abilities of the seeker to be really effective. Remember, there is no substitute for practice. How each person interprets the ogham when using this technique will be personal and heavily reliant on inner vision, intuition, as well as the support of spirit guides and allies.

Fionn's Window Circle Ceremony

This simple ceremony picks up from the last chapter's discussion of Fionn's Window. The ceremony may be used as a meditative and visionary technique or to create a sacred space in which the practitioner is surrounded by a grove of ogham trees and sigils. The sacred space may be used for spellwork, healing, shamanic journeying, or other purposes.

First gather anything you would like to have in your completed circle. This may include your ogham staves, or if you are able, you may hold each sigil in your memory to effectively draw with energy around your space. Calm and centre yourself, drawing in energy from the earth.

When you are ready, turn your attention to the north. Facing that direction, hold the ogham stave for birch or its image in your inner vision. Call upon the assistance of the ogham beith, and place the ogham stave upon the ground in front of you or draw the ogham in the air. As you do this, see in your inner vision that the ogham sigil flashes with power for a moment.

Next, turn your attention to the east and repeat the process with the ogham for hawthorn, huath. Then turn to the south and do the same with the ogham for blackberry, muin. Finally, turn to the west and do the same with pine, ailm. You have now cast the first of the five circles.

You then turn again to the north and do the same with the next ogham, rowan/luis; then oak/duir in the east; ivy/gort in the south and so on until you have gone through the whole ogham and cast the circle with five layers. For the purposes of this ceremony, you may choose to ignore the forfeda or include them in their positions as you are guided or feel. Their inclusion or absence makes subtle changes in the energy of the circle, but they are not essential.

When the five circles are cast, take a moment to breathe and feel into the space. Lie on your back. Using your inner vision, see the oghams surrounding you, spiralling around and forming the walls and roof of a Celtic roundhouse. Beneath you is the sacred earth and the underworld. Far above is the star realm, the heavens. If you are able to have a fire or candle in your sacred space, take a moment to consider this sacred fire as the hearth and gathering point of your space in the middle world. All prayers and acts of magic made here rise past your ogham guardians and allies to interface with the gods above you in the upper world, like smoke rising softly through the roof from your hearth and heart fire. Remember, a roundhouse does not have a smoke hole but rather a central ridgepole that is sometimes used to hold up the thatched roof which spirals around it. You in the centre of your space are in the position of the centre ridgepole, the World Tree, able to ascend and descend to the otherworld at will, guided and accompanied by your ogham spirit allies. Take a moment to reflect on this, building up the image of a roundhouse around you in your inner vision, and be open to any insights that spirit may offer you. What does your inner roundhouse look like? How does it feel?

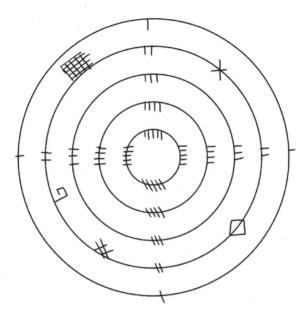

Figure 8: Fionn's Window

You may also like to call upon Fionn at this time to guide you with his insight. He may also be called upon here for protection, should you ever feel it is necessary.

You may create this sacred space to work in, journey in, or meditate in as often as you like or are guided.

Each of the five circles will function slightly differently, together forming more of an energetic spiral than a static circular enclosure. The practitioner should feel this out personally, but loosely speaking they create a sacred space together with protection and access on different levels of the world tree. With regards to this sort of practice, experience is far more valuable than verbal description; it is a matter of using our subtle senses and experience with regards to the many layers of its application.

When closing the circles after use, each ogham cast and invoked should be thanked and removed or "closed" by wiping over with the hand in reverse order. Thus the ceremony always begins and ends with beith, the birch.

Tree Charms, Crafts, Spells, and Potions

In this section we will look at how to apply our knowledge of the ogham trees for magical purposes, be it for healing, spells, or as shamanic tools.

If it is to be the most effective, all magic involving trees should make use of our relationship with individual tree spirits, taking into consideration ethical and environmental considerations as well. In this way our spiritual and magical work are part of a seamless flow, drawn out of our relationship to the earth and all forms of life who dwell within it, in whatever form. There is no need to dominate or bind spirits to perform our will—an attitude which has been popular amongst magical practitioners of the past. Conversely, to draw only from reserves of personal power should also be avoided.

It is both counterproductive and abusive to acquire or use items from the natural world merely as a form of spiritual consumerism, as one would go shopping for a loaf of bread. Many natural, beautiful, magical items can now be found for sale—wands, staves, and ogham sets to name a few—and while many of these are bought and sold with great respect for their natural resources, the relationship with their indwelling spirits, the source of their power cannot be bought. No doubt this relationship can be developed over time by those willing to put the care and respect into the task, but that is an additional matter. Instead, rather than seeing the earth, its resources, and its diverse spiritual inhabitants as beings to use for our gain, we should always aim to come from a place of kinship and compassion—a term rarely used in much Pagan practice that nonetheless is key to effective magic. Should our work be in accord, we align ourselves to the flow of nature and can make use of the will and power of our spirit kin. We are part of a collective that becomes far more powerful than the sum of its individual parts. In this way we have nature behind us, and if we are lucky we may steer manifestation into providing according to our requests, hopefully having evolved our desires in the light of the bright knowledge of poetic vision, as emanations of the earth herself.

Magic with our tree kin and all the green world does not conform to rules and dogma but instead becomes most effective when we use our sense of innate connection to guide us and inspire our work. Leaves, wood, roots, seeds, and the flowers of trees and plants all have a long history of magical use; when we work in a traditional manner, our work benefits from the time-worn energetic paths that have been made before us, also serving as sources of power and support. Thus the collective lore found in the ogham is a very useful guide that can greatly assist us, but it cannot replace our own sense of relationship with individual trees we encounter. Our relationship with and attention to the tree we are working with should be our greatest tutor and will often guide us to work in new or forgotten ways that simply cannot be found or effectively described in spell books. For this reason, readers are encouraged to always remember that true magic is an act of co-creation, allowing the flow of nature and the threads of the greater web to steer us into the most effective course.

For those using tree and plant matter for ingestion in any way, it is always important to consult a reliable herbal, a qualified herbalist, and use common sense. Always be sure that you have correctly identified the plant you are using to be sure of its effects.

The following spells and charms can therefore be seen as an effective starting place for your practice; over time it will evolve and see additions as your relationship with the tree spirits around you grows and develops. Use your intuition and any guidance you receive to finesse your own way of working with these traditional techniques together with your tree spirit allies.

Birch Besom

Used for energetic cleansing, as well as assisting shamanic flight by dancing around your space with it, there is a vast amount of folklore around the world concerning broomsticks. They are a powerful household magical ally, with many uses besides sweeping. When one propped against the wall falls to the floor, be warned—you can expect company or a change of fortune!

First, gather a birch staff equal to your own height (with the tree spirit's permission), and drill a hole approximately six inches from the bottom. Insert another birch stick or peg into this to help bind the twigs. Next, (again with the spirit's permission), gather broom or birch twigs. Bind them tightly to the staff using twine or thin copper wire. Hold it out from the body and ask the tree spirits to bless and charge it as instructed earlier. Decorate with flowers or other magical items, and refresh them at least once a year, thanking the broom for its work during that time.

Work with your broom to sweep away negativity. Brooms should be blessed and honoured at least once a year and can be energetic doorways for use in ceremony. They can also be "turned"—held upright and turned clockwise—to mark the turning of the season.

Rowan Berry Charm Bracelet

Protective rowan berry bracelets or necklaces are very easy to make. With careful treatment, rowan berries dry quite well, and the charm will last for several months or as long as the thread keeps. When it snaps or the berries fall away, the magic is no longer needed; the berries can be buried or given to the earth.

You will need rowan berries, red thread, and a needle.

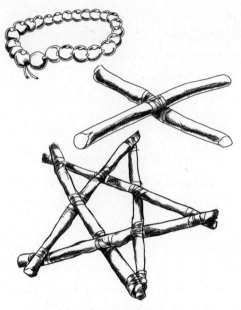

Figure 9: Rowan Charms

First you will gather berries. Find a rowan tree that feels right and spend some time with it before asking its permission. Only gather berries if you feel that permission has been granted. You may need to visit several times (or visit several trees) to build a relationship with the tree spirit first.

When you have gathered the berries, you may prefer to make this charm within a magic circle or other sacred space to help focus your intent.

Take the threaded needle, and gently string the berries on to it one at a time, talking gently to the rowan spirit as you go, thanking it for its help, and perhaps discussing why you feel you need help if there is a specific issue.

When you are done, tie it onto your wrist, or tie the ends together, first ensuring it is long enough to slip on. Holding it in your hand, take three slow deep breaths, gathering your intent. Say aloud:

Rowan tree, rowan tree,
here I ask a boon of thee:
Keep me safe from hurt and harm
and lend your magic to this charm!

You may like to repeat this chant for several minutes to let the power build. When you feel it is right, exclaim "So it shall be!" The spell is complete. Thank the rowan again for its assistance before closing your circle or sacred space.

Rowan Red Thread Cross

Rowan crosses are very old charms. They can be sewn into clothing, carried in your pocket, hung over doors and windows, or placed under pillows. The equal-armed cross is an ancient symbol called a sun wheel, and it was later adopted as the Celtic cross. A rowan pentacle makes a suitable alternative.

As with rowan berry charms, this magic is the most effective when a relationship has been formed with the tree spirit first and permission has been given to gather the twigs. Fallen twigs are fine to use. The easiest is to make a cross with two three-inch twigs; it is portable and can be placed discreetly around the home or in clothing; from there it's a matter of choice, practicality, and intuition.

When you have gathered your twigs, you may choose to make the cross whilst in your circle or sacred space to focus your intent, although traditionally these were made by the woman of the house whilst seated by the fire.

Embroidery thread is best to use for this, as it is slightly thicker than cotton. Whatever you choose, take your thread and tie the two pieces together in the centre, winding around and around so that the thread provides spacing between the two cross pieces. Remember to thank the rowan spirit as you work. You may choose to use the same words used for the rowan berry bracelet to help build the power.

Always treat the spirit of the tree respectfully as a helpful friend, and build your relationship with the tree over time, gathering from the same tree each year if you are able.

Alder Shield

Alder shields are useful for protection when shamanic journeying or for placing around a sacred space. They can range from very plain and simple to highly decorated in a variety of ways.

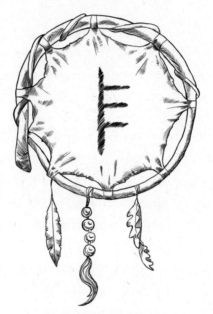

Figure 10: Alder Shield

When gathering alder wood, remember to seek permission from the alder spirit before beginning, and perhaps make it an offering of blessed spring water or song. You need a long, thin, whippy piece of alder you can bend into a circle of whatever size you wish. Tightly bind the circle with embroidery thread.

You can then create either a Celtic cross, sun wheel, or four directions design by crossing two further pieces of wood and binding them into the circle, or you may choose to make a latticework with multiple vertical and horizontal pieces bound onto the hoop. Alternatively you may choose to make and attach a circular piece of hide, cloth, or paper decorated with ogham or images of your animal allies, guides, or other designs relevant to your personal practice.

You can also add feathers, stones, or other items, hung from threads around its edge or tied to its central crosspiece. The important thing to consider when making a spirit shield is that it has your personal energy and intention put into its construction—this is far more important than making it look perfect or professional.

Whilst making your alder shield, repeatedly call to the spirit of the alder to assist you and bless your work. Take your time and remember that you are engaged in a sacred activity. You may also want to cleanse and bless your work with sage or mugwort smoke or blessed spring water. Before use or before placing it somewhere in your sacred space and after constructing the shield, ask that the spirit of the alder bless and empower your shield.

Hawthorn Charm Bag to Ease an Aching Heart

This is a basic formula for charm bags and spell bottles that will work well for other aims as well, making use of other trees, plants, etc. Always be sure to have the plant spirits' support for best results.

You will need a charm bag or bottle; hawthorn leaves, flowers, or berries, depending on the season; rose petals, and vervain, all gathered with the plants' and tree spirits' permission. If you must buy them, spend time with each to contact their spirits, and ask that they bless your work using your own words and intuition. Place everything together with a small lock of your hair and charge the ingredients by seeing the plant and tree spirits around you, assisting and energising your charm. You may also like to use the following chant that came to me for this purpose:

Heart be healed, heart be calm,
heart be safe now from all harm.

Repeat until you feel the charm is done. Thank the plants for their help and kinship. Place the charm somewhere safe and out of the way. In nine months' time, return the herbs to the earth when their work is done.

Oak and Acorn Spell

This spell will increase your personal power, and it works well after soul retrieval ceremonies to help restore it and keep you set on a path that is better for you, more fortunate, healthy, and positive.

You need spring water, a leafy oak twig or small branch, some acorns, a small piece of cotton cloth cut from your clothing, and red thread.

Gather the wood and water with the tree's permission and the water spirit's blessing. Dip the leafy branch in the water with the acorns, and leave for as long as possible. Then use the water and the leafy branch to asperge your space, dipping the branch and flicking and sprinkling the water all through your energy field, and over your bare skin. Add the water and the leaves to a ritual bath to further cleanse yourself, and infuse your energy with the oak's spirit. When you are done, wrap the leaves in the cloth, tie with red thread, and bury together with the acorns in the earth. You will find renewal, strength, and inner sovereignty return to you within the next three months.

Holly King Holly Wreath

A holly wreath is an excellent decoration for the winter solstice that at the same time provides protection from the spirits of storm and cold, through the darkest, longest night.

Figure 11: Holly Wreath

Gather a whippy piece of holly, preferably with berries, remembering to ask permission of the tree spirit first. When you have gathered the holly, hold it up to the sun and call to the holly king for blessing and protection, to empower your work. Use your own words or try these:

Holly King, lord of the winter sun, I call to you! Bless my work
this day, and lend your blessing and power to this, my charm.
I gather and welcome the holly into my home this night, this day,
and every night and every day, until the new sun returns!
May my heart and hearth fire burn bright until the spring!
Bless me and my kin in thought and deed, Holly King!

Bind the holly wreath into a circle using red thread or more decorative red ribbon. You may then choose to add further decoration as you wish. When you have finished, hold the wreath up to the winter sun, and say:

My work is done, may you bless and charge this with your power, Holly King, lord of the winter sun!

Visualise the sun's rays infusing every leaf and twig, until it glows in your inner vision. Hang on your door, hearth, or use as a table setting with a blessed red candle in the middle.

Blackberry Money Charm

Seek out a blackberry bush and ask its permission to gather a few leaves as well as its assistance in your spell. Taking the leaves and a small, deep blue cloth, wrap a coin or note of the highest denomination possible within the leaf and cloth, binding it with deep blue thread to make a small parcel. As you tie the coin in the leaves, hold them in your hands and ask the blackberry to assist you in drawing good luck and prosperity to you. The following chant may help you:

Figure 12: Blackberry Charm

Blackberry, blackberry, hear me now
grant me gold, with never a frown.

Repeat as many times as you wish until you sense the blackberry spirit has charged your charm. Place in a small pouch, or wrap with cloth and place in your purse or wallet.

Elderflower Anointing Water

Elderflower water is good for the skin, and if magically charged by the Elder Mother, will assist in attracting faeries and gaining the sight.

Figure 13: Elderflower Water

Use fresh spring water wherever possible. Gather the elderflowers with the elder tree's permission, and wrap in green cloth until ready for use, the fresher the better. Place the elderflowers in a stainless steel or enamel pan (never iron or aluminium) and cover with the water. Cover and gently simmer for ten minutes. Then simmer on the lowest possible setting for a further ten. Take a wooden or a silver spoon used only for magical purposes or a suitable wand, and stir clockwise nine times, asking in your own words that the Elder Mother bless and charge your potion. Do this slowly and with intent. When you are ready, return the lid to the pot, turn off the heat, and leave overnight, ideally upon your altar or other sacred space.

The next day, strain through a muslin or kitchen towel at least two or three times, to get rid of all herbal matter, and bottle. Add 50 percent alcohol or witch hazel as a preservative if you wish, or store in the fridge. It will keep without preservative for two weeks to a month.

Use this potion to anoint the eyelids or apply to the heart or pulse points. Alternatively it works well as a magically charged facial toner that is good for beauty spells.

Heather Goddess Poppet

A poppet is a special doll used for magic and healing. Sometimes it is used to represent and form a link with a specific person, but it can also be blessed and charged and used as a representative of various gods and goddesses. Heather is an excellent plant to work with to encourage the presence of benevolent goddesses in your life, and it can also help ease fears and loneliness.

To make a heather poppet, gather some sprigs of heather asking its permission first. Using red or white thread, bind them together with another sprig as a cross piece about a third of the way down to make a humanoid goddess figure. Magically charge this poppet with your intent and bless it with spring water. Invoke your chosen goddess, asking her to empower it. Wrap in white or purple cloth overnight, and remember to honour it regularly with offerings of food and drink. This poppet can then act like a worry doll to tell your troubles to, as well as a magical being that may guide and advise you, should you enter into dialogue with it whilst in meditation or using your inner vision.

After a time it may feel right to thank it and give it some final offerings before returning it to the earth. You could also recharge it by invoking the goddess once again.

Ogham Vibrational Essences

Vibrational essences can be used for healing, space clearing, and energising. They can be given safely to animals, plants, and children as they are so gentle and contain no herbal matter, only the vibrational, spirit energy of the tree or plant used. Vibrational essences are a vast subject and can be made in a variety of ways. Ogham tree vibrational essences can be made infused with the extra energetic signature of their accompanying ogham sigil.

Ogham tree essences are best made during the full moon, whether or not you choose to infuse them with moonlight. You will need fresh spring water, a glass bowl, and a piece of paper upon which is inscribed the relevant ogham sigil drawn with conscious intent in as sacred a manner as possible. You will also need a sterilised dark glass bottle for storing. You may also decide to use brandy or glycerine as a preservative.

First choose the ogham tree or plant you wish to work with in order to make the essence. Use your intuition and any guidance you may receive from communion with the plant itself. Also try to select one that is in good and vibrant health, in leaf, and preferably in flower (if appropriate).

When you feel you have the plant's permission, pour some water into the bowl or glass. Placing the ogham sigil beneath it, find a place in the branches, or amongst the leaves or the roots in which to position the bowl. Leave to charge, energise, and infuse in sunlight—and if it feels appropriate, moonlight—for twelve to twenty-four hours. During this time, the plant spirit will send some of its energy and presence into the water. Do not worry if it rains, as this is an extra spirit gift for your essence that will add extra power.

When it is time, collect the bowl and paper and thank the tree or plant. Store the water in the dark glass bottle, and top up if desired with 50 percent alcohol or glycerine to preserve. Label carefully, including the ogham sigil.

Vibrational essences are usually taken by placing a few drops on the tongue or in water. Alternatively they can be placed in a bowl upon the altar, sprayed around a space, or asperged (sprinkled) around an area for cleansing and blessing, as well as anointed on the brow or on candles for magical workings. They are also excellent for offerings and tree healing, where the essence of the same species can be used to anoint and water the tree concerned.

Ogham Tree Tinctures

Many of the trees and plants mentioned in this book have parts—bark, berries, and flowers—that can be taken medicinally. However, great care should *always* be taken to ensure that you have both correctly identified the plant you wish to use, and have thoroughly researched its effects, especially if you have any underlying health conditions or are intending to treat children. With due caution, homemade tinctures are easy to make and effective. When gathering plant material, always ask the plants' permission and the land owner, where relevant.

You will need a dark glass jar or bottle sterilised using tablets or boiling water, and either brandy or vodka with as high an alcohol content as possible. Take your plant matter and crush with a pestle and mortar or or cut it up knife, a process that is especially important with barks and tough leaves. Place in the jar and pour enough alcohol to cover completely. Leave in a cool, dark place for a month, and then strain and bottle in another sterilised container. With research and practice, you can combine plants to make more sophisticated tinctures for specific medical complaints and health issues.

Particularly useful and safe ogham tree tinctures are hawthorn for stress and elderberry for coughs and colds. Nonalcoholic tinctures, called elixirs, can be made in the same way using honey. As before, use enough to completely cover the plant material.

They will keep best in a cool, dark place for several months or years depending on the strength of the alcohol used. Elixirs will happily keep for many months, but should always be checked before use.

Conclusion

Humanity's relationship with the trees is ancient and transcends all times and cultures. We have always held them sacred, and rightly so. Trees have always been the friends of humanity, lending their bodies to make tools, building material, and fuel. They are also our magical and healing partners, not only with regards to human needs, but also for the earth herself.

Today our relationship with the trees is more important than ever before, as our planet endures more pollution and deforestation than in our long history together. So many of us have grown distant from nature, but our need for the wild green world will never leave us. I therefore encourage you, dear reader, to re-remember your relationship with the trees around you—any and all species. They are noble spirits with much to teach us, and they offer their gifts so freely. They support so much of the material world and also teach us the value of standing still, of growing deep roots in the sacred, rich, dark soil, and of reaching our branches high, towards the light.

Honour the trees. Plant them, sow their seeds, protect them, and nurture them in whatever way you can, just as our ancestors did. Seek silence, and learn to listen to their wisdom—the voice of the wind in the branches, the creak of the woods, and their promptings that stir in your own heart. You will be richly rewarded.

May the blessings of our tree kin be upon you and every generation to come!

Appendix:
The Ogham and the
Correspondances at a Glance

Please see next page.

1. Beith/Birch—Beginnings/cleansing (healing, protection)

2. Luis/Rowan—Protection/vision (protection, warning)

3. Fearn/Alder—Defence/shielding (protection, encouragement)

4. Saille/Willow—Harmony/inspiration (dream work, healing)

5. Nuin/Ash—Strength/empowerment (empowerment, protection)

6. Huath/Hawthorn—Challenge/love (love, healing the heart)

7. Duir/Oak—King/fate/sovereignty (protection, guidance)

8. Tinne/Holly—Energy/life force (protection, vivacity)

9. Coll/Hazel—Wisdom/knowledge (inspiration)

10. Quert/Apple—Wholeness/the soul (healing)

11. Muin/Blackberry—Harvest/manifestation (empowerment, encouragement)

12. Gort/Ivy—Support/community (encouragement, support)

13. Ngetal/Broom/Fern—Energetic hygiene/preservation (shielding, disguise)

14. Straif/Blackthorn—Magical power (empowerment, constraint)

15. Ruis/Elder—Sacrifice (healing/inspiring)

16. Ailm/Scots Pine—Perspective/far sight (teaching, cleansing)

17. Onn/Gorse—Fertility/eroticism (vivification, inspiration)

18. Ur/Heather—The goddess/earth (healing, support)

19. Eadha/Aspen—Movement/change/crossing over (attunement, communing)

20. Idho/Yew—Infinity (dissolution, communion, healing)

21. Ebadh/White Poplar—Crossing over/spirit allies/soul midwifery (guidance, support)

22. Oir/Spindle—Fate and destiny/the weaver goddesses/choosing the life to come (empowering)

23. Uilleann/Honeysuckle—Memory/past life recall/healing ancestral wounds (healing, grounding)

24. Iphin/Gooseberry—Ancestral energetic legacies/vision/fertility, vitality (healing, energising)

25. Eamhancholl/Witch Hazel/Wych Elm—Otherworld contact/faerie/magic (empowerment, increased vision)

26. Phagos/Beech—Sovereign goddess of the land/magical knowledge/ancestral knowledge (inspiration, vision, support)

Appendix:
How to Plant a Tree

Trees can be planted for a whole host of reasons, least of which is the earth's needs for them now more than ever. However, many people feel they don't have the space or the means. In fact, it is possible to grow trees of all shapes and sizes to fit almost everyone's circumstances and space.

Growing from Nuts and Berries

The best time to try this method is early autumn, September and October. Some seeds such as oak, beech, chestnut, horse chestnut, and sycamore do best planted straight away. Ash seeds should gathered and sown early in August. Always be sure to correctly identify and label what you have gathered. Seeds found on the ground or those gently shaken from a branch are best—never tear seeds off of a tree. When you get seeds home, put them in some water to test their fertility. Discard those that float; these have been hollowed by insects or rot.

Most seeds need a period of cold in order to germinate. This process can be as simple as placing the seeds in a plastic bag with a little gritty and slightly damp compost or leaf mould and leaving them in a fridge for a month or more. Check them periodically, as some may begin to sprout.

Sprouted seeds can be gently removed and potted. In the northern hemisphere, you can alternatively place seeds in compost in a pot outdoors over winter. Place the pot in a sheltered location where it will not get too much rain. Make simple prayers to the spirits of the trees that your seeds will sprout.

Growing On

Trees grown from seed can be potted into small pots with gritty compost for a few months. Keep an eye on them so their roots don't become constricted, but try not to pot them into bigger containers or out into the ground until the following winter at least, when they will be dormant and less likely to be damaged. Keep them out of full sun and heavy rain. They will do fine against a shady wall, but also make sure they don't dry out.

Planting a Tree

The process for planting a larger young tree, a small year-old seedling (called a "whip"), a tree that is "bare rooted," and one covered in soil is basically the same. First prepare the site where the tree will be planted: dig and loosen compacted soil. Make a hole roughly two feet wider than the circumference of the roots. Check the soil you are planting in—if it gets very waterlogged, add grit for drainage. If the soil is poor, add organic compost to feed the tree as it gets established. Gently dusting the roots with some mycorrhizal fungi helps the tree draw nutrients from the soil and attunes its immune system to its environment.

Consider whether the tree will need a stake to support it in high winds. If needed, position the stake at the same time as planting, at a 45 degree angle and at a depth of about two feet. See that it reaches no more than a third of the tree's height. Attach any stakes to the tree with a tree tie so they do not rub against the tree's trunk.

Place the tree in the hole, and gently fill it back in, leaving the soil level with the base of its trunk. Be sure to tamp it down carefully to discourage air pockets. Avoid compacting the soil.

From time to time, tune in to the spirit of your tree, whether it is in a pot or fully grown somewhere. Try to be sensitive to its subtle communications as well as its environment. Occasionally it may need pruning or other practical activities. If it does, communicate these matters to the tree first to lessen its shock and disturbance. From time to time you may sense its needs; do your best to support and protect it. The best green allies we have are those we nurture with care.

Bibliography

Bacon, E. *Archaeology: Discoveries in the 1960s.* Lincoln, UK: Praeger, 1971.

(no author) "Bawming the Thorn" *Appleton Village Portal* (Cheshire, UK). http://www.appletonthorn.org.uk/bawming-day.

[Bernes, Juliana]. *The Book of Saint Albans* (1486). London: Elliot Stock, 1881.

Calder, George, ed. *Auraceipt na n-Éces, The Scholars' Primer.* Edinburgh, UK: Grant, 1917.

Cambrensis, Giraldus. *Description of Wales* (1195). Edited by Ernest Rhys. London: J. M. Dent and Co, 1908.

Carmichael, Alexander. *Carmina Gadelica, Volume 2.* http://www .sacred-texts.com/neu/celt/cg2/cg2108.htm.

Carney, James. *The Invention of the Ogam Cipher. "Ériu"* 22. Dublin, IRL: Royal Irish Academy, 1975.

Carr-Gomm, Philip, and Stephanie Carr-Gomm. *The Druid Plant Oracle.* New York: St. Martin's Press, 2007.

Chambers, Robert. *Popular Rhymes of Scotland.* London: W & R Chambers, 1870.

Child, Francis James. *The English and Scottish Popular Ballads, Volume 1.* Mineola, NY: Dover, 2003.

Cleaver, Alan, and Leslie Park. "Beating the Bounds." *Strange Britain.* http://www.strangebritain.co.uk/traditions/bounds.html.

Coomaraswarmy, Ananda K. *The Door in the Sky.* Princeton, NJ: Princeton University Press. 1997.

Culpeper, Nicholas. *Culpeper's Complete Herbal.* London: Foulsham, 1939.

(no author). "Darradarljod: The Battle Song of the Valkyries." Accessed 24/4/12. http://www.orkneyjar.com/tradition/darra.htm.

(no author). "Did You Know? Fraoch Leann (Heather Ale)." Accessed http://www.rampantscotland.com/know/blknow_heatherale.htm.

Dio, Cassius. *Rome.* Translated by Herbert Baldwin Foster. New York: Pafraets, 1905. (Kindle edition.)

Dollinger. André. "Ancient Egyptian Plants: The Willow." http://reshafim.org.il/ad/egypt/botany/willow.htm.

Drury, Nevill. *The Dictionary of the Esoteric.* London: Watkins, 2004.

Ellis, Peter Berresford. *A Dictionary of Irish Mythology.* London: Oxford Reference, 1991.

Euripides. *The Bacchae.* Translated by Gilbert Murray. Bartleby.com, 2001.

Fox, Cyril. *A Find of the Early Iron Age from Llyn Cerrig Bach, Anglesey.* Cardiff, UK: National Museum of Wales, 1945.

Frazer, James George. "The Relics of Tree Worship in Modern Europe." Chapter 10 in *The Golden Bough.* http://www.sacred-texts.com/pag/frazer/gb01000.htm.

———. "The King of the Wood." Chapter 1 in *The Golden Bough.* http://www.sacred-texts.com/pag/frazer/gb00103.htm.

Gerard, John. *Gerard's Herbal* (1633). [London?], UK: Velluminous Press, 2010.

Graves, Robert. *The Greek Myths, Part 1*. London: Pelican Books, 1975.

———. *The White Goddess*. London: Faber and Faber, 1990.

Green, Miranda J. *Dictionary of Celtic Myth and Legend*. London: Thames & Hudson, 1997.

Gregory, Lady. *Irish Myths and Legends*. Philadelphia: Running Press, 1998. First published 1902, publisher unknown.

Grieve, Maud. *A Modern Herbal*. Surrey, UK: Merchant, 1973.

Grimm, Jacob. *Teutonic Mythology, Vol. 4*. London: J.S. London, 1888. First published in 1835 by Shallybass.

Gundarsson. Kveldulf. *Elves, Wights, and Trolls*. Bloomington, IN: iUniverse, 2007.

Gwynn, Edward, translator. *The Metrical Dindsenchas* (1905). http://www.ucc.ie/celt/online/T106500D.html.

Ida, Bobula. *The Great Stag: A Sumerian Divinity* (1953). Reprint from *The Yearbook of Ancient and Medieval History*. http://www.stavacademy.co.uk/mimir/greatstag.htm

Jorgen, Moe, and Peter Christen Asbjornsen, eds. *Fodor's Normandy, Brittany and the Best of the North*. Accessed 7/4/12. http://books.google.co.uk/books?id=JbyMN6oZK8MC&.

Keightley, Thomas. *The Fairy Mythology: Illustrative of the Romance and Superstition of Various Countries*. London: G. Bell, 1892.

Kinsella, Thomas, translator. *The Táin*. London: Oxford University Press, 2002.

[no author]. *Larousse Encyclopaedia of Mythology*. London: Batchworth Press, 1959.

Lucan. *The Pharsalia*. Translated by H. T. Riley. First published in 1853 by H. G. Bohn, London. (Kindle edition.)

Lust, John. *The Herb Book*. New York: Bantam, 1986.

MacNeill, Eoin, ed. *Duanaire Finn: The Book of the Lays of Fionn, Part I*. London: David Nutt for the Irish Texts Society, 1908.

(no author). "Madron Well and Baptistry." Pendeen, Cornwall, UK. Accessed 12/10/12. http://cornishancientsites.com/Madron%20Well%20%26%20Baptistry.pdf

McManus, Damian. *A Guide to Ogam*. Maynooth, IRL: An Sagart, 1991.

Maier, Bernhard. *Dictionary of Celtic Religion and Culture*. London: Athenaeum Press Ltd., 2000.

Matthews, Caitlín, and John Matthews. *The Aquarian Guide to British and Irish Mythology*. London: Aquarian Press, 1988.

Matthews, John. *The Celtic Shaman*. London: Rider, 2001.

Matthews, John, and Will Worthington. *The Green Man Tree Oracle*. New York: Barnes and Noble, 2003.

Murray, James A. H., ed. *The Romance and Prophecies of Thomas of Ercledoune*. Somerset, UK: Llanerch, 1991.

Murphy, Gerard, translator. *Dunaire Finn: The Book of the Lays of Fionn, part II*. London: David Nutt for the Irish Texts Society, 1908.

O'Donovan, John, translator. *Cormac's Glossary*. Calcutta: Irish Archaeological and Celtic Society, 1868.

Page, R. I. *Norse Myths*. Austin, TX: University of Texas Press, 1990.

Pliny. *Natural History*. Heinemann MacMillan, 1949–1954. http://www.masseiana.org/pliny.htm#BOOK XVI.

Rackham, H. Jones, W. H. S. Jones, and D. E. Eichholz, translators. *Pliny: Natural History,* book 16, chapter 95. Cambridge, MA: Harvard University Press, 1938.

Rohde, Eleanor Sinclair. *The Old English Herbals*. Newstead, AUS: Emereo Classics, 2010.

(no author). "Seahenge." Lynn Museum, Nowich, Norfolk, UK. http:// www.museums.norfolk.gov.uk/view/NCC095944

Shakespeare, William. *Henry IV, part I*. Edited by Stephen Greenblatt. Norton Shakespeare, 1st ser. London: Norton, 1997.

Sigfusson, Saemund. *The Elder Eddas*. Translated by Benjamin Thorpe. London: Norroena Society, 1906.

Sikes, Wirt. *British Goblins*. London: EP Publishing, 1973.

Spence, Lewis. *The Fairy Tradition in Britain*. Whitefish, MT: Kessinger, 1995.

Squire, Charles. *Celtic Myth and Legend*. https://archive.org/stream /celticmythlegend00squi#page/n0/mode/2up. London: Gresham Publishing, 1905.

Stokes, Whitley, translator. *Lives of the Saints, from the Book of Lismore*. London: Clarendon Press, 1890.

Stokes, Whitley, ed. "The Prose tales in the Rennes Dindsenchas" in *Revue Celtique XV*. Paris: Librarie Emille Bouillon, 1894.

———. "The Edinburgh Dinnsenchas" in *Folklore 4* (1893). http:// www.ucd.ie/tlh/trans/ws.fl.4.001.t.text.html.

Tacitus, Cornelius. *The Annals*. Translated by J. C. Yardley. London: Oxford University Press, 2008. (Kindle edition.)

Tegnér, Esaias. *Frithiof's Saga: A Legend of the North*. Stockholm: A Bonnier, 1839.

(no author). "The Forestry Commission Scotland: Fortingall Yew." Accessed 13/7/13. http://www.forestry.gov.uk/forestry /INFD-6UFC5F.

(no author). "The Tragic Death of Fergus mac Leide." www
.ancienttexts.org/library/celtic/ctexts/fergusmacleide.html.

(no author). "The Heritage Tree Database: Hawthorn." Co. Clare,
Ireland. http://www.treecouncil.ie/heritagetrees/395.htm.

Varner, Gary R. *The Mythic Forest, The Green Man and the Spirit of
Nature.* New York: Algora, 2006.

Westwood, Jennifer, and Jacquelline Simpson. *The Lore of the Land: A
Guide to England's Legends, from Spring-heeled Jack to the Witch of
the Warboys.* New York: Penguin, 2005.

Wilde, Wilde. *Ancient Legends, Mystic Charms, and Superstitions of
Ireland.* London: Chatto and Windus, 1902.

Williams, Mike. *The Shaman's Spirit: Discovering the Wisdom of
Nature, Power Animals, Sacred Places and Rituals.* London:
Watkins, 2013.

Index

GET MORE AT LLEWELLYN.COM

Visit us online to browse hundreds of our books and decks, plus sign up to receive our e-newsletters and exclusive online offers.

- Free tarot readings • Spell-a-Day • Moon phases
- Recipes, spells, and tips • Blogs • Encyclopedia
- Author interviews, articles, and upcoming events

GET SOCIAL WITH LLEWELLYN

Find us on [f]   🐦 @LlewellynBooks
www.Facebook.com/LlewellynBooks

GET BOOKS AT LLEWELLYN

LLEWELLYN ORDERING INFORMATION

Order online: Visit our website at www.llewellyn.com to select your books and place an order on our secure server.

Order by phone:
- Call toll free within the US at 1-877-NEW-WRLD (1-877-639-9753)
- We accept VISA, MasterCard, American Express, and Discover.

Order by mail:
Send the full price of your order (MN residents add 6.875% sales tax) in US funds plus postage and handling to: Llewellyn Worldwide, 2143 Wooddale Drive, Woodbury, MN 55125-2989

POSTAGE AND HANDLING
STANDARD (US):(Please allow 12 business days)
$30.00 and under, add $6.00.
$30.01 and over, FREE SHIPPING.

CANADA:
We cannot ship to Canada. Please shop your local bookstore or Amazon Canada.

INTERNATIONAL:
Customers pay the actual shipping cost to the final destination, which includes tracking information.

Visit us online for more shipping options. Prices subject to change.

FREE CATALOG!
To order, call
1-877-
NEW-WRLD
ext. 8236
or visit our
website